## PACE UNIVERSITY
## MORTOLA LIBRARY
### Pleasantville, N.Y. 10570
### Telephone (914) 993-3380

# Marketing in Developing Countries

EDITED BY G.S. KINDRA

ST. MARTIN'S PRESS
New York

Printed in Great Britain
First published in the United States of America in 1984

Library of Congress Cataloging in Publication Data
Main entry under title :

Marketing in developing countries.

   Includes bibliographical references and index.
   1. Marketing – Developing countries – Addresses,
essays, lectures.  I. Kindra, G.S. (Gurprit S.),
1954-
HF5415.12.D44M37   1984    381'.09172'4      84-15149
ISBN 0-312-51531-6

# CONTENTS

iii

# FIGURES

# TABLES

*To B.A. Nilausen*

# FOREWORD

Philip Kotler

A recent issue of *The Economist* carried the following advertisement: 'Postgraduate Diploma & M. Com. Degree in Marketing for Industrialising Countries.' The ad went on to read:

> For the third year, we offer two postgraduate instructional courses in marketing specifically developed and designed for students from the industrializing countries of the Third World. We recognize that planners in such countries (a) wish to protect their country's future standard of living by reducing dependence on the extraction and export of raw materials, and see the acquisition of marketing skills as an essential prerequisite for developing a viable, modern commercial sector (b) wish to achieve these aims with the minimum of damage to culture and traditions.[1]

The nine-month program is sponsored by the University of Strathclyde in Glasgow, Scotland.

This may be the only program of its kind today. At other universities we will occasionally discover single courses devoted to 'marketing in economic development', or find that several sessions of the standard course on international marketing may be devoted to 'Third World countries'. But the University of Strathclyde is the first to offer a nine-month program of concentration in this area. We will certainly see more courses of this kind offered in the years to come.

It has been two decades since Drucker[2] and Rostow[3] wrote their classic articles singling out marketing as a major force for economic change in the developing countries. Yet most business people and government officials in developing countries know little about marketing. Economic planning decisions are made largely by government economists who know little about marketing. Their assumptions about economic behavior are too simplistic to guide national economic planning. And company business planning in these countries suffers from too much product-and-production orientation.

Marketing skills played a major role in helping today's leading economies arrive at their current levels of development. Among the most important factors in the growth of the US economy have been the large number of 'frontier' entrepreneurs, the large pool of ambitious sales-people, the extensive use of advertising media to promote products and services, the mass use of credit permitting people to buy more than their incomes would allow, and so on. Many of these institutions were copied in Japan after Admiral Perry opened trade with Japan a little more than one hundred years ago; and the Japanese government played a crucial role in selecting those industries that would spearhead Japan's drive toward world trade leadership.

Developing economies need to import modern marketing ideas; and marketing is the match that will ignite the economic takeoff. The government's role is crucial in this connection, and must play its four major roles – planner, facilitator, regulator and entrepreneur – in a way that demonstrates market-based thinking and action:

(1) As planner, the government must define where the developing economy should move in the world trade picture. Many developing economies are dependent on raw material exports and therefore sub-ject to volatile demand and price fluctuations. The government must search for value-adding opportunities so that the economy is less de-pendent upon world commodity prices. But the determination of at-tractive market opportunities requires careful marketing research and data analysis, and not simply reliance on broad economic statistics.

(2) As facilitator, the government needs to create and kindle entre-preneurial energy in the society. Substantial investments must be made in the infrastructure of education, health, transportation and communication. In addition, the government must develop export-promotion programs to encourage companies to undertake more exports. It must also initiate actions to modernize the wholesale and retail sectors of the economy.

(3) As regulator, the government must establish rules for fair deal-ings between business firms and their customers, and between business firms and each other. Yet the government should not over-regulate, for this would sap business drive and lead talented people to play 'safe' roles as bureaucrats rather than as risk-takers. The government should be liberal in its treatment of foreign multi-nationals, because these companies bring in marketing expertise, challenge inefficient competitors, innovate new products, and provide much energy for change.

(4) As entrepreneur, the government should determine those busi-nesses and industries which it will own and/or operate. One clear

arena for state enterprises are those industries that are basic but which private capital will not run or run well. Another arena is where state enterprises might increase competition in industries lacking a competitive spirit, and where prices are too high.

Thus government must create an environment in which entrepreneurship is developed, stimulated and rewarded. Once started, an entrepreneurial culture creates its own momentum. Eventually, less government is needed because the society has acquired built-in energy and capital that is not dependent on government initiative. This is the condition that allows the 'withering away of the state'.

Professor Kindra deserves praise for assembling this unique collection of original articles on the role of marketing in development. This book represents one of the first collections of its kind, and promises to whet one's appetite for further work in this area. The readings will be of interest to company executives and marketers, to government officials, and to economists and academics. While marketing is not a total panacea for successful economic development, it has a lot more to conribute than has so far been perceived.

## Notes

1. *The Economist*, 30 April 1983, p. 127.
2. Peter F. Drucker, 'Marketing and Economic Development', *Journal of Marketing*, January 1958, pp. 252–9.
3. Walt. W. Rostow, 'The Concept of a National Market and its Economic Growth Implications', in Peter D. Bennett (ed.), *Marketing and Economic Development*, American Marketing Association, Chicago, 1965, pp. 11–20.

# PREFACE

It has often been mentioned by academic faculties in developing countries that textbooks, readings and cases used in their courses are of Western origin; that the usefulness of such material is limited in scope, particularly when colleges and universities are increasingly pressurized by their respective governments and societies to emphasize issues and problems that relate directly to local needs and aspirations. My contact with management executives in one such country, Sri Lanka, also indicated a dire need for 'localized' material for the practical use of managers in the markets of their domain.

The lack of marketing vitality in developing countries results from misconceptions regarding its nature and application. That marketing can play a stimulative role in economic and social development by promoting social goals such as birth control, education, investment, hygiene, etc., needs to be communicated to students, managers and bureaucrats of developing countries. The prevalent image of marketing in these countries, one of a wasteful, parasitic and socially irrelevant activity, must be corrected with arguments and examples.

All chapters in this book, therefore, strive to meet the dual objective of establishing the role of marketing in the development of aspiring societies, and providing relevant reading material for the student of marketing in developing countries. Furthermore, the book provides an excellent insight for Western communities interested in understanding the Third World perspective.

The concepts of 'underdeveloped', 'less developed', or 'Third World' are used interchangeably in this book. All such notations, in various chapters, apply to countries that are dependent on the West for industrial and technological know-how, and whose inhabitants desire the facilities and comforts of modern life.

I take this opportunity to express my gratitude to all of the contributors to this book. I also wish to thank Peter Sowden of Croom Helm, Publishers, London, for his diligent efforts in producing this book.

My special thanks are due to Professor Philip Kotler of Northwestern University for his continued support and inspiration.

Thanks are extended to Louise Moreau, Irene Turmel, Diane Fontaine and others at the University of Ottawa faculty secretarial staff for their ever cheerful assistance.

As student and teacher of marketing, I am pleased to bring together this unique collection of papers as a contribution to the modern literature on international marketing.

G.S. Kindra
University of Ottawa

# 1 INTRODUCTION: MARKETING IN DEVELOPING COUNTRIES

## G.S. Kindra

In this introductory chapter we attempt to establish the rationale for this book, and provide summaries of the various chapters.

In the world of the 1980s the developing nations aspire, more than ever, for economic growth and better standards of living. Although economic development is normally associated with increases in *per capita* income, for the purpose of this book it includes social advancements as well. Emphasis on intrinsic and aesthetic values, the existence of (relative) leisure, the elimination of drudgery, and a marked reduction in interreligious, interethnic and intercaste friction are some outcomes envisaged within the realm of development.

In most less developed countries (LDCs) today there is a general dissatisfaction with growth models based on capital formation and productivity improvements. An increasing number of such nations are tacitly recognizing the link between marketing and development. More importantly, perhaps, international aid organizations are actively encouraging programs based on demand-manipulation. This appears to be done under the assumption that increased consumption will lead to higher employment and thus aggregate incomes — resulting in further increases in consumption as well as investment. (The desired level of savings and investment could be finetuned by employing marketing or demarketing.) The Canadian International Development Agency (CIDA) and the Agency for International Aid have funded a number of such research and training programs in several countries. Sri Lanka, the small island-nation of South Asia is currently benefiting from one such program sponsored by CIDA. The editor, during a recent assignment in that country, found a keen awareness among the senior managers in the private and public sectors, of the potential role of marketing in the development of their key industries.

Chapters 2, 3 and 4 shed light on the validity of assumptions underlying demand-manipulation aid programs. In doing so, these chapters have explored in depth the link between marketing and economic development.

In Chapter 2 Dr Nikhilesh Dholakia presents the reader with a broad,

1

analytic view of the future of marketing in LDCs and its impact on the world system as a whole. The purpose of his article is to highlight the alternative developmental options available to LDCs and to analyze the nature of the marketing system under each development strategy. Dholakia's argument is organized along the following steps:

(1) *The LDCs of the Future*
(2) *The Future of the LDCs*
(3) *Marketing in the LDCs*
(4) *Future of Marketing in LDCs*
(5) *Implications for the World System*

Arguing that LDCs are contemporaneous with the developed world (and not at a lower 'stage' of development), Dholakia suggests that LDCs are not forever playing 'catch up' with the marketing system of the developed world — even though selected indicators may be interpreted in this way. It means that LDC marketing systems face challenges and problems that will not be resolved by economic growth alone. Whichever model of development a country follows — be it miracle export, autonomous growth, or the minor world model — fresh perspective will be needed to foster appropriate marketing systems for LDCs.

In Chapter 3 Dr Hamid Etemad starts by examining the reasons as to why marketing remains badly neglected in the development process. He suggests that marketing has a potent role to play in economic development, and puts forward a process of organizing for more efficient and accelerated development in which user's satisfaction and value play a central role.

Etemad argues that if the evolutionary path of marketing management practices in the highly developed countries has any bearing on the problem of economic development, it must be the movement from supply-side orientation to demand and marketing orientation, and finally to a strategic orientation which combines all influential elements including demand and supply. In short, the outmoded supply-and-production oriented, inward-directed model of economic development should be combined selectively, and eventually replaced by outward, strategic, and demand-manipulation oriented strategies. A model for economic development with the latter orientations is proposed and its policy implications examined.

Chapter 4 attempts to build bridges between marketing and the emerging meanings and strategies of development. This chapter is structured into the following major sections:

(1) *Aspects of Marketing* Marketing broken down into component aspects for the purpose of relating these to development.
(2) *Views of Development* Exploration of the alternative meanings and concepts of development.
(3) *Theories of Development* Examination of theories as to what causes development or underdevelopment.
(4) *Agent of Development* The question of which agency should play what role in the process of development.

The authors suggest that in the years to come development is likely to become the top item on the global agenda — not because of the Malthusian spectre of hungry teeming millions, as was once widely believed — but because of the realization that the problems of development — stagnation, poverty, environmental decay, alienation, cultural homogenization, inequity, unresponsive institutions, etc. — are not just problems of the Third World alone. Within this context, marketing people should evolve alternative marketing concepts suitable for the variety of development trajectories found in the world of today.

Today countries like India, China, Egypt and Brazil are gaining cognizance of the fact that marketing has a key role to play in the advancement of social programs relating to family planning, adult education, hygiene, etc. However, trained personnel are lacking, and the very idea of how marketing can help needs to be communicated to the various responsible groups and individuals. (China has recently concluded a long-term agreement with Canada on the transfer of knowledge in various areas, including marketing.)

The trading field is generally recognized as the breeding ground for entrepreneurs. In the West these risk-takers played an important role in the creation of necessary conditions for the industrial revolution. Also, studies of industrialists in LDCs indicate that a large majority of them moved from various trading occupations (Moyer and Hutt, 1978). But this move is the result of a general dislike of the trading class in many LDCs. Therefore, although marketing helps create the necessary entrepreneur class, the educators in LDCs are constantly faced with the difficult task of eliminating the stigma and misconceptions related to marketing, and of training potential risk-takers to direct the transition from agriculture to industry.

In the second section of the book five chapters provide suggestions, examples and models for marketing action in the Third World. In

Chapter 5 Professors Mahmoud and Rice discuss the problems of marketing in Egypt and focus on selected environmental issues such as economic conditions, bureaucratic problems, demographic characteristics, the infrastructure and the socio-cultural context. While Egypt is typical of many developing countries and is therefore usefully employed as an example, the paper indicates the idiosyncrasies in Egypt's environment that are of particular interest to marketers. The authors also provide an extensive list of possible solutions to various problems encountered by multinational marketers in Egypt. They conclude that the difficulty of marketing in Egypt is in recognizing the problems; dealing with the problems is an easier task. The success of the multinational marketer, therefore, will be measured by his/her ability to appreciate environmental differences and to adopt geocentric policies.

In Chapter 6 Professor Hung provides the reader with a fascinating example of how history, geography, topography, demography, government policies and political conditions interact to shape the marketing environment of a country. The first section of this chapter provides a brief historical account of the Hong Kong economy and its industrialization in the postwar years; and this is followed by an examination of the present industrial structure. The last part of the chapter deals with a survey of the marketing-related perceptions of foreign manufacturers operating in Hong Kong and a discussion of the important market characteristics.

Professor Hung also delves into the future of the economic miracle of Hong Kong, and suggests that although Britain may retain Victoria Island and the Kowloon Peninsula, the possible loss of the New Territories after 1997 will have far reaching implications.

Chapter 7, by Professor Françoise Simon-Miller, looks at the African market, and develops the idea of syncretic marketing practices which incorporate some Western-type products without using them as perfect substitutes for local African goods. Focusing on Ivory Coast and Nigeria, the author provides several examples of how present marketing practices of local as well as foreign-owned firms, might be modified to ensure a balanced Afro-centric approach that leads to psycho-cultural compatibility. Artificial market-control methods should be gradually abandoned in favor of decentralized development which would lead to better integration of the dual African economy. Simon-Miller goes on to point out that widespread dysfunctions in the present consumption patterns will be minimized through increased flexibility and efficiency in price, product and promotional planning.

Dr Ruby Roy Dholakia, in Chapter 8, looks at the alternate views of man for designing strategies that seek to influence and control human behavior. The various assumptions of program designers reflect their belief about why individuals should conform, and how they can be made to conform. She suggests that the view of man as *Homo consumens* can be used to explain consumption-enhancing activities of traditional marketing programs.

While relevant research is sparse, it is possible to identify five models of man that can be used to develop family-planning programs. The author has assembled these models from a consideration of individual, social and cultural influences on family-planning behavior. Labelled the macro, social, rational, risk-aversive, and psychoanalytic model of man, each of these views differ on their reasons for holding a particular position on family planning. While there can be considerable overlap in the traditional socio-economic characteristics of these models, their interaction creates a set of motivations that determine family-planning behavior.

Drawing on the models of man approach in Chapter 9, Kindra, Dholakia and Pangotra further explore the process of marketing birth control in LDCs, and shed light on the possible role of the public sector in the process. They suggest that six courses of action are open to any LDC in response to its population problems: (1) to do nothing; (2) to employ a mass-communication strategy; (3) to provide services directly; (4) to manipulate the balances of incentives and disincentives; (5) to shift the weight of social institutions and opportunities; and (6) to coerce behavior-modification through various forms of direct sanctions. Looking specifically at the family-planning program in India, the authors provide insight into some of the reasons for the relatively disappointing performance of the program. By focusing on India, where the public sector has been involved with the largest and the oldest family-planning program in the world, various conflicts and problems common to most LDCs are brought out. Kindra *et al.* suggest that a marketing-management approach to the task of family planning is necessary for improvements in program performance. One approach to the management of birth-control marketing is discussed under the so-called Sketch Plan framework. This approach is based on the recognition that acceptance of a small family norm is interwoven with the freedom to make that choice. This is an important point because even though segments of the LDC population will accept the small-family concept, they are often deprived of the means and objective motivation for accomplishing the same. The suggested framework for planning the marketing of birth control in LDCs emphasizes that strategies be aimed at the three-dimensional goal of increasing the population's desire, ability and capability toward acceptance of the small-family norm and the practice of birth control. It is also implied that, in consideration of the wide geographical variations in population growth, *per capita* income and the level of development in general programs should be designed in a segmented manner to suit the nature of each group.

It is estimated that in India, while the Green Revolution has produced a grain surplus, up to 10 percent of the output is lost to rodents and spoilage, while the consumer often spends 50 percent of his income on food. A fully developed system of distribution that efficiently matches consumer needs with production should eventually lower costs and thus the price paid by the consumer — thereby freeing more discretionary income for pursuits like education, hygiene, and even leisure.

The development of an efficient distribution system, by necessity, will bring about a more reliable communication system, which in turn will facilitate social intercourse and efficient exchange of views among the geographically dispersed channel members. This is the starting point of a developmental process whereby interreligious, intercaste and interethnic frictions will give way to a dialogue of mutual interest and understanding.

A well-developed macro-marketing system also instills a sense of purpose and ethics. In many LDCs it is fairly common practice for small businessmen — be it a clothing merchant, fruitseller or any street hawker — to cheat in relation to quality, quantity and price standard. The editor encountered a reticent fishmonger in Sri Lanka who, upon being discovered in tipping the scales variously with his arm and toes, simply refused to conduct a fair exchange. Any economy needs standards of ethics and integrity if it is to thrive. In an environment where humanity is too preoccupied with daily existence to worry about workmanship, marketing can create a sense of business norms and the rightness and wrongness of commercial actions.

Chapters 10 to 14 make up the third and final section, and this part of the book is more analytical in nature — with implications for government planners, business educators and operating multinationals. Chapter 10 discusses the critical task of marketing education in the Third World, stresses the need for modifications of marketing-course content, and makes recommendations to the educators. Highlighting the fallacy of the assumption that essentially North American marketing ideas can be readily transplanted into the LDC environment, Professors Ross and McTavish suggest that the 'similar path' model of development is a misrepresentation of reality, based as it is on the questionable assumption that LDCs are evolving and will continue to evolve in the same manner as developed countries.

The three important dimensions of marketing are micro/macro, profit sector/non-profit sector, and positive/normative. From the viewpoint of the Third World marketing educator, it will be useful to know how and to what extent each element of the three-dimensional model of marketing applies. Are the macro-marketing concerns broadly similar to those found in the developed world, or are there important differences? What are the special problems of non-profit-sector marketing, or of the individual entrepreneur?

These and similar issues are examined in detail. It is argued, for example, that the educator must try to strive for an understanding of why certain practices and institutions exist, before evaluating their usefulness for marketing. The educator must recognize that the basic orientation of marketing revolves around consumer satisfaction — against a background of strong state involvement. Making a strong case for product adaptation in the content of marketing education in LDCs, the authors extend several recommendations to the educator.

The chapter concludes by observing that a great deal of product adaptation, market knowledge, and customer sensitivity is required — particularly because the yardstick of profitability is not the only measure used to gauge the performance of companies.

Professors Jorgenson, Hafsi and Kiggundu, focusing on the five major types of firms in LDCs in Chapter 11, explore the issue of market imperfections and its implications for multinationals as well as LDC-based firms. In developing economies, the authors point out, one finds imperfect markets and thin organizational networks. The number of organizations is small relative to total population, and the distribution (of organizations) is highly skewed toward many small-size firms, few medium-size organizations, and a very few large foreign and state-owned organizations. Is size related to change? Are structural types related to growth and development? Is centralization desirable over decentralized firms in LDCs? These and similar issues are examined in this chapter. Jorgensen *et al.* also look at various catalysts of organizational change and examine the nature of their effect. They begin by outlining the more general catalysts that affect all organizations, and conclude by discussing structural change within specific types of organizations.

In Chapter 12 Etemad develops a general model of comparative marketing. Features of this model are discussed in detail, and shortcomings of descriptive marketing (which covers most of the past literature on comparative marketing) are pointed out. To further explore the implications of the model, two examples are analyzed. The author also provides the reader with a comprehensive review of comparative marketing literature from a historical and methodological perspective.

A major contribution of this chapter lies in its elucidation of a concise statement of comparative marketing which can be used as a model for carrying out 'comparative analysis'. Etemad suggests careful decomposition of marketing and marketing environments into their components at different levels of analysis. A statement of environmentalism must be established (between the marketing and marketing-environment component) before any 'comparative analysis' is carried out. This is necessary because a contextual or environmentally adapted marketing strategy stands a greater chance of success than does a marketing program that has not fully absorbed these effects. This assumes an even greater importance in international marketing, where the contextual effects of a foreign environment can play a critical role in the success or failure of a multinational.

Maheswaran's Chapter 13 explores the phenomenon of state enterprises – from a marketing perspective. The author looks at various rationales for the existence of a state-owned enterprise (SOE), and provides a useful classification of SOEs. Examining the cases of Korea, Venezuela, Cyprus, Malaysia, Sri Lanka, Bangla Desh, India and Indonesia, the author examines the extent of SOE participation in the economic development of those countries.

SOEs have been set up for a variety of reasons including economic, political and motivational. The marketing policies and procedures of these organizations are likely to vary according to the type of industry and the nature of its competition. A SOE operating under monopolistic conditions, for example, will adopt a pricing policy based on objectives other than competitive parity or brand loyalty. Essentially, the marketing strategies of SOEs will be determined by the nature of competition and the priority of social versus commercial objectives. Marketing strategies for both monopoly and competition-oriented SOEs are examined under conditions of social orientation as well as commercial orientation.

The final chapter, 14, by Kaynak is useful because it looks at the current problems of marketing research in LDCs, and provides suggestions and ideas on how to effectively conduct the same in the Third World environment.

The author develops the argument that marketing research has an important role to play in LDCs. Yet for these countries there are socio-logical, psychological, cultural and technical complexities involved that make the process challenging and complicated.

In summary, the book examines the role of marketing from a descriptive as well as a prescriptive aspect. The role of marketing in the economic development of an aspiring society is established in the first section of this book. The five chapters which comprise the second part look at various examples and models of marketing action in LDCs — focusing particularly on Egypt, India, Hong Kong and Africa. The issue of family planning is also examined in detail from a marketing perspec-tive. The third section examines the critical role of marketing education in LDCs, provides guidelines on conducting effective marketing re-search, and examines state-owned enterprises from a marketing per-spective. This final section also develops a formal model of comparative marketing, and provides important insights into the theory of market imperfections and organizational structures in LDCs.

## Reference

Moyer, R. and Hutt, M. *Macromarketing*, John Wiley & Sons, New York, 1978, pp. 11–14

# 2 MARKETING IN LESS DEVELOPED COUNTRIES: ITS NATURE AND PROSPECTS

Nikhilesh Dholakia

Marketing — concepts, practices, institutions — has been so dominantly a Western phenomenon, in fact for the most part an American phenomenon, that the discussion of marketing in underdeveloped areas is at best a peripheral concern in mainstream marketing. If we are concerned, however, about the future of the world system, then such a peripheral view is disastrous. This is because the less developed countries of the Third World represent the 'underdeveloped' frontier — in terms of consumption patterns, natural resources, human resources, industrialization, technology and environment. The wherewithals for growth and development, as well as the avenues for growth and development, are likely to be found increasingly in the LDCs. How the LDCs should develop is likely to be one of the hottest political issues in the next century.[1] The future of not only the LDCs but the entire world system would depend on the trajectory of development that the LDCs take. This is not because the LDCs are politically and economically central in world affairs. Rather, it is because the problems are so immense and the prospects are so dim that the concerns of the LDCs would force their way to the top of the global agenda, sooner or later.

The debates regarding the LDCs are carried on along well-known economic, political and social dimensions — trade, investment, aid, materials, technology, growth, equity, autonomy, ecology, needs, etc. Marketing plays a major or minor role in all these dimensions. Yet, *marketing issues* receive scant attention in discussions on world order (United Nations, 1980; Dholakia and Dholakia, 1982) and development strategy (Hilger, 1977; Etemad, 1982). This paper presents a broad, analytic view of the future of marketing in the LDCs and its impact on the world system as a whole. Its purpose is to highlight the alternative developmental options available to LDCs, and to analyze the nature of the marketing system under each development strategy. The argument is organized along the following steps:

(1) *The LDCs of the Future* Which countries will be the LDCs of the future? Will the composition of the LDC bloc change significantly in

10

the near future?

(2) *The Future of the LDCs* What will be their character? What are the dominant characteristics of LDCs today? Are these likely to persist?

(3) *Marketing in the LDCs* What form does marketing in LDCs take?

(4) *Future of Marketing in the LDCs* What developmental trajectories are the marketing systems in the LDCs likely to take? What options are available and what forces will shape the choices?[2]

(5) *Implications for the World System* How would choices of marketing systems in the LDCs affect the rest of the world? What policies should the developed countries follow with respect to marketing in LDCs?

The perspective of this paper is future-oriented in the sense of investigating tendencies, possibilities and options. The paper eschews the temptation, however, to make speculative, crystal-ball predictions. The emphasis is on relationships — past and emerging — which would influence the future of LDC marketing.

## Main Characteristics of LDCs

Lack of development in the LDCs is reflected in low incomes, poverty, illiteracy, poor health, inefficient industry and agriculture, non-existent social security, cultural atrophy, social anomalies, low political participation, onerous bureaucracy and several other deficiencies (for a classic study, see Adelman and Morris, 1973). Conventional development economics has long held these conditions to be a 'state' or 'phase' to be overcome (Rostow, 1978). The development problem is one of getting the growth engine started — and then things take care of themselves. In recent years this view has broken down, not so much because of critiques from more 'planning'-oriented economists (Myrdal, 1970; Bauer, 1972), but because of its invalidation by the stark reality of the LDCs (Nugent and Yotopoulos, 1979). It is being grudgingly recognized, even by Western-dominated international agencies (World Bank, 1975), that critical political economic analysis often provides clearer insights into the nature of underdevelopment. Using such analysis and examining several economic indices Weisskopf (1972) finds that underdevelopment in the contemporary LDCs is reflected in and associated with:

- Large gap between developed countries and LDCs (Donges, 1977).
- Much worse internal income distribution in LDCs in comparison to developed countries (Adelman and Morris, 1973).

• Dependence on few export goods, mainly primary commodities, for foreign-exchange earnings.
• Persistent dualism — large pre-capitalist sectors coexisting with modern sectors.
• Political and economic power concentrated in a small, cohesive elite.
• Local capitalists and governments highly dependent on developed-country counterparts.

In summary, the LDCs are not at a lower stage of development — they are contemporaneous with the developed world but in a dependent way (Frank, 1979; Sunkel, 1979). If we accept this proposition then there is an important point of departure as far as analysis of marketing systems is concerned. It implies that LDCs are not forever playing 'catch up' with the marketing systems of developed countries, even though selected indicators may be interpretable in this way. It means LDC marketing systems face challenges and problems that will not be resolved by economic growth alone. Fresh perspective will be needed to foster appropriate marketing systems for LDCs.

## LDCs of the Future

At present most of the world's countries and most of the world's people are in the LDCs (Ward, 1962; Myrdal, 1970; Colman and Nixson, 1978). Is the composition of this group of countries likely to be any different as we enter the twenty-first century? There are many reasons to believe that this would not be the case:

(1) Large gaps exist between developed countries and the LDCs. Fritsch (1978) cites the following ratios between developed countries and the LDCs: *per capita* income 30 : 1, energy consumption 10 : 1, R and D expenditure 300 : 1. The inequalities between developed countries and LDCs have been growing in the recent past (Weisskopf, 1972; Shilling and Carter, 1978). Even if LDCs grew at somewhat higher rates than developed countries, a large gap would persist at the turn of the century (Pajestka, 1972).
(2) Development is a multidimensional concept (Seers, 1970; Hunter, 1971). Not only several economic variables but many social, cultural, and political variables are involved in the process of 'development' (Adelman and Morris, 1973). Hence, even if some LDCs (such as a few OPEC nations) managed to reach developed-country levels on a few

dimensions (e.g. *per capita* income), it is unlikely that they would achieve a comprehensive developmental profile corresponding to the developed world.[3]

(3) Recent history shows that the time frame for comprehensive development is rather long — spanning several decades if not centuries. This is borne out by the experience of the USSR, Japan, and a handful of other countries which have managed the transition from underdevelopment to development in the first half of this century. By the commencement of the next century, it would be surprising if even half a dozen more countries make this transition.

The membership, composition and relative status of the LDC bloc, therefore, are unlikely to change in the near future. For marketing, this implies that 'LDC marketing' is likely to be a persistent, significant and widespread phenomenon. It cannot be ignored, nor brushed aside as an antiquated form of marketing, on the basis of deterministic growth-stage theories (Baran and Hobsbawm, 1961). We can safely assume that LDC marketing will continue to be distinct from marketing in the developed countries, well into the twenty-first century.

**Future of the LDCs**

Although the composition of the LDC bloc may not change in the near future, its nature (economic, social, political, etc.) certainly will. While it is easy to visualize the future *composition* of this group of nations, it is extremely difficult to foresee the forms that the economies, societies and politics of the LDCs will assume. This is because critical choices face the LDCs regarding developmental stategies (Pajestka, 1972; Miles, Cole and Gershuny, 1978; Amin, 1979; Galtung, 1979). The criteria for such choices are being constantly debated (Donges, 1977; Miles, Cole and Gershuny, 1978; Evans, 1979; Sebastien, 1979), and the pressures to sway LDCs in different directions are numerous (Weisskopf, 1972; Hansen, 1979). Given these complexities, it is useful to structure the analysis as follows:

(1) Extrapolation of tendencies, assuming *status quo* conditions prevail.
(2) Exploration of alternative development strategies.

*Extrapolating Status Quo*

What future can be expected for the LDCs assuming business-as-usual or *status quo* conditions? Weisskopf (1972) finds three disturbing trends:

(1) Increasing subordination of LDCs to the corporations and governments of the developed Western world (see also Colman and Nixson, 1978; Chs. 9 and 10).
(2) Increasing internal inequality within most LDCs (Adelman and Morris, 1973).
(3) Inadequate growth because of resource mobilization and utilization problems.

In spite of ideological differences, scholars of varying persuasion agree that things look bleak for the LDCs when *status quo* conditions are simply extrapolated (Cole, 1978; Galtung, 1979). This gives rise to what Pajestka (1972) calls the 'impossibility hypothesis' − things cannot continue for the LDCs in this dismal way without endangering world peace. Something must give.

*Alternative Development Models*

Assuming that avoiding devastating conflicts is a global goal, it can be surmised that LDCs as well as other countries would desperately look for alternative development strategies. At least three alternative strategies to *status quo* are possible:

(1) The miracle export model: some countries would try to emulate the strategy of Taiwan and South Korea and become export bases for the developed nations. This so-called East Asian model (Cline, 1982) is popular among the Asian countries and is being tried also in LDCs elsewhere.
(2) The autonomous development model: variously called the non-capitalist model (Weisskopf, 1972), the autonomous model (Amin, 1979), the socialist model (Pajestka, 1972). The basic features of this model are disengagement from the world capitalist system (Morehouse, 1979), reliance on appropriate technologies (Sebastien, 1979), and collective self-reliance by the Third World countries (Hveem, 1978; Floto, 1980). Countries like Cuba, Yugoslavia, Vietnam, Algeria, Tanzania and North Korea have tried this model for some time − with mixed results. Several new emerging nations or revolutionary regimes − Angola, Mozambique, Nicaragua, Zimbabwe − may also be attracted to it.[4]
(3) The minor world model: some countries with large industrial bases (e.g. Brazil, India) would try to emerge as regional economic powers. This model is obviously open only to those countries which can take advantage of their large industrial base and market size. In practice,

Table 2.1: Three Development Models: Alternatives to *Status Quo*

| Model | Examples/Likely examples | Main advantages | Main disadvantages | Conditions favoring adoption |
|---|---|---|---|---|
| *Miracle exporter* | South Korea, Taiwan, Singapore, Hong Kong, Sri Lanka | Rapid export growth<br><br>Rapid transfer of technologies that are becoming unprofitable in high-wage countries<br>High levels of investment by transnational corporations | High dependency on developed market economies<br><br>Lop-sided growth: urban consumer goods oriented, exports set priorities | Developed industrial base, workforce<br><br>High political economic integration with Western markets<br><br>Mobilizative, authoritarian regime |
| *Autonomous* | Cuba, Yugoslavia, Vietnam, North Korea, Algeria | Autonomous developmental goals<br>Attempts towards balanced, equitable development<br>Mutual assistance among such countries | Risk of isolation from world<br><br>Risk of lagging in technology<br><br>Likely dependence on Soviet bloc | Revolutionary and mobilizative ethos<br>Decentralized political and economic system<br>Capabilities in appropriate technologies<br>Widespread education |
| *Regional power* | Brazil, India, China | Relative regional dominance<br><br>Relative autonomy of developmental policy<br>Fairly diversified economic system | Moderate to high dependency on developed market economies<br>Geopolitical conflicts likely<br>Likelihood of becoming 'second class' industrially and technically | Large country size and domestic market<br>Large and diversified industrial base<br>Military strength<br>Independent scientific and technical capabilities |

the strategy would either lean towards export-led growth or towards autonomous development.

Table 2.1 summarizes these development models which constitute alternatives to the continuation of *status quo*. The table presents the characteristics of such models and conditions favoring the adoption of such models.

It is reasonable to expect that by the turn of the century sufficient numbers of LDCs would have chosen development strategies considerably different from the currently dominant ones. In other words, these models would have significant numbers of adherents to make each model a competing developmental system with its particular set of priorities, internal structures and processes, and external relations. Superimposed on economic dualism (unlikely to disappear in most countries), these alternatives models would present highly complex business environments. For example, a country may adopt a 'miracle export' strategy for its urban-industrial sector, but favor an autonomous, self-reliant strategy for its rural sector.[5] Analytical and practical challenges to marketing in countries following these different models of development can be expected to be formidable.

## Nature of Marketing in the LDCs

Whatever developmental trajectory an LDC takes, its marketing system will be affected by it. Any discussion of the future of LDC marketing systems, therefore, must take into account the developmental strategy as well as the present nature of marketing.

Scholars who have examined marketing in the developing world have been influenced by orthodox development economics and particularly by the 'stages-of-development' view (Rostow, 1978). Thus, they have commented on the emergence of particular institutional forms and marketing processes at certain stages of development (Moyer, 1964; Slater, 1968; Douglas, 1971; Arndt, 1972). While the emergence of supermarkets, department stores, containerized transport, broadcast advertising, etc. are empirically valid facts, these do not constitute sequential stages of development. Such a linear view of development of marketing systems ignores the fact that the LDCs have started from a different base from the developed countries, have usually experienced long periods of foreign domination, and have followed economic development paths quite different from those followed by the advanced market economies (Etemad, 1981).

The orthodox development theory has been widely challenged and often invalidated (Nugent, 1979). There is, however, too little questioning of the traditional views of marketing and development (for exceptions, see Goldman, 1974, 1975; Hilger, 1977). It can be assumed, however, that LDC marketing systems exhibit dependent, inequitable and stagnant characteristics similar to LDC economies in general. Parallel to the features of underdeveloped economies identified by Weisskopf (1972) and others (e.g. Griffin, 1969; Dos Santos, 1973; Frank, 1979; Furtado, 1979), the marketing systems of LDCs are characterized by:

(1) *Development Gaps* Throughputs, service levels, institutions, etc. of LDC marketing systems lag behind those of the developed countries by substantial factors (Arndt, 1972; Bandhari and Vora, 1979). The average retail store in Iran, for example, employed less than two people and had an annual sales of about $11,000, compared to employment of over five people and sales of over $80,000 for the average British retail store (United Nations, (1979), Table 146).

(2) *Lack of Equity* Marketing institutions are highly inequitable in the services provided and prices charged to low-income and high-income consumers (Goldman, 1974; Bandhari and Vora, 1979). In India, for example, there are less than two drugstores for 1,000 rural people compared to almost twenty per 1,000 urbanities (Bandhari and Vora, 1979).

(3) *Non-diversified Exports* International marketing expertize and/or manufacturing capabilities are lacking to develop a diversified export base. East Asian exceptions apart, the LDCs essentially remain suppliers of primary commodities, trade terms for many of which are deteriorating or highly fluctuating (Hassan, 1978; United Nations, 1979). In those few countries where industrial exports have expanded, a heavy price has been paid in terms of political and economic dependence on powerful buyers (Bennett and Sharpe, 1979; Wynn, 1982). Also, a few low-technology goods dominate the manufactured exports of LDCs, with textiles accounting for about 30 percent (United Nations, 1980, p. 1130).

(4) *Persistent Dualism* Large sectors of the economy remain 'non-marketized' in the sense of being outside market systems. When 'markets' are interpreted broadly to include social services such as health and education, substantial rural sectors of the LDCs are simply not touched by such service delivery systems (Dholakia and Firat,

1975). Also, in the conventional economic sectors, pre-capitalist institutional forms proliferate in the rural areas. For example, the larger village merchant is typically a retailer of urban manufactured goods, a purchaser of rural output, and a moneylender to rural enterprises, all combined into one person (Khurana, Balakrishnan, Dholakia and Moulik, 1981). Interestingly, the remotest pre-capitalist rural enclaves are efficiently linked to the major urban trading centers for purposes of commodity exports or expanding the markets for urban manufacturers. Dualism, therefore, is selective — it is quickly overcome when integration into world markets is desired by the powerful domestic or transnational firms.

(5) *Monopolistic Power* Market concentration and brand dominance are even more pronounced in the LDCs than in the developed countries. In most manufactured goods, foreign brands or local brands with foreign collaboration are dominant, often having near monopoly. For non-branded commodities, powerful wholesalers dominate the system. In Indonesia, for example, fresh-produce trades are dominated by large wholesalers who, although numerous, are cohesive because of kinship ties.

(6) *Dependent Structures* Any institution which practices or preaches modern marketing is heavily independent on Western counterparts. Subsidiaries of transnational corporations, affiliates of transnational corporations, advertizing agencies, consulting firms, business schools, etc. engage in heavy borrowing of marketing tools and concepts. The traditional institutions (such as indigenous wholesalers or media), which have outdated but 'appropriate' marketing technologies, are heavily dependent on foreign-controlled or assisted markets for goods and marketing services. In agricultural trade, international aid agencies such as the World Bank often exercise decisive influence because they assist in agricultural development projects. This is also true for the service sector — for example, the significant foreign involvement in family-planning services in LDCs.

The picture that emerges, therefore, is not of a 'lagged' marketing system which is merely trying to 'catch up'. It is the picture of a complexly developed and dependent marketing system which thrives on inequity and lacks impulses for self-sustained development. Such marketing systems have been resilient, adaptive to economic conditions, and even fairly low-cost in performing their marketing functions (Sorenson, 1978; Bandhari and Vora, 1979). These systems have been generally incapable, however, of bringing about major innovations in products, customer services, marketing methods, communications media, or market-research techniques. In most cases the indigenous marketing systems of the LDCs have not been able to come up with market expansionary strategies, either domestically or internationally. Thus, the typical LDC marketing system merely performs a system maintenance function — it can neither spur rapid economic development, as some marketing scholars advocate (Etemad, 1982), nor generate appropriate products and services that would benefit the mass of population (Sen Gupta, 1975).

## The Future of Marketing in the LDCs

Since the LDC marketing systems reflect, and to some extent influence, the general character of LDC economies, the future of such marketing systems would naturally be tied to the future of these economies. If the current situation were merely extrapolated, an intensification of *status quo* conditions would be observed. Specifically, with respect to marketing, one is likely to observe:

(1) *Increasing Dependence* In the manufacturing sectors of Third World countries, foreign influence is already high and can be expected to increase further (Colman and Nixson, 1978, Ch. 9). The twin tendencies of: (a) choice of Western technologies, and (b) emulation of Western consumption patterns, ensure that marketing systems for manufactured goods are modeled after, and dependent on, the Western marketing systems. The trading structure, however, is much more resistant to foreign influence than the manufacturing system. The experience of some Latin American countries and certain South East Asian countries — which have been under greater Western influence than the rest of the LDCs — shows that foreign distributional forms do eventually penetrate the market (Slater, 1968). American retail chains and franchises have entered these markets. In most of Asia and Africa, however, trade is traditional and proprietary (see, for example, Sorensen, 1978). These represent a natural expansionary frontier for the corporate retailing firms of the Western world. Under *status quo* assumptions, penetration of foreign capital in the distributive sector would increase, and so would the dependence of LDC marketing systems. Similar developments can be expected with respect to advertising, market research, new products, new technologies, and new managerial techniques.

(2) *Increasing Inequality* In Latin American countries, the contrast between modern, affluent, urban, marketing structures and traditional, poor, rural marketing structures is very sharp. The contrast, though great in absolute terms, is not as sharp in the relatively underdeveloped countries of Asia and Africa.[6] To the extent Latin America projects the image of the future for many Asian and African marketing systems, greater inequalities in urban versus rural distribution can be expected (Dholakia and Dholakia, 1978). The intensification of inequality is observable in other aspects of marketing as well. In India, for example, print advertising directed at an affluent urban minority is getting increasingly intense and sophisticated, although literacy rates and print-media circulations remain abysmally low. There is, thus, a widening gap between the marketing system that serves the rich urbanites and the one that serves the rural poor (Sen Gupta, 1975).

(3) *Continuing Stagnation* Marketing systems in the Third World have been notoriously opportunistic — serving the proximate, high-margin, luxury-item consumers to the neglect of remote, low-margin, necessity-item consumers (Sen Gupta, 1975). Consumer-goods companies have attempted to expand distribution to rural areas only after 'green revolutions' have created a sizeable rural elite. In this way, marketing has responded — usually belatedly — to growth factors. It has rarely been the source of growth impulses. If anything, some marketers have been detractors of growth by frittering away resources in hoarding goods and in speculative activities. This passive, non-stimulative, stagnation-inducing role of marketing can be expected to continue under *status quo* assumptions.

The question is whether the LDCs would continue to tolerate *status quo* conditions, especially as the internal and external inequities continue to intensify. In some countries, the groups that stand to benefit from the *status quo* would try to maintain it. The continuation of dependent, inequitable and passive marketing systems might be tolerated or even encouraged. In many countries, however, the contradictions of such marketing systems would force changes. Just as alternative development strategies are being experimented with in the LDCs, so are alternative marketing institution and strategies being tried. Table 2.2 illustrates the match between alternative development strategies and alternative marketing systems. It shows that the countries opting for the 'miracle export' model would permit a large relatively unfettered role for foreign manufacturing and distributing companies. Those countries striving for 'regional power' status would attempt partial

Table 2.2: Relationships Between Developmental Strategies and Marketing

| Marketing system characteristics | 'Miracle export' model | Developmental strategy (alternative to *status quo*) | |
| --- | --- | --- | --- |
| | | 'Autonomous' model | 'Regional power' model |
| Integration into world market | Integration and dependence | Autonomous with selective links | Integration but regional dominance |
| Typical international marketing firm | Affiliate of TNC* from developed market economy | State trading co. or producer's marketing cooperatives | Local TNC – public or private |
| Typical domestic marketing firm | Affiliate of TNC from developed market economy | Public sector or self-managed companies | Local big corporation |
| Urban retail structure | Penetration of foreign chains, franchises | Consumer cooperative, state agencies, licensed private operators | Growth of local chains |
| Rural retail structure | Traditional outlets | Multipurpose cooperatives, state agencies | Traditional outlets, some cooperatives |
| Product policy | Importation of foreign products and technology | Appropriate technology, highly adapted products | Imitation and adaptation of foreign products, technology |
| Marketing communications | Promotion of foreign brands; culturally alien communication sources and situations | Mobilization, consumer education, product information, culturally relevant sources and situations | Protection and promotion of local brands |
| Media | Private – highly commercial | Most public – selectively commercial | Private and public – moderately commercial |
| Pricing | Relative freedom to set prices | Controls on the majority of products | Control on 'essential' products |

* TNC: Transnational Corporation

Table 2.3: Illustrative Marketing Strategy Differences for a Mass-consumption Item in Countries Adopting Two Distinctive Developmental Models

| Marketing strategy variable | Description of marketing strategy likely to be used in segments | |
|---|---|---|
| | Type A country | Type B country |
| Objective of market development efforts | For a given level of market development investment, maximize the net return to the firm | For a given level of market investment, maximize need satisfaction, subject to financial viability constraints for the firm |
| Basis for delineating market segments | Socio-economic status of consumers, response-sensitivity to marketing mix elements | Need for the type of product or service being marketed |
| Basis for selecting market segments | Select the segments with the highest short-run profit potential, considering market situation and competitive conditions | Select segments on the basis of need saliency |
| Product positioning | Position the product to maximize preference in the selected segments | Position the product to maximize acceptance and use in the selected segments |
| Pricing strategy | Price at a level that will maximize profits | Price at a level that will maximize reach among high-need segments |
| Distribution strategy | Adequate coverage of selected segments | Intensive coverage of high-need segments |
| Promotional strategy | Incentivize trial and enhance brand image in the chosen segments | Communicate product benefit, availability, and use information |
| Market-research strategy | Monitor consumer preference and perceived brand image | Monitor need satisfaction, consumer wellbeing |

insulation from foreign influence and at the same time promote indigenous enterprise. The countries adopting the 'autonomous' course would attempt to disengage from the priorities and imperatives of the world market while maintaining selective links with it. Such countries would face the greatest challenge in designing and operating their market systems. The experience of developed countries would be of very limited value. A large amount of innovation and experimentation would be required to evolve marketing institutions, practices, and concepts appropriate to their socio-economic conditions. Table 2.2 also outlines the broad characteristics of the distribution structures, communication methods, and product policies under each of the three developmental models.

## Marketing Strategies and Concepts

It is evident that the 'autonomous' model represents the greatest challenge for marketing strategists and scholars. The familiar marketing management concepts, which have largely originated in the USA, can be fairly easily adapted to the needs of an LDC adopting the 'miracle export' model. It is difficult to visualize what forms marketing strategy would take under the autonomous model. Table 2.3 outlines the likely strategic postures of a firm marketing a mass-consumption item under two very distinct developmental models. It is apparent that conventional marketing wisdom offers very little guidance for strategy formulation in type-B country. It is equally apparent, however, that the strategic task is not beyond the capabilities of contemporary management science. Practice and research in marketing need to develop so as to better meet the requirements of LDCs adopting the 'autonomous' model.

## Impact on the World System

It is impossible to 'forecast' the impact of changes in LDC marketing on the world system as a whole. One reason for this is that the choice of alternative developmental strategies by the LDCs cannot be predicted. It is possible, however, to *analyze* the impact on the world system if the *status quo* conditions continue or if one of the alternative developmental strategies is adopted.

The developed countries of the world have benefited from the *status quo* and would continue to do so, to the extent *status quo* is not disturbed. Under these conditions, the developed countries have had:

(a) access to raw-material resources located all over the world, (b) a favorable division of labor by manufacturing certain goods in low-wage countries, (c) a good market for mature technologies and consumer products in the LDC, (d) much higher returns on investments in the LDCs, and so on. All these have contributed to continued high growth and rising living standards in the developed countries. The *status quo*, however, is inherently unstable. LDCs are challenging the subordinate role in the world order. The debate on the New International Economic Order shows that the LDCs want a restructuring of trade and investment patterns. Even more seriously, the internal inequalities in the LDCs are increasing to the point where violent conflicts become inevitable. Border conflicts, civil wars, insurgencies, terrorism and repressive regimes are the manifestations of the rising internal contradictions. In other words, *status quo* or 'business as usual' is likely to be unusually bad business in the long run.

The choice of the 'miracle export' model has been proposed as one answer to these problems. This model entails a new international division of labor in which the LDCs become a giant low-technology manufacturing base while the Western countries develop high-technology, automated, service economies. The sweatshops and smokestacks are transferred to the LDCs while a cybernetic idyll prevails in the West. There are some obvious benefits for the LDCs as far as industrial development is concerned. The question is to what extent a dependent industrialization contributes to the alleviation of the problems of underdevelopment. In all probability, the urban-rural disparities would increase. Also, the LDCs might not want to sacrifice their environment as a price for such dependent industralization. The industrial working class in LDCs, as it became increasingly conscious of wage differentials, would be likely to repudiate such a system. The problems in the developed world might be equally severe. High-technology firms, service industries, and companies accustomed to obtaining products from foreign sources might gain in terms of profits and markets. Traditional low-technology industries with established domestic manufacturing facilities would be adversely affected. Organized labor would be up in arms against 'runaway shops' if attempts were made to close down domestic plants. Protectionist pressures would sharply rise. Unemployment as well as business failures would become endemic. It is also questionable whether the international trading system could handle the pressures of all LDCs becoming 'miracle exporters'. Cline (1982) has shown through a simulation that the world trading system would collapse, if all the LDCs followed East Asia's 'miracle export' model.

The 'regional power' model would have consequences somewhat similar to the 'miracle export' model. Additionally, the transnational corporations of the West would face intense competition from the LDC firms (Heenan and Keegan, 1979). The importance of the 'regional power' model, however, is minimized by the fact that very few LDCs have the capability to implement this model.

The 'autonomy' model appears unfavorable to Western countries in the short run. LDC markets for many luxury goods and some inappropriate technologies would be shut out. Similarly, it would be difficult to use LDCs as sources of low-technology manufactures, though not impossible. Prices for raw materials might rise as LDCs sought better control of resources and follow conservation policies. These effects are likely to be extremely short run and, under appropriate international conditions, not severe at all. For example, Western firms are beginning to obtain manufactured goods from an autonomous country, viz. China. The procedures may not be as simple as in the case of Taiwan or South Korea, but China represents a much more attractive source in the long run because comparative manufacturing wages in China are likely to be low for a long time. Similarly, commodity agreements could be reached to ensure fair prices and production rates for LDC commodity producers. Finally, in the long run, autonomous policies would ensure equitable economic and social development in the LDCs. This would not only promote world peace, but would also open up market opportunities world-wide for industries and institutions in the 'basic need' sectors such as nutrition, clothing, housing, health care, education, communication and transportation. For the marketing discipline, the challenges of designing socially responsive and developmentally oriented marketing systems and programs would bring about a conceptual renewal and fresh, new paradigms.

## Notes

1. In keeping with the theme of this book, the term LDC is used. It should be noted that this does not represent an endorsement of the 'stages' view of development.

2. In this paper the term marketing is used primarily in an institutionalist sense — it refers to marketing system of a country as a whole (see Arndt, 1981, for a recent elaboration of this perspective). Marketing institutions (structures), actions (practices), and ideas (concepts) are mutually related (Dholakia and Dholakia, 1982). Hence the discussion is not confined to marketing institutions only.

3. 'Development' is a multidimensional construct that includes growth, equity, sectoral development indicators, regional development indicators and social

indicators. The last are extremely important because that is how people 'feel' development — in marketing terminology, this is what the 'consumers' of development are interested in buying.

4. In the present bipolar world, dominated by two superpowers, disengagement from the world capitalist system often ends up as dependence on the Soviet Union. This is true to varying degrees for all the countries cited under this model, with the possible exception of Yugoslavia. This should not detract from the model itself — an ideal-type that is difficult to follow given the way the work is structured at present.

5. This is roughly what South Korea has been attempting to do in recent years. For a description of the South Korean self-reliance movement as it applies to rural areas, see Saemaul Undong (1980).

6. Latin America is much more heavily integrated with developed market economies than are Asia or Africa. For example, about 51% of the entire stock of foreign (transnational) investments in the world is in Latin America while only about 25% is in Africa and 23% in Asia, including the Middle East (see Colman and Nixson, 1978, Table 9.1).

# References

Adelman, Irma and Morris, Cynthia T. *Economic Growth and Social Equity in Developing Countries*, Stanford University Press, Stanford, Ca., 1973

Amin, Samir 'Toward an Alternative Strategy of Autocentered Development', in Geo. Modelski (ed.), *Transnational Corporations and World Order*, W.H. Freeman, San Francisco, 1979

Arndt, Johan 'Temporal Lags in Comparative Retailing', *Journal of Marketing, 36*, October 1972, pp. 40–5

—— 'The Political Economy of Marketing Systems: Reviving the Institutional Approach', *Journal of Macromarketing, 1*, Fall 1981, 36–47

Baran, Paul A. and Hobsbawm, E.J. 'The Stages of Economic Growth: A Review', *Kyklos*, Fasc. 2, *14*, 1961, 234–42

Bauer, P.T. *Dissent on Development*, Harvard University Press, Cambridge, 1972

Bennett, Douglas and Sharpe, Kenneth E. 'Transnational Corporations and the Political Economy of Export Promotions: The Case of the Mexican Auto Industry', *International Organization, 33*, Fall 1979, 177–201

Bhandari, L. and Vora, M.N. 'Indian Distribution System: Role of Private Trade', in N. Dholakia and R. Khurnana (eds), *Public Distribution Systems: Evolution, Evaluation, and Prospects*, Oxford and IBH, New Delhi, 1979, pp. 42–60

Cline, William, R. 'Can the East Asian Model of Development be Generalized?' *World Development, 10*, no. 2, 1982, 81–90

Cole, Sam 'The Global Futures Debate 1965–1976', in C. Freeman and M. Jahoda (eds), *World Futures: The Great Debate*, Universe Books, New York, 1978, pp. 9–49

Colman, David and Nixson, Frederick *Economics of Change in Less Developed Countries*, John Wiley & Sons, New York, 1978

Dholakia, Nikhilesh and Firat, A.F. 'The Role of Marketing in the Development of Nonmarket Sectors and Conditions Necessary for Success', in D. Izraeli, D.N. Izraeli and F. Meissner (eds), *Marketing Systems for Developing Countries*, John Wiley & Sons, New York, 1975

—— and Dholakia, Ruby R. 'A Comparative View of Public Policy Toward Distribution', *European Journal of Marketing, 12*, no. 7, 1978, 541–53

—— and —— 'Marketing in the Emerging World Order', *Journal of Macromarketing, 2*, Spring 1982, 47–56

Donges, Jurgen B. 'The Third World Demand for a New International Economic Order: Governmental Surveillance versus Market Decision Making in Trade and Investment', *Kyklos*, Fasc. 2, *30*, 1977, 235–58

Dos Santos, T. 'The Crisis of Development Theory and the Problem of Dependence in Latin America', in H. Bernstein (ed.), *Underdevelopment and Development: The Third World Today*, Penguin, New York, 1973, pp. 57–80

Douglas, Susan P. 'Patterns and Parallels of Marketing Structures in Several Countries', *MSU Business Topics, 19*, Spring 1971, 38–48

Etemad, Hamid 'A Comparative Time Path Analysis of World Markets', Presented at Annual Meeting of the Academy of International Business, Montreal, October, 1981

—— 'Marketing: The Catalyst in Economic Development Process', Presented at Seventh Annual Macromarketing Seminar, University of Colorado, Boulder, Co., August 5–8, 1982

Evans, David 'International Commodity Policy: UNCTAD and NIEO in Search of a Rationale', *World Development, 7*, March 1979, 259–79

Floto, Eduardo 'Towards Third World Collective Self Reliance', *International Foundation for Development Alternatives Dossier, 18*, July/August 1980

Frank, Andre Gunder *Dependent Accumulation and Underdevelopment*, Macmillan, London, 1979

Fritsch, Bruno 'The Future of the World Economic Order', in W. Michalski (ed.), *The Future of Industrial Societies*, Sijthoff and Noordhoff, Alphen aan den Rijn, The Netherlands, 1978, pp. 45–55

Furtado, C. 'Elements of a Theory of Underdevelopment – The Underdeveloped Structures', in H. Bernstein (ed.), *Underdevelopment and Development: The Third World Today*, Penguin, New York, 1979, pp. 33–43

Galtung, Johan 'The New International Economic Order and the Basic Needs Approach', *Alternatives, 4*, March 1979, 455–76

Goldman, Arieh 'Outreach of Consumers and the Modernization of Urban Food Retailing in Developing Countries', *Journal of Marketing, 38*, October 1974, 8–16

—— 'The Role of Trading-up in the Development of the Retailing System', *Journal of Marketing, 39*, January 1975, 54–62

Griffin, Keith *Underdevelopment in Spanish America*, Allen & Unwin, London, 1969

Hansen, Roger D. *Beyond the North-South Stalemate*, McGraw-Hill, New York, 1979

Hassan, M.F. 'International Trade and World Economic Order', *Third World Review, 4*, Spring 1978, 73–85

Heenan, D.A. and Keegan, W.J. 'The Rise of Third World Multinationals', *Harvard Business Review, 57*, January/February 1979, 101–9

Hilger, Marye T. 'Theories of the Relationship between Marketing and Economic Development: Public Policy Implications', in P.D. White and C.C. Slater (eds), *Macromarketing*, University of Colorado, Business Research Division, 1977, pp. 333–50

Hunter, J. 'What is Development?' Overseas Development Council, Communique on Development Issues, no. 8, April 1971.

Hveem, Helge *The Political Economy of Third World Producer Associations*, Universitetsforlaget, Oslo, 1978

Khurana, R., Balakrishnan, K., Dholakia, N. and Moulik, T.K. *Management of Decentralized Sector: Case of Handlooms*, Oxford and IBH, New Delhi, 1981

Miles, Ian, Cole, Sam and Gershuny, Jay 'Images of the Future', in C. Freeman and M. Jahoda (eds), *World Futures: The Great Debate*, Universe Books, New York, 1978, pp. 279–342

Morehouse, Ward 'Third World Disengagement and Collaboration: A Neglected Transitional Option', in J. Ramesh and C. Weiss (eds), *Mobilizing Technology for World Development*, Praeger, New York 1979, pp. 74–81

Moyer, Reed 'The Structure of Markets in Developing Countries', *MSU Business Topics, 12*, Fall 1964, 43–60

Myrdal, Gunnar *The Challenge of World Poverty*, Vintage, New York, 1970

Nugent, Jeffrey B. and Yotopoulos, Pan A. 'What has Orthodox Development Economics Learned from Recent Experience?', *World Development, 7*, June 1979, 541–54

Pajestka, Jozef 'The Three Socio-Economic Systems Towards the End of the 20th Century', in J.H. Bhagwati (ed.), *Economics and the World Order: From 1970s to the 1990s*, Free Press, New York, 1972, pp. 79–99

Rostow, W.W. *The World Economy: History and Prospect*, University of Texas Press, Austin, Texas, 1978

*Saemaul Undong* Republic of Korea, Ministry of Home Affairs, Seoul, 1980

Sebastien, Luis de 'Appropriate Technology in Developing Countries: Some Political and Economic Considerations', in J. Ramesh and C. Weiss (eds), *Mobilizing Technology for World Development*, Praeger, New York, 1979, pp. 66–73

Seers, Dudley 'The Meaning of Development', *International Development Review*, no. 1, 1970, 1–10

Sen Gupta, Subroto 'The Elite Barrier to Consumer Goods Marketing', *R.K. Sirkar Memorial Lecture*, Advertising Club, Calcutta, 1975

Shilling, John and Carter, Nicholas 'The Outlook for Developing Countries', in N.M. Kamrany (ed.), *The New Economics of the Less Developed Countries*, Westview Press, Boulder, Co., 1978, pp. 23–50

Slater, Charles C. 'Marketing Processes in Developing Latin American Countries', *Journal of Marketing, 22*, July, 50–5

Sorensen, O.J. 'A Conceptual Framework for Analysis of Government Intervention in the Distributive Trade in Ghana', Working Paper Series 78–4, University of Ghana, School of Administration, February 1978

Sunkel, Osvaldo 'Big Business and "Dependencia"', in George Modelski (ed.), *Transnational Corporations and World Order*, W.H. Freeman, San Francisco, 1979

United Nations *Statistical Yearbook 1978*, United Nations, New York, 1979

—— *1979 Yearbook of International Trade Statistics*, United Nations, New York, 1980

Ward, Barbara *The Rich Nations and the Poor Nations*, W.W. Norton, New York, 1962

Weisskopf, Thomas E. 'Capitalism, Underdevelopment and the Future of the Poor Countries', in J.H. Bhagwati (ed.), *Economics and the World Order: From the 1970s to the 1990s*, Free Press, New York, 1972, pp. 43–77

World Bank *The Assault on World Poverty*, The Johns Hopkins University Press, Baltimore, 1975

Wynn, Sam 'The Taiwanese "Economic Miracle"', *Monthly Review, 33*, April 1982, 30–40

# 3 IS MARKETING THE CATALYST IN THE ECONOMIC DEVELOPMENT PROCESS?

Hamid Etemad

## Introduction

In order to understand underdevelopment one has to examine its main features and the reasons for its persistence over time to provide a proper perspective for further analysis. Underdevelopment is characterized differently in different countries, and research in Economic Development (ED) has established a wide range of varying reasons for lack of, or slow rate of economic growth over time. The presence of a set of characteristics and the lack of others are regarded as underlying underdevelopment. Although they manifest themselves differently, all emanate from lack of efficiency, undefined or poorly defined direction (or orientation) and poor organization. The main purpose of this paper is, therefore, to show:

(1) that the traditional literature on economics and economic development does not clearly specify a universally applicable process to lead to growth and development, and to stop or to slow down the rampant extent and gap of underdevelopment (the extent of this gap is indicated in Table 3.1); and,
(2) that modern marketing, both at macro and micro levels, is a potent vehicle that can organize, orient, augment and accelerate economic development.

The objective of this paper is not to refute or to deny the role of influential 'factors' in the process of development, as they are reviewed in the next section, but instead it is to advocate that marketing as a concept, doctrine or theory, possesses enhancing characteristics that can improve the process of development regardless of the country's state of current-factor endowments.

The chapter comprises two main parts. Part I examines the role of so-called 'factors' in ED. A comparison of economic principles, leading to current ED theories with that of marketing is presented next. The effects of 'trade' and 'second best' theories on ED completes the first part.

Table 3.1: The Development Gap, by Groups of Countries

| | Low-income countries | Lower middle-income countries | Upper middle-income countries | High-income countries | Developing countries | Developed countries |
|---|---|---|---|---|---|---|
| Mid-1979 population (millions) | 1,131.7 | 1,443.6 | 597.0 | 1,146.4 | 3,244.5 | 1,074.2 |
| Average per capita GNP (1979) | $176 | $454 | $1,347 | $6,300 | $597 | $6,468 |
| Average PQLI[a] | 41 | 64 | 69 | 93 | 57 | 94 |
| Average birth-rate (per 1,000) | 38 | 27 | 35 | 16 | 32 | 15 |
| Average death-rate (per 1,000) | 16 | 10 | 9 | 9 | 12 | 9 |
| Average life expectancy (years) | 49 | 60 | 61 | 72 | 56 | 72 |
| Average infant mortality-rate (per 1,000 live births) | 132 | 75 | 85 | 21 | 96 | 18 |
| Average literacy rate | 35% | 56% | 71% | 97% | 52% | 99% |
| Average per capita education expenditures | $4 | $12 | $41 | $280 | $18 | $286 |
| Average per capita military expenditures | $5 | $28 | $52 | $297 | $29 | $300 |

Note: a. Each country's PQLI (Physical Quality of Life Index) is based on an average of life expectancy at age one, infant mortality and literacy.

Source: John Sewell, *The United States and World Development: Agenda for 1980*, Praeger Publishers New York, NY, 1980.

In Part II contributions of marketing to ED along with the short-comings of some selective ED theories are briefly compared and brought to perspective. A model based on marketing principles is proposed, and its ED-enhancing features are analyzed. The last section of Part II consists of a summary and concluding notes to this chapter.

## Part I

Literature on economic development is numerous, massive and well beyond the scope of this paper. Excellent surveys (Hahn and Matthews, 1964), textbook treatment (Burmeister and Dobel, 1962) and theoretical expositions (Solow, 1970; Scitovsky, 1954 and 1962) are presented elsewhere. Despite the volume of work in the area, there is no strong conceptual concensus as to what constitutes underdevelopment, what are the main causes, and why it persists over time. There is strong agreement, however, that the process of economic development is not an accidental phenomenon (Balasa, 1980).

*The Role of 'Factors' in Economic Development*

Several 'factors' are reported to have played an influential role in economic development in some of the developing countries and the following presents a list and summary of the main arguments. To avoid conveying universal applicability the exceptions are also pointed out.

(1) *Effective Market Size* The size of a country influences the country's potential for exploiting economies of scale, and the extent to which competition can be adopted in the early stages of growth. Inward or outward orientation of economic development policy, however, interacts strongly with the size factor. An inward orientation in a small country may lead to high concentration, slow down economic growth, and hence cause *relative* underdevelopment. Conversely, extreme outward orientation (e.g. transforming the industrial structure toward export platform) nullifies the country's small domestic-size factor. The small countries of Benelux and Scandinavia have traditionally been free traders. They have enjoyed, and are still enjoying, a high standard of living. In contrast, Brazil, the developing country with one of the largest domestic markets, turned inwards in mid-1960, and that led to her slower growth-rate. India still continues to pursue her inward orientation (Balassa, 1980; Havrylyshyn, 1981; Kuznets, 1960; Robinson, 1961, 1965; Science Council of Canada, 1981).

(2) *Natural Resource Endowment* A country's endowment of natural resources can influence its economic growth and industrialization by providing it with raw materials and natural resources for further processing or exports. This, in turn, can generate additional funds for capital formation and economic development. A rich endowment, however, must be viewed as a mixed blessing. For it may originally increase wage-rates in the endowed industries which can generally spread to the rest of the economy and push production costs higher than might otherwise be the case. Exportation of endowed resources can positively influence the balance of payments, which may cause an upward pressure on the exchange-rate and lead to lower import prices in the local currency. This may also lead to increased consumption of imports as comparative costs begin to shift away from domestic products and in favor of imports. Should the income effect of rich endowment result in higher factor-input costs, the exportation of manufactured material is bound to suffer. A combination of lower exports and higher imports can slow down further future growth-rates. Therefore, a sole dependence on endowment may impede long-range and broadly based economic development.

As compared to bauxite, iron ore and other natural resources, the case of oil exporting countries is very special, as it has resulted in *limited* diversification in these countries. Nevertheless, oil earnings have adversely affected the international competitiveness of manufacturing industries in Venezuela and Mexico (Chenery, 1964; Claque and Tanzi, 1972). Lower income from oil, however, mainly due to the recent worldwide recession, has dampened the rate of diversification and exportation in these countries, while their necessary imports (basic and infrastructural needs) have remained the same or increased. The adverse balance-of-payments pressures of the situation have resulted in currency depreciation, spending cutbacks, and lower growth-rates (e.g. Mexico).

(3) *Favorable Geographical Location* Although the advantages of location in terms of easy access to other markets cannot be denied, regional integration of closely located markets in Latin America led to a high-cost area which subsequently contributed to slow economic growth-rates in the region.

While the economic development of Denmark, the Netherlands and Norway are attributed to their favorable geographical location and access to nearby European markets for manufactured products, isolated countries like Japan, Taiwan and South Korea have done very well with respect to manufacturing exports, not withstanding their distant locations (Bruno, 1962; Viner, 1952; Mead, 1955).[1]

(4) *Preferential Ties to Large Industrial Countries* The evidence on the effects of preferential ties on ED is mixed. On one hand, preferential ties are expected to create preferential access to large industrial markets for exports, imports and foreign direct investment. The former French colonies in Africa are reported to have benefited from their special status in France and in turn with the European market. On the other hand, Japan, Taiwan, Korea and Singapore have not enjoyed preferential access to US or European markets, despite heavy US foreign direct investment in the latter three countries (Bruno, 1962).[2]

(5) *Political and Social Conditions* The effect of a country's political and social conditions on its economic development can be only assessed in retrospect. There are successful and unsuccessful economies under democratic and dictatorship systems. The evidence here is extremely mixed. Stable political and social conditions are necessary — but not sufficient — for growth, as they allow for planning and orderly conduct. Additionally, external financing of growth or foreign direct investment — as stimulants to ED — require minimum political risk and highly stable conditions. Most rapidly developing countries have enjoyed stability (e.g. Japan, Korea, Malaysia, etc.). The governments providing for such conditions, however, are not all democratic. Indeed, they cover a wide political spectrum. Therefore, it is the stability of social and political conditions (and not the ideological inclination) that is necessary and highly influential in economic development (Clark, 1957; Deutsch, 1961).

(6) *Educational Background* Educational level and background in a country are reported to be one of the major factors contributing to economic development. Education is also viewed as investment in human capital, although it may not become productive in the short run or in the usual span of time for non-educational investments. Most highly developed and developing countries enjoy a high level of education. Exceptional cases, however, were Chile and Uruguay in the 1960s. These countries exhibited poor economic growth-rate, despite their high educational levels as measured by the Harbison-Myers education index (Harbison and Myers, 1964, 1965). The effect of education on ED is studied extensively. The general concensus is that it has a very positive effect, as can be witnessed by the works of Claque and Tanzi, 1972; Clark, 1957; Hagen, 1957; Harbison and Myers, 1964, 1965; Harbison, Maruhnic and Resnick, Gutman, 1965; Schultz, 1965.

(7) *Foreign Aid* The contribution of foreign aid to economic development is at best mixed. The proponents of foreign aid argue that foreign aid should be treated as a massive infusion of capital, food, equipment

and know-how to the recipient countries that could not generate them domestically, and therefore, it must have a positive and stimulative effect. While this may be the case in theory, reality does not strongly support it. The difficulty is due to the fact that one cannot observe or measure for the purpose of comparison a country's own economic development in the absence of aid.

Opponents of foreign aid, on the other hand, argue that aid has become an instrument of the donor's foreign policy, and more often than not, has a political as opposed to, or instead of, an economic impact. Misallocation of resources, the increased cost of industrial production and unwanted or less desirable technology (e.g. inappropriate technology) are among the undesirable features that are attributed to the 'tying' of the aid. In some cases, foreign aid has offset military spending. This is certainly the case for Korea, Taiwan and some of the Central American countries. The literature in aid and ED is massive, mixed and inconclusive. For example, see Adelman and Chenery, 1966; Chenery and Carter, 1973; Griffin and Enos, 1970; Hirschman, 1958, Ch. 3; Hirschman and Bird, 1968; Papanek, 1972.

(8) *Foreign Direct Investment* Foreign direct investment (FDI) is accepted as a contributing factor to economic development (Calvet, 1981; Papanek, 1972; Pearson, 1969; Weisskopf, 1972). The theories of foreign direct investment overlap with those of economic development, and address many common issues that are well beyond the scope of this chapter.[3]

Although the policy-decision of allowing foreign direct investment to enhance economic-development goals rests with recipient countries, the effective control of FDI does not appear to be within their reach. Hence, the adoption of different policies have led to different sets of responses from foreign investors. Nevertheless, there is a general agreement on the positive and short-run effects of FDI (e.g. in terms of income, employment, transfer and diffusion of technology, balance of payment) on economic development in the host country. The long-run effects of FDI, however, do not enjoy the same support.

(9) *Other Factors* Factors affecting ED are not limited to the above list. The contributions of other factors — anywhere from the availability of entrepreneurial talent and risk-taking capacity to capital formation and savings rates — are extensively examined elsewhere (for example, see Balassa, 1980; Houthakker, 1961, 1965; Landau, 1971; Lluch and Powell, 1973; Mikessel, 1966; Mikessel and Zinser, 1973; Papanek, 1962).

**Part II**

*The Role of Marketing in Economic Development in Perspective*

The decade of the 1950s must be marked as the beginning of organized efforts in the systematic study of marketing's role in ED.[4] Holton (1953) studied Puerto Rico's marketing system, and showed that marketing activities could have a positive impact on ED. In Fisher's (1954) study of marketing structure and economic development, he found that tertiary production and employment tended to grow faster than economic growth-rate. This finding provided a corollary to the frequently suggested improvements to traditional channels of distribution, and started a series of research in the marketing of services and the role of tertiary employment in ED. Bauer's (1954a, 1954b) study of trade patterns in former British West African colonies, Bauer and Yamey's (1954) subsequent research on the economic impact of marketing reform on ED, and Baldwin's (1954) study of cocoa markets in Western Nigeria reconfirmed the impact of marketing on ED. Bauer and Yamey (1957) followed up their research by studying underdevelopment. Drucker's (1958) keynote speech on the role of marketing in ED culminated the pioneering efforts of marketers in that decade. Definitive studies like that of Galbraith and Holton (1955) in Puerto Rico had shown substantial inefficiency and waste in the marketing system which adversely affected the process of ED. For example, they illustrated that a redesigning of the system could result in savings of up to 19 percent in the island's food bill (Galbraith, Holton, 1955, pp. 177–98). By implication, the resulting extra purchasing power, or the capital formation associated with savings of such magnitude, could be a strong stimulant to the ED process. That is, the corresponding income-generating process (when the savings are spent) through income multiplier mechanism, or the readily available capital base (when the savings are invested) through investment multiplier process would have had unparalleled effects on the ED process.

In the next two decades (1960s and 1970s) ED-related literature in marketing flourished. Every aspect of the work was scrutinized, although a comprehensive review of the literature is well beyond the scope of this chapter. The broad outline of the work, however, falls into the following general categories:

(1) Impact of marketing at theoretical and macro levels;
(2) impact of marketing on regional or national markets;
(3) sectoral impact of marketing;

(4) impact of marketing at the micro and functional level;
(5) normative impact; and,
(6) impact of comparative marketing.

The discipline of comparative marketing was not formally and explicitly associated with the impact of marketing on ED. Its implications, however, mainly due to the comparative nature of it — i.e. explicit comparison of marketing systems, subsystems or processes across countries at different levels of economic growth and development — had, and will have, an indirect impact. Boddewyn's (1981) comprehensive review of comparative marketing literature has addressed most of the pertinent issues, and in the interest of time and space they will not be repeated here. One point, however, must be noted — that most comparative marketing studies are deficient in capturing and taking into account the context of their comparison, as the forefathers of comparative marketing (e.g. Bartels, 1963, 1968) had advised and advocated.[5]

In summary, marketing-oriented studies of ED addressed specific regional, sectoral and functional aspects of ED as well as the theoretical and normative dimensions. Marketing orientation of these studies, however, distinguished them from economically oriented studies (or theories) and led to the study of a different set of problems and resulted in varying recommendations. A comparison of some of the differences is presented below.

### Marketing-oriented versus Economic-oriented Studies of ED

Comparison of marketing-oriented studies of economic development with that of economic-oriented studies reveals the former's important advantages.

(1) *Organizational and Informational Function* Developing countries suffer from massive inorganization mainly due to lack of pertinent information. As Drucker states:

> [The] essential aspect of underdeveloped economy and the factor, the absence of which keeps it underdeveloped, is the inability to organize economic effort and energies . . . to convert self-limiting static system into creative, self-generating organic growth. (1958, p. 255.)

Marketing creates a 'network, through which information can flow among the many firm units forming interrelated activities necessary to produce the final consumer product' (Higgins, 1979, p. 769) or achieve its final industrial objectives. Farm planting or industrial-manufacturing decisions, for example, cannot be made in a vacuum. Pertinent information is required. This information must convey the requirements of other links in the production-distribution channel. To provide such vitally required information to different members of the production-distribution channel, an information network and hence an organization, anywhere from highly formal and structured to informal and implicit, is necessary. In fact, market-oriented production-distribution systems provide the structure for transmitting and using such vital information and feedback, and can lead to optimal production and distribution decisions. As a result, only demanded products are produced, and the cost of inventory and wastage are minimized. Conversely, under the state of an imperfect information or production-oriented system, the probability of a perfect functioning of a series of tasks — ranging from a reasonable and efficient allocation of resources, market clearing at reasonable prices and adding of social value to rewarding of the efficient system and punishing of the inefficient — is much lower. That is mainly due to the fact that market orientation of such systems, in responding to market needs far outclasses the *assumption* that production-oriented systems are fully capable of collecting market information. Even for those instances for which the above assumption holds true, the production-oriented producers are less likely to give prominence to market consideration over production consideration. Some of the main features of market and production-oriented systems of production-distribution are compared and illustrated in Table 3.2.

(2) *Entrepreneurial Talent and Capital Accumulation* Marketing orientation in a production-distribution network in developing countries can stimulate entrepreneurial talent and accumulation of capital. In a study of the 250 leading industrialists of Pakistan, who controlled 50 percent of Pakistan's industrial capacity, Papanek (1962) found that a full 45 percent of them moved into industry directly from trading (i.e. distribution) occupations. Furthermore, Papanek reported that 69 percent of all capital involved in industrial production was controlled by these (and other) ex-traders, some of whom were formerly involved in export-import as well as internal trading. In the study of West African traders, Bauer and Yamey (1957, p. 263) came to similar conclusions.

Bauer's and Yamey's similar study in Malaya reconfirmed their earlier findings. Most of the Pakistani industrialists, as Papanek reported,

Table 3.2: Comparison of Different Economic Development (ED) Orientations with Different Orientation in Marketing and Management's Evolutionary Path

| | ED with production/supply-side orientation | ED with marketing orientation | ED with strategic orientation |
|---|---|---|---|
| Concept | | | |
| Focus/Emphasis | Increasing physical production capacity | Social Welfare<br>  buyer satisfaction<br>  marketing and distribution | Complete societal welfare |
| Ends/Objectives/Criteria | High return to capital investment<br>Increased production<br>Utilization of resources<br>Higher *material* possession | Maximization of social or buyer satisfaction to lead to higher objective productivity<br>Fair return to all productive factors | Maximized social welfare subject to global welfare constraints<br>Fair return to all productive factors local and foreign |
| Means for accomplishing the ends | Installing new production capacity by:<br>  capital investment through increased savings, decreased consumption<br>Protective tariff and non-tariff barriers<br>Import substitution<br>Foreign borrowings<br>Inward orientation | Strong marketing orientation by:<br>  emphasizing comparative advantage<br>  encouraging competition<br>  increasing choice<br>  increasing discrimination possibilities<br>  decreasing protective barriers<br>Establishing incentive systems subsidies to local producers subsidies to exporters<br>Open international market operation<br>Selective outward orientation on goods with comparative advantage | Integrated, coordinated, strategic international decision-making<br>Emphasis on comparative advantage<br>Regionally or internationally integrated production-distribution system<br>Complete environmental consciousness<br>Social and global responsibility<br>Fair international competition and trade<br>Integrated inward-outward orientation |
| Prominent issues over-riding others | Supply-side issues<br>  production, capacity | Marketing orientation<br>Comparative advantage | Law of comparative advantage |
| Relatively ignored or de-emphasized issues | Social Welfare<br>Consumer satisfaction<br>Marketing and distribution<br>Demand-side issues<br>Competition<br>Benefits of trade<br>Exports | Nationalism<br>Local sourcing and local-content requirements<br>Across-the-board local production<br>Import substitution<br>Supply-side issues | Nationalism |

brought into industry the missing ingredients — i.e. their marketing experience, entrepreneurial talent and accumulated capital from trading. As these studies show, efficient marketing intermediaries have been instrumental in ED, and that there is no reason to believe that their positive contribution ceases in the later stages of economic development. It is very important to note that this is contrary to the popular belief that marketing intermediaries are 'parasites' that 'drag' and hamper economic development. In fact, a modern and efficient distribution system can be instrumental in eradicating spot or regional shortages or abundances, and hence minimize waste and disparity, which are amongst the symptoms of underdevelopment.

(3) *Overhaul of Outmoded Pricing System* Development of marketing can play a profound role in overhauling the traditional or outmoded system of pricing. Most developing countries seem to be plagued with primitive price schedules based primarily on their perceived inelastic demand-and-supply schedules. In the absence of an efficient system of production-distribution to equalize spot and regional shortages, abundances and disparities, local producers feel and then act as 'natural monopolies'. Pseudo-monopolistic behavior and its associated distortions in the pricing system, can be harmful to economic development for it fails to allocate the scarce resources efficiently. It is also bound to suboptimize consumer and societal satisfaction and value.

Small market size may at times make it necessary to allow for protected (or regulated) monopoly producers. But an efficient and widespread system of distribution can help to limit the extent of monopolistic practices, and hence minimize the harmful effects in the society. In the absence of production monopolies, an efficient system of production-distribution can force prices close to their competitive level. This, in turn, helps to optimize the allocation of resources, rewards the efficient producer-distributor, and punishes the inefficient. Therefore, this process is capable of rationalizing production, increasing the system's overall efficiency and/or productivity, and, above all, it can maximize social welfare (in terms of physical, material as well as psychic satisfaction).

(4) *Systematic Incentives for Innovativeness, Inventions and Efficiency* Economic development in LDCs is hampered by a massive class structure and traditional or social rigidities. An efficient system of marketing provides incentives for people to break away from those traditional molds and social barriers. Market mechanism provides tangible incentives which can reward successful risk-takers and innovators. Market mechanism also offers clear and inescapable opportunities for breaking

out of the socially lower-status jobs (e.g. middleman) and joining the ranks of higher-status positions (e.g. industrialist or businessman). Bauer (1954), Bauer and Yamey (1957) and Higgins (1959) provide numerous examples of such opportunities and incentives which emanated directly from marketing orientation. The attractiveness and reachability of higher-status positions ought to be the ultimate driving force for people to try to achieve them.

(5) *Flexibility in Scale* An integrated system of production, distribution and marketing can be carried out at any level, and does not require massive industrial or social projects. Stated differently, marketing concepts are as applicable to small or private projects as they are to large private or public ones, but their focus and their constituency will be obviously different. In small projects, a firm or an entrepreneur must focus on the wants and needs (or desires) of a small market or segment. In large projects, investors (public or private) may consider the welfare or satisfaction of a much larger market segment, the whole market, or even the whole country (e.g. in the case of social overhead capital investments). In all cases the principles remain the same -- they are the basic triad of marketing: crystalizing demand, guiding production, and creating discrimination possibilities.

(6) *Promotes Small Enterprises and Identifies Potential ED Agents* Marketing can be the most accessible 'multiplier' of entrepreneurial and managerial activities in the underdeveloped areas. Economic development is not a fact of nature. As Balassa put it, 'accident de parcourse', mainly due to the use of inappropriate policies, can easily stop it (1980). To initiate, promote and manage the process of ED and to avoid 'accident de parcourse', entrepreneurial and managerial talent and expertise are badly needed; and that is precisely one of the most underdeveloped resources in the underdeveloped areas. As Drucker (1958, p. 256) put it, 'Economic development is the result of the action, the purposeful, responsible, risk-taking action of men as entrepreneurs and managers.' He further wrote: 'Certainly it is the entrepreneur and manager who alone can convey to the people of these countries an understanding of what economic development means and how it can be achieved' (p. 256).

This is a profound statement for it recognizes that the people of the developing countries are an integral part of the process. In fact, they must feel that economic progress is for them, and must see their role in the process. By implication then, ED planners should be able to integrate people and markets into the process and allow them to actively incorporate themselves into, and support or influence the course of development, as opposed to becoming the mere subjects in an economic development experiment.

In summary, marketing as an underlying structure, philosophy or orientation for economic development does not suffer from the above-mentioned difficulties that have hindered economic literature's contribution. But instead, marketing system can be employed as a *catalyst* to bring together all influential and economic agents — small or large and private or public — to adopt marketing orientation as the unifying ED strategy. Adoption of this orientation accomplishes three major tasks:

(1) results in maximum satisfaction of, and value for their respective constituencies (e.g. consumers, industries, markets, or the whole country);

(2) guides production and distribution in minimizing waste and inefficiency; and above all,

(3) encourages the continuation of the system, by rewarding the efficient and productive and punishing the inefficient.

The final result of such a process is that more efficient agents, in a pareto-optimal sense, are rewarded relatively highly, which motivates them to have even higher efficiencies and/or greater productivities; and the inefficient are forced eventually to leave the market place. This will impact ED very positively. On the consumption side, consumers try to maximize their material (e.g. better goods and services), social (e.g. higher prestige or social class), and psychic (e.g. higher satisfaction and lower cognitive dissonance) welfare by working harder to acquire their high priority (in terms of attractiveness) items. Hirschman has made the following succinct observation:

Some products of modern industrial civilization — flashlights, radios, bicycles, or beer — are always found sufficiently attractive to make people stop hoarding, restrict traditional consumption, work harder, or produce more for the market to acquire them. (1958, p. 53)

Hence, if producers can find those 'sufficiently attractive' goods and services[6] and bring them to the right market place at the right (reasonably affordable) price,[7] workers will work harder and/or produce more to acquire them,[8] which in turn, at the aggregate level, results in a higher level of aggregate demand, to be satisfied by higher aggregate supply — simultaneously or gradually.

*Organizing for Economic Development*

One of the fundamental questions that a development economist or planner is always faced with is: how to organize for economic development. Contrary to the voluminous literature on ED, the field does not present a blueprint or a set of systematic procedures for economic development. In 1958 Hirschman wrote:

> economists have not been able to construct, much less agree on a single and unbroken chain of causes and effects that would neatly explain the transition from 'under development' to development. (p. 50)

Not much seems to have changed. They still suffer from a myopic view of demand, market and exchange mechnism in developing countries. Dholakia and Firat (1976) emphasize that demand and purchasing behavior in underdeveloped countries are not homogeneous; the means for exchange of information are inadequate; facilities for resolving disparities and differences are poor; and marketing activities are still outmoded and inefficient. Slater (1968, 1976) came to a similar conclusion that lack of pertinent information, poor transportation facilities, and underdeveloped distribution systems are still plaguing the developing countries. In addition to the above problems, many questions still remain unresolved. For example, which sector must be developed first? What orientations should it adopt? Should a sector be developed to the level of self-sufficiency or should it go beyond? Should the benefits of exporting from the more developed sectors be invested in further technological support of the sector, or should they be rechanneled to finance the revitalization of the other sectors, or the rest of the country? Should a country adopt an 'inward' or 'outward' orientation? And so on. This is an agenda for future research in this area, and direct answers to the above questions are well beyond the scope of this paper. Instead, it proposes a new marketing-oriented paradigm for organizing ED efforts. The paradigm attempts to avoid the shortfalls of economic modeling, and incorporates all the six aspects of a marketing-oriented process discussed earlier.

*A Marketing-oriented Model for Economic Development: A Strategic Model* The process of economic development is bound to affect a society's functioning and way of life. The newly created opportunities create upward mobility and run against the fabric of traditional values and established social classes; and along with them traditional market segments go through a state of flux and transition. The whole society gradually adopts a new system of values, and in a sense crosses its old traditions and culture. Therefore, a case can be made that the cross-cultural model (e.g. Sheth and Sethi, 1977) of market (or consumer) behavior is highly capable of capturing the transitional period and providing useful suggestions. Cultural change does not occur in isolation, other dimensions of the socio-economic and political life change along with it. The applicability of a cross-cultural model increases when one recognizes the inevitable evolution of socio-political dimensions along with cultural and economic change. This has strong implications for market segmentation and market-oriented models. For example, in comparison with 'social class' segmentation — in which products are neutral and segments static — the implications of cross-cultural models are far reaching. In fact, in a dynamic and changing society, social classes are not static, and products do not remain necessarily neutral.

A three-category classification is suggested by Sheth and Sethi, namely: consumption-substitution, new-want-creating, and income-adding product categories.

In the consumption substitution category new products introduce added variety and choice to the market place. The consumer is already familiar with the basic-product class, and may derive added marginal utility and satisfaction only by substituting one variety for another.

In the new-want-creating category, at least two subcategories must be noted: (i) complementary products, and (ii) products that satisfy new contingencies. For the former, possession and use of the product improves and enhances an existing product or process, and to that extent this category of products enhances the productivity and efficiency of existing products or production processes, and result in improved overall output (higher or better, however defined). Hence, production, distribution and use of this product category must be encouraged.

For the latter subcategory, however, as Sheth and Sethi put it: 'The purchase is made because a new need has arisen due to change in buyer's social situation.' (p. 384)

The possession and use of this type of product may indeed cause a change in buyer's perceived social class (or situation). 'Prestige and status' products fall into this category. Marketing-oriented economic planners should be careful about this category, for some luxury or non-essential products may qualify as prestige and status-enhancing products.

The income-adding product category 'includes all products that may have positive effect on the buyer's income' and the income may subsequently affect the consumer's 'standing in the social milieu.' (Sheth and Sethi, 1977, p. 385.)

*Classification of Products for Economic Development* In contrast to the traditional economic view of product classification in which products assume broad-range but narrow economic definitions (e.g. investment to consumption, perishable to durable, elastic to inelastic, substitute to complement, etc.), the model proposed here adopts a marketing-oriented product classification. This view is similar to that of Sheth and Sethi's (1977) classification of products in their model of cross-cultural consumer behavior as reviewed briefly above.

Classification of products plays an important role in the ED process, as one of the main questions in ED is: Which products should be encouraged and which ones should be discouraged, taxed, or disallowed in a marketing-oriented system of product distribution? Although a direct and specific answer to the above question is highly desirable, given the diversity of different settings (e.g. in different countries) such a specific answer may not be generally applicable and therefore will not be attempted in this paper. However, instead of identifying the specific good or services (at micro level), a criterion for identification, and the classification of a broad class of products with ED-augmenting potentials (at macro level) seems to facilitate the process. In fact, the model proposed here utilizes a three-category classification to address the above question about the class of products that should be selected to lead off the ED process. The categories are:

(1) *Positively Charged Goods and Services (PCGS)* This category of products can positively influence and augment ED's process unequivocally (e.g. fertilizers, farm machinery, power tools, etc.).

(2) *Neutrally Charged Goods or Services* This class of products has no positive or harmful effects on ED (e.g. manual tools, small household appliances, etc.).

(3) *Negatively Charged Goods or Services (NCGS)* This set of products can potentially (but not necessarily) impede ED (e.g. purely luxurious and unnecessary goods).

Two points must be noted:

(1) That goods and services includes industrial products and processes

as well as consumer goods and services.

(2) That the above three-category classification is intended to capture the two extreme and mid-point of a continuous-product continuum.

*Classification of People for the ED Process* Another important question in a marketing-oriented ED process is: What group or class of people should be encouraged or challenged to participate actively in the process? The identification of a class or group of people to lead the ED process has its roots in the market-segmentation theory. Market-segmentation theory, based partially on the theory of a discriminating monopolist maximizing his profits, is the primary motivation for the marketers to match different products (or classes of product(s)) to different market segments (or groups of people) to maximize marketing efficiency. Increased marketing efficiency is usually the result of matching of a product to a market segment or a product class to a market, which makes possible a fine tuning of marketing strategies for each targeted market segment, in contrast to a general approach for the entire population. Analogically, the matching of an ED-augmenting product to people (or product classes and market or population segments) should yield higher efficiencies than the general, free-market allocations. For this simple reason a classification of population (or segmentation) will be presented below.

Although it is not necessary and may not be useful to identify the specific characteristics of market segments in terms of their detail profiles, it is possible to present a criterion for a broad classification of people with ED-augmenting potentials. Once this is done, the 'matching' of classes of products to classes of people to form binary pairs — parallel to product to a market segment at micro level, or product class to a market at macro level — is a much easier task. Therefore, this paper proposes a three-category classification similar to that of the products presented above. The basic dimension involved in the classification is desire for upward mobility in terms of achieving higher standards of living, higher income, higher social status, etc. At one extreme of this dimension would be the highly upwardly mobile segment (UBS) with a high potential for achieving success and higher standards in all dimensions. The other extreme could represent that segment of the population which has very little desire for achieving higher standards and prefers the *status quo*. Stated differently, the population is viewed as a continuous continuum in terms of desire for achievement and upward mobility which can be segmented (along that continuum) into several segments within the above two extremes.

The task of assigning different product groups to different segments of the population is not an easy one, as it involves two fundamental issues of welfare and normative economics — i.e. equity and pareto optimality.

Equity refers to a normative and somewhat philosophical concept of the equitable distribution of ED benefits across different segments of the population. Fundamentally, it is a distributional problem. At one end of the spectrum the advocates of radical economic doctrines argue for equitable distribution or re-distribution before economic growth. almost to the exclusion of efficiency. At the other end of the spectrum are those who advocate an expedient and efficient growth regardless of its distributional consequences.

Pareto optimality is a theoretical statement referring to the relative state of parity (in terms of comparative statics) between entities under examination. A pareto-optimal case in ED, for example, is a case in which everyone is at least as well off after the ED process as compared to his initial state before the process. It suffices to note that these two issues have plagued the literature of ED for some time, and no easy resolution seems to be in sight. This paper will not support or refute the position of either of the doctrines. Instead, it leaves the final resolution of the issues to markets and to a lesser degree to national coordinating and planning agencies. Although the functioning and philosophical orientation of these agencies can affect the initial sequencing of events, the parallel structure of the model presented below favors an outcome close to natural market choice in terms of assignment of tasks or allocation of resources.

*The Model* The function of the model is based primarily on the theory of market segmentation as mentioned before. The model has *three* structural blocks as follows:

(1) A block characterizing segmentation of products (goods and services) in terms of their propensity to contribute to economic development. This block is presented in the left side of Figure 3.1 and is entitled PCGS (positively charged goods and services).

(2) A block characterizing segmentation of people in terms of their propensity to influence and augment economic development. This block is represented on the right side of Figure 3.1 and is entitled UMMS (upwardly mobile market segments).

(3) A block characterizing all the planning and coordination necessary for smooth implementation of the ED process. This task is partly done

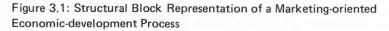

Figure 3.1: Structural Block Representation of a Marketing-oriented Economic-development Process

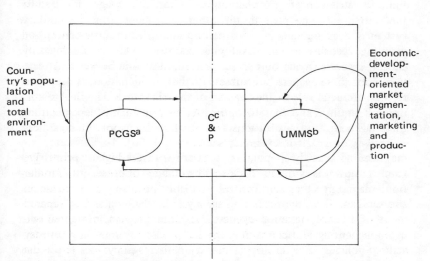

Notes: a. PCGS = Positively charged goods and services (goods and services that possess a high propensity of augmenting ED).
b. UMMS = Upwardly mobile market segments (market segments that possess high propensity to achieve higher standards).
c. C & P = Coordination and planning (coordinating and planning agencies may perform this task).

by planning and coordinating agencies, and partly done by market participants, and is represented by the middle block of Figure 3.1.

The connecting arrows on Figure 3.1 are representative of the dynamic nature of the model; for the definition, functioning and the relation of the three blocks are all mutually dependent on each other – i.e. a change in a market segment, and hence a block, affects all other parts.

One attractive alternative is that the management of production, distribution and marketing of highly positive charged goods and services be assigned to (or voluntarily picked up by) the people with the highest potential for achievement of higher standards or upward mobility. This alternative, however, may result in a further skewing of the distribution of income, social status, etc. in favor of one segment at a cost to others – i.e. in favor of already rich, well educated, privileged and hence relatively upwardly mobile. Similar to any allocation or assignment scheme, this alternative has its own distributional characteristics. As mentioned previously, distributional problems have caused and continue to cause concern for planning and coordinating agencies, leading them to prefer one plan to the other — ranging from a voluntary system of free markets in industrialized countries to more centralized planning agencies in the developing countries. One would logically expect that the goals, objectives, philosophical orientation and functioning of these agencies are subsets of that of the nation, as they start to play a crucial role in the shaping of the ED course. The final resolution of 'equity' and 'pareto optimality' is also highly dependent on these agencies and institutions (for further discussion of goals and objectives of ED, for example, see Slater, 1976). To illustrate, one may assume that the population segment with the highest propensity to move upwards is the most desired candidate for possession, production, management and/or control of highly positively charged goods and services. Then the regulating agency (e.g. planning agency, department of finance, taxation agency, etc.) can play an influential role in implementing and controlling the ED process by imposing countervailing policies. For example, the regulating agency can encourage the production and distribution of positively charged goods and services to help increase aggregate production and distribution, resulting in the creation of additional wealth and well-being, on one hand; and on the other hand, through a redistribution taxation system help the poor, undereducated and the underprivileged to increase their potential for upward mobility.

In order to achieve the goals of the economic development plan, and to have an orderly transitional process, the government may decide to proceed in stages to revise its goal-induced policies. Specifically, the government should develop a set of priorities and a system of incentives with respect to positively charged products and different segments of the population.

A system of incentives (e.g. grants, subsidies and loans) to create industries which produce or complement positively charged products should help the process of economic development. With respect to agriculture, as an example, agricultural machinery and fertilizer industries are good augmenting industries. To encourage and perhaps force farmers to use or increase the use of fertilizers (up to the optimal level) to increase their production, efficiency and income, is an example of policies which can help to increase economic upward mobility. A combination of both sets of programs (i.e. production of PCGS and incentives for higher usage) should result in higher agricultural

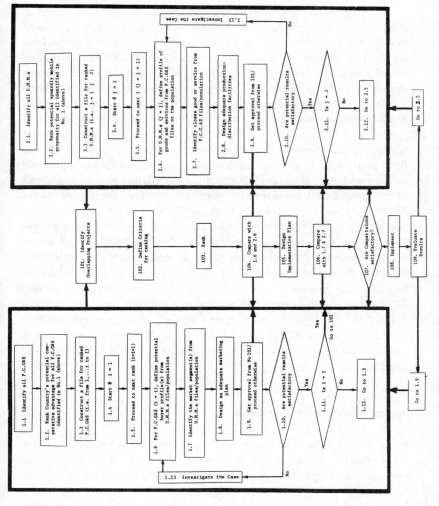

Figure 3.2: Planning Flow Chart for Marketing-oriented Economic Development

P.C.G&S = Positively Charged Goods and Services (goods and services that enhance ED)

U.M.M.S. = Upwardly Mobile Market Segments (market segments that enjoy potentially high propensity to move upwardly)

49

production, higher productivity per farm (or farmer), higher purchasing power leading to higher material well-being for farmers, and perhaps a stimulant of the whole society. The 'demonstration effect' is bound to take hold (Shapiro, 1965, p. 416). When that happens, even in the absence of a governmental system of incentives, all those segments who have been possessing a high *propensity* to move upwards will find those goods and services and strive to achieve upward movement. A typical and simplified example for the strategic planning of such a systematic economic development process is given in Figure 3.2 as a flow chart. Specifically, the process leading to the ranking of goods and services and their associated *ideal* market/population segments in terms of possession and management of productive and distributive means for such products is depicted on the left side of Figure 3.2. The right side of the figure presents a parallel scheme for the ranking of people in terms of their upward mobility and their associated *ideal* set of goods and services that can help them to realize their desired level of mobility. In the middle section of Figure 3.2 some of the coordinating and planning functions of such institutions or agencies are depicted. The heavy solid lines are representative of a multiple-function manifold − i.e. they take the information or feedback, and direct the function to the proper box within each of the blocks. Without the use of such multiple-function manifold lines, the figure would be unnecessarily complicated.

### Summary and Concluding Notes

From a comprehensive review and comparison of economic development-oriented literature in marketing, and that of economic and economic development, the following conclusions emerge:

(1) Marketing is seen as the final outcome rather than an ongoing process. This is mainly due to the myopic view of underdevelopment symptoms as well as a lack of full appreciation of marketing's potent role in ED. Underdevelopment is seen primarily as shortage of supply, and marketing as creator of demand. Within that frame of thought there is obviously very little room for any marketing contribution. This paper argues that it is equally plausible that those marketing practices that cause increases in demand and consumption can be also directed to promote and achieve other ED goals, e.g. higher savings and investments.

(2) Although underdevelopment and the conditions which cause it are viewed differently, they all emanate from certain common characteristics such as: lack of efficiency, poorly defined directions, undefined or underdefined orientation, inadequate factor endowments, poor organizations, and underdeveloped markets and marketing institutions.

The main objective of this paper — that marketing can be a potent catalyst in ED — is in response to the two conclusions above and their apparent discrepancies, which are reviewed in the paper. In fact, this paper has argued that marketing practices can result in organizing, augmenting, and accelerating economic development. Furthermore, this paper has taken the position that all the building blocks for implementing a marketing-oriented economic development are currently available, but they are not systematically deployed. To illustrate, this paper presents a model for the systematic implementation of a marketing-oriented ED process. The model offers a potent but flexible set of procedures for accommodating a wide range of circumstances.

## Notes

1. The advantages of geographical location can be clearly understood by studying countries at the crossroads of trade and commerce throughout history. A more modern version is captured by membership of a common market, for example the EEC. For the detailed advantages of customs unions see Viner, 1950 and Mead, 1955.

2. Old colonial ties are examples of preferential ties. Former British colonies still receive preferential treatment in the Commonwealth countries. Israel is also a recipient of US preferential treatment. See Bruno, 1962.

3. The effects of foreign direct investment on ED overlap with that of the theory of FDI and multinational firms. For a window to this massive literature see the review paper by Calvet, 1981.

4. 1950 as a starting point for a selective review of the literature carries no special significance; and is not intended to create the impression that the decade of 1950 is the true beginning of such works.

5. For a more detailed discussion of this and related issues see Etemad, 1980, 1982 and Chapter 12 of this book.

6. The finding of 'sufficiently attractive' goods and services is within the reach of 'crystalizing and identifying incipient or latent demand' which is one of the principal functions of marketing.

7. The delivery of sufficiently attractive goods and services to the right location and at the right time and price, is the end result of the marketing's organizing and optimizing function.

8. The creation of incentives for people to work harder (resulting in higher output in and by itself) for the purpose of buying sufficiently attractive goods and services, is also the consequences of marketing's discriminating and rewarding functions. That is, people work harder to buy better products and turn away from

not-so-attractive products. Thus, they force the issue of meritorious rewarding resulting in higher output and more efficient allocation of resources from less attractive to more attractive products and services.

# References

Adelman, I. and Chenery, H.B. 'Foreign Aid and Economic Development: The Case of Greece', *Review of Economics and Statistics*, February 1966, 1–19

Balassa, Bela 'The Process of Industrial Development and Alternatives Development Strategies', *Essays in International Finance*, no. 141, Princeton University, Princeton, NJ, 1980, 1

Baldwin, K.D.S. *The Marketing of Cocoa in Western Nigeria with Special Reference to the Position of Middlemen*, Oxford University Press, London, 1954

Bartels, Robert (ed.) *Comparative Marketing: Wholesaling in Fifteen Countries*, Richard D. Irwin, Homewood, Ill., 1963

—— 'Are Domestic and International Marketing Dissimilar?' *Journal of Marketing*, July 1968, 56–61

Bauer, P.T. 'The Economics of Marketing Reform', *Journal of Political Economy*, vol. LXII, June 1954a, 210–35

—— *West African Trade: A Study of Competition, Oligopoly, and Monopoly in a Changing Economy*, Cambridge University Press, Cambridge, England, 1954b

—— and Yamey, Basil *The Economics of Under Developed Countries*, University of Chicago, Ill., 1954

Boddewyn, Jean 'Comparative Marketing: The First Twenty-five Years', *Journal of International Business Studies*, Spring/Summer 1981, 61–79

Bruno, M. 'Interdependence, Resource Use, and Structural Change in Israel, Bank of Israel Research Department', *Special Studies*, no. 2, Jerusalem, 1962

Burmeister, E. and Dobell, A.R. *Mathematical Theories of Economic Growth*, Macmillan, London, 1962

Calvet, A.L. 'A Synthesis of Foreign Direct Investment Theories and Theories of the Multinational Firm', *Journal of International Business Studies*, Spring Summer 1981, 43–59

Claque, C. and Tanzi, V. 'Human Capital, Natural Resources and the Purchasing Power Parity Doctrine: Some Empirical Results', *Economica Internationale*, February 1972, 3–17

Clark, C. *The Condition of Economic Progress*, Macmillan, London, 1957 (3rd edn)

Chenery, H.B. 'Land: The Effects of Resources on Economic Development', in K. Berrill (ed.), *Economic Development with Special Reference to East Asia*, St Martin's, NY, 1964

Deutsch, K.W. 'Social Mobilization and Political Development', *American Economic Review*, September 1961, 493–514

Dholakia, N. and Firat, F.A. 'The Role of Marketing in the Development of Nonmarket Sectors and Condition Necessary for Success' in Israeli *et al.* (eds), *Marketing Systems for Developing Countries*, John Wiley & Sons, New York, 1976, pp. 50–62

Drucker, Peter F. 'Marketing and Economic Development', *Journal of Marketing*, January 1958, 252–9

Etemad, H. 'Are Domestic and International Markets Dissimilar?: A Review and Extension', ASAC-IB proceedings, Halifax, NS, May 1980

—— 'World Product Mandating in Perspective', proceedings of ASAC-IB, Ottawa, May 1982

Fisher, Allan 'Marketing Structure and Economic Development: Comment', *Quarterly Journal of Economics*, vol. LXVIII, February 1954, 151–4

Galbraith, John K. and Holton, R.H. *Marketing Efficiency in Puerto Rico*, Harvard University Press, Cambridge, Mass., 1955

Griffin, K.B. and Enos, J.L. 'Foreign Assistance: Objective and Consequences', *Economic Development and Cultural Change*, April 1970, 313–27

Gutmann, P. 'The Anatomy of Economic Growth', in P. Gutmann (ed.), *Economic Growth*, Prentice Hall, Englewood Cliffs, 1965, pp. 27–9

Hagen, Everett 'The Process of Economic Development', *Economic Development and Cultural Change*, April 1957, 202–4

Hahn, F.H. and Matthews, R.C.O. 'The Theory of Economic Growth', *Economic Journal*, December 1964

Harbison, F.H., Maruhnic, J. and Resnick, J. *Quantitative Analysis of Modernization and Development*, Princeton University, Princeton, NJ, 1970, pp. 58–73

—— and Myers, C. *Education, Manpower and Economic Growth*, McGraw-Hill, New York, 1964

—— and —— *Education: Country Studies in Economic Development*, McGraw-Hill, New York, 1965

Havrylyshyn, Oli 'Trade among Developing Countries: Theory Policy Issues, and Principal Trends', World Bank Staff Working Paper No. 479, World Bank, Washington DC, 1981, pp. 18–20

Higgins, Benjamin *Economic Development*, W.W. Norton and Co., New York, 1959

Hirschman, Albert O. *The Strategy of Economic Development*, Yale University Press, New Haven, 1958

—— and Bird, R.M. 'Foreign Aid – A Critique and Proposal', *Essays in International Finance*, no. 69, Princeton University Press, Princeton, NJ, July 1968

Holton, Richard H. 'Marketing Structure and Economic Development', *Quarterly Journal of Economics*, August 1953, 344–61

Houthakker, H.S. 'An International Comparison of Personal Saving', *Proceeding of International Statistical Institute* (32nd session, part 2), 1961, Tokyo, pp. 56–9

—— 'On Some Determinants of Savings in Developed and Under Developed Countries', in E.A.G. Robinson (ed.), *Problems of Economic Development*, MacMillan, London, 1965

Kuznets, S. 'Economic Growth and Small Nations', in E.A.G. Robinson (ed.), *Economic Consequences of the Size of Nations*, Macmillan, London, 1960

Landau, L. 'Saving Function in Latin America', in H.B. Chenery (ed.), *Studies in Development Planning*, Harvard University Press, Cambridge, Mass., 1971

Lewis, W.A. *The Theory of Economic Growth*, Allen & Unwin, London, 1955, pp. 274–83

Lluch, C. and Powell, A. *International Comparison of Expenditure and Saving Patterns*, IBRD Development Research Center, 1973

Mead, James E. *The Theory of Customs Union*, North-Holland Publishing Co., Amsterdam, Holland, 1955, pp. 35–41

Mikessel, R.F. 'Public Foreign Capital for Private Enterprise in Developing Countries', *Essays in International Finance*, no. 52, Princeton University, Princeton, NJ, April 1966

—— and Zinser, J.E. 'The Nature of Savings Function in Developing Countries: A Survey of Theoretical and Empirical Literature', *Journal of Economic Literature*, March 1973, 1–26

Papanek, G.F. 'The Development of Entrepreneurship', *American Economic Review*, vol. LII, no. 2, 1962, 54

—— 'The Effect of Aid and Other Resources Transfers on Savings and Growth in Less Developed Countries', *Economic Journal*, September 1972, 934–50

Pearson, L.B. *Partners in Development*, Praeger, NY, 1969, pp. 99–123

Schultz, T. 'Investment in Human Capital', in P. Gutmann (ed.), *Economic Growth*, Prentice Hall, Englewood Cliffs, 1965, pp. 125–42

Science Council of Canada 'Multinational and Industrial Strategy: The role of World Product Mandates', in Dhawan, Etemad and Wright (eds), *International Business: A Canadian Perspective*, Addison-Wesley, Don Mills Ontario, 1981, pp. 582–7

Scitovsky, T. 'Growth – Balanced or Unbalanced?' in M. Abramovitz (ed.), *Allocation of Economic Resources*, Stanford University Press, Stanford, 1959

—— *Economic Theory and Western European Integration*, Unwin University Books, London, 1962, pp. 20–32

Sethi, S.P. and Etemad, H. 'Marketing: The Missing Link in Economic Development?' in J. Hampton and A. van Gent (eds), *International Marketing in the 1980s: Problems and Challenges*, New York, Praeger, 1983

Sewell, John *The United States and World Development: Agenda 1980*, Praeger Publishers, New York, 1980

Shapiro, S.J. 'Comparative Marketing and Economic Development', in G. Schwartz (ed.), *Science in Marketing*, John Wiley & Sons Inc., New York, 1965, pp. 398–429

Sheth, N.N. and Sethi, S.P. 'A Theory of Cross Cultural Buyer Behaviour', in A.G. Woodside, J.H. Sheth and P.D. Bennett (eds), *Consumer and Industrial Buying Behaviour*, North-Holland, New York, 1977, pp. 369–89

Slater, C.C. 'Marketing Processes in Developing Latin American Societies', *Journal of Marketing, 32*, July 1968, 50–3

—— 'A Catalyst for Development', in Dov Israeli and Dafna N. Israeli (eds), *Marketing Systems for Developing Countries*, John Wiley & Sons, New York, 1976, pp. 3–17

Solow, R.M. *Growth Theory: An Exposition*, Oxford University Press, New York, 1970

Viner, Jacob *The Custom Union Issue*. Endowment for International Peace, New York, 1950

Weisskopf, T.E. 'The Impact of Foreign Capital Inflow on Domestic Savings in Under Developed Countries', *Journal of International Economics*, February 1972, 25–38

## Further Reading

Alderson, W. *Dynamic Marketing Behavior*, Irwin, Homewood, Ill., 1965

Bennett, Peter D. 'The Role of Government in the Promotion of Efficiency in the Retail Marketing of Food Products in Greater Santiago, Chile', in Peter D. Bennett (ed.), *Marketing and Economic Development*, American Marketing Association, 1965, pp. 105–9

Collins, N.R. and Holton, R.H. 'Programming Changes in Marketing in Planned Economic Development', *Kyklos*, vol. XVI, 1963, 123–35

Cook, Hugh L. 'Observations on Market Structure and National Economic Development in the Philippines', *Journal of Farm Economics*, vol. XLI, August 1958, 500–18

Dell, Sidney *A Latin American Common Market?* Oxford University Press, London, 1966, pp. 70–80

Domar, F.D. 'Expansion and Employment', *American Economic Review*, vol. 47, 1947

Etemad, H. 'Towards a Generalized Model of Comparative Marketing', in J.

Hampton and A. van Gent (eds), proceedings of *International Marketing in the 1980s: Problems and Challenges*, The Netherlands School of Business, July 1982

Gehrels, Franz and Johnston, Bruce F. 'The Economic Gains of European Integration', *Journal of Political Economy*, August 1955

Hamid, Hakima 'Marketing and Business Practices in Afghanistan', *Middle East Journal*, vol. XIV, Winter 1960, 87–93

Harrod, R.F. *Towards a Dynamic Economics*, Macmillan, London, 1948

Holton, Richard H. 'Economic Development and the Growth of the Trade Sector in Italy', *Banca Nazionale del Lavoro*, vol. XV, September 1962, 240–58

Kahlon, A.A. and Reed, Charles, E. 'Problems of Marketable Surplus in Indian Agriculture', *Indian Journal of Agricultural Economics*, vol. XVI, January–March 1961, 46–50

Keynes, John Maynard *General Theory of Employment, Interest and Money*, Macmillan, London, 1963

Kindleberger, C.P. *Economic Development*, McGraw-Hill, New York, 1958, pp. 106–8

Malthus, Thomas *Principles of Political Economy*, William Pickering, London, 1936

Martin, Lee R. 'Some Marketing Problems in Pakistan and India', *Journal of Farm Economics*, vol. XLI, December 1959, 1323–6

McClelland, D.C. *The Achieving Society*, Van Nostrand, Princeton, NJ, 1961

—— and Winter, David G. *Motivating Economic Achievement*, Free Press, New York, 1969, pp. 309–37

Meissner, Frank 'Capital and Technical Cooperation Programs for Agricultural Marketing in Developing Countries of Latin America', in Israeli *et al.* (eds), *Marketing Systems for Developing Countries*, Wiley, New York, 1976, pp. 31–49

Mill, John Stuart *Principles of Political Economy*, The Colonial Press, London, 1900

Mintz, S.W. 'The Jamaican Internal Marketing Pattern: Some Notes and Hypotheses', *Social and Economic Studies*, vol. IV, March 1955, 95–103

—— 'The Role of the Middleman in the Internal Distribution System of a Caribbean Peasant Economy', *Human Organization*, vol. XV, Summer 1956, 18–24

—— 'Markets in Haiti', *New Society*, vol. I, March 1963, 18–19

Nicossia, F.M. *Consumer Decision Process*, Prentice Hall, Englewood Cliffs, 1966

Nurske, Ragnar *Problems of Capital Formation in Under Developed Countries*, Oxford University Press, New York, 1952, pp. 61–75

Ricardo, David 'On Economic Growth', in S. Baffa (ed.), *On the Principles of Political Economy and Taxation*, Cambridge University Press, Cambridge, 1959

Robinson, E.A.G. (ed.) *Economic Consequences of the Size of Nations*, Macmillan, London, 1960

—— (ed.) *Problems of Economic Development*, Macmillan, London, 1965

Rostow, W.W. 'The Concept of a National Market and Its Economic Growth Implications', in P.D. Bennett (ed.), *Marketing and Economic Development*, American Marketing Association, Chicago, 1965, pp. 11–20

Samli, A. Coskun 'Wholesaling in an Economy of Scarcity', *Journal of Marketing*, vol. XXVIII, July 1964, 55–8

Schooler, R. 'Marketing in the Central American Common Market', in P.D. Bennett (ed.), *Marketing and Economic Development*, American Marketing Association, Chicago, 1965, 116–17

Sherbini, Abdel Aziz 'Marketing in the Industrialization of Under Developed Countries', *Journal of Marketing*, vol. XXIX, January 1965, 28–32

Singer, Hans 'Social Development — Key Growth Sector', *International Development Review*, March 1965

Slater, Charles C. 'The Role of Food Marketing in Latin American Economic Development', in P.D. Bennett (ed.), *Marketing and Economic Development*, American Marketing Association, Chicago, 1965, pp. 30–7

—— and Walsham, G. 'A Systems Simulation Model of the Kenyan Economy', *Omega, The International Journal of Management Science, 3*, May 1975, 557–67

—— and Jenkins, D. 'Systems Approaches to Comparative Macro-Marketing', in G. Fisk and R.W. Nason (eds), *Macro-Marketing: New Steps on the Learning Curve*, Graduate School of Business Administration, University of Colorado, Boulder, 1979, pp. 371–80

Smithies, A. 'Rising Expectation and Economic Development', *The Economic Journal*, June 1961

Solomon, M.R. 'The Structure of the Market in Under Developed Economies', *Quarterly Journal of Economics*, vol. LXII, August 1948, 519–37

Thorelli, H.B. 'Political Science and Marketing', in R. Cox, W. Anderson and S.J. Shapiro (eds), *Theory in Marketing: Second Series*, Richard D. Irwin, Homewood, Ill., 1964

Westfall, R. and B., Jr. and Harper, W. 'Marketing in India', *Journal of Marketing*, vol. XXV, October 1960, 11–17

Wind, Yoram 'The Role of Marketing in Israel', *Journal of Marketing*, vol. XXXI, April 1967, 53–7

# 4  MISSING LINKS: MARKETING AND THE NEWER THEORIES OF DEVELOPMENT[1]

Nikhilesh Dholakia and Ruby Roy Dholakia

The discipline of marketing has shown a relatively low level of interest in the problems of development. The low level is reflected in both the limited *quantity* of marketing scholarship in this area as well as the unappealing *quality* of much of the work on marketing aspects of development. This is unfortunate. Concepts which have a marketing flavor — consumption, markets, life-styles, choice behavior, distribution systems, etc. — are quite central in development theories and projects. Depending on the context and perspective, marketing is often held to be the villain or the vital ingredient in the process of development.

This chapter examines the links between marketing and the newer theories of development. The 'newer' theories are the variety of perspectives on development which have evolved as a result of the failure of the neoclassical economic models to bring about substantial development in the Third World. The newer theories also reflect a convergence of the concepts of classical political economy, present-day ecological concerns, and the search for psychosocial (rather than just economic) values by the peoples in the industrialized as well as Third World countries. At present, such newer theories and concepts of development tend to be eclectic, multidisciplinary, and somewhat tentative. Yet such concepts are catching the imaginations of organizations ranging from grass-roots movements to international aid agencies. As a result, the very notion of development is undergoing a redefinition.

This chapter, which attempts to build bridges between marketing and the emerging meanings and strategies of development, is structured into the following major sections:

(1) *Aspects of Marketing* This section breaks down marketing into component aspects for the purposes of relating these to development.
(2) *Views of Development* Exploration of the alternative meanings and concepts of development is carried out in this section.
(3) *Theories of Development* Examination of theories as to what causes

development or underdevelopment is explored here.

(4) *Agent of Development* This section addresses the question of which agency should play what role in the process of development.

In each of sections 2, 3 and 4, the development issues raised in that section are related to the marketing aspects outlined in section 1. In this way the conceptual links between marketing and development are strengthened.

## Aspects of Marketing

Like development, marketing is a multifaceted subject; it can be viewed narrowly as activities that occur in the transfer of goods and services from producers to consumers, or broadly as all processes by which a society meets its consumption needs (for definitional reviews, see Kotler, 1981, Ch. 1; Hunt, 1976; Fisk, 1980). The broader the conception of development, the broader should be the definition of marketing. From a developmental perspective, the relevant aspects of marketing can be viewed at four levels. It is useful to assess the relationship of marketing to development at each of these levels.

### Society Level

With economic growth, the overall importance of marketing in society changes. Tertiary and service activities — many of which are marketing activities — expand in number, size and complexity. The share of such activities in the national product rises. Questions of distribution and marketing costs assume considerable salience (see, for example, Cox, Goodman and Fichandler, 1965). The infrastructures for physical distribution and marketing communications expand and become differentiated. Also, public policies oriented to marketers and consumers evolve and take sophisticated forms. In short, with growth the character of the overall marketing system changes (Layton, 1982). Variables pertaining to the overall size, share, differentiation, cost, etc., of the marketing system (see Table 4.1, column A) are of great importance in understanding the links between marketing and development.

### Sector Level

Sectorial shifts from agriculture to manufacturing to services are usually associated with economic growth. Even within a sector, and specifically within industries, the competitive structure, the diversity of products

Table 4.1: Aspects of Marketing Relevant to Development

| A<br>Country-level<br>aspects | B<br>Sector-level<br>aspects | C<br>Channel-level<br>aspects | D<br>Consumer-level<br>aspects |
|---|---|---|---|
| Overall size of market | Competitive structure | Channel structure | Values |
| Share of marketing in national product | Diversity of products | Channel innovations | Life-styles |
| Differentiation of market | Types of marketing strategies | Power distribution | Power and consciousness |
| Physical distribution infra-structure | Financing of marketing activities | Economic viability | Buying/consuming methods |
| Communication infrastructure | | | |

offered, the type of marketing strategies used, and the way marketing activities are financed can vary. It should be noted here that the model of marketing implicit in marketing textbooks is characterized by:

- Large, rivairous, oligopolistic firms
- Price-making flexibility
- Differentiated products
- Segmented markets
- Reliance on positioning and communication strategies

It is evident that such a model of marketing is not universal but characterizes a particular economic formation, viz. the major industrial sectors of the Western economies. The use of such a model for the developing economies of the Third World, therefore, is quite inappropriate. In investigating the relationship between marketing and development, it is necessary to know the sectoral aspects of marketing and development (see Table 4.1, column B). Specifically, the marketing models associated with decentralized sectors, dualistic sectors, state-controlled sectors and other sectoral types peculiar to Third World countries need to be investigated.

*Channel Level*

As conduits for the flow of goods, information and money, channels occupy a special place in marketing systems. Channel changes are closely linked with economic changes as evidenced, for example, in the 'wheel of retailing' phenomena (Markin and Duncan, 1981). The following channel-level aspects are very pertinent in exploring how marketing relates to development:

- channel structure
- innovations in channels
- distribution of power in a channel
- economic viability of various channels

While the emergence of mass retailing channels is somewhat related to the level of economic development, there is no unilinear relationship, and it is certainly inappropriate to treat mass retailing as an indicator of development. Instead, studies of the variety of retail and wholesale forms actually prevalent in Third World countries are needed.

## Consumer Level

There are significant human impacts of the process of development. In the sphere of consumption, changes might occur in consumers'

- values
- life-styles and consumption patterns
- consciousness
- buying and consuming methods
- power

It is important to understand how the consumer transforms as his socio-economic context transforms. Such changes represent the micro aspects of marketing relevant to development.

## Views of Development

In a general sense, 'development seems to imply *positive* change, i.e. improvement of position' (Hettne and Wallensteen, 1978, p. 53). Until the 1960s most development experts and planners equated development with economic growth. While development and growth are certainly not semantic equivalents, the belief was that growth would bring about general socio-economic well-being through a trickle-down of benefits. Economic prosperity was also supposed to bring about political democracy of the Western variety. Although the growth performance of Third World countries in the two decades following World War II was reasonably good (Bell, 1980), the benefits hardly reached the mass of the population. Adelman (1980) points out that the pace of urbanization far outstripped that of industrialization, inequities led to bloody civil strife in some countries, trickle-down effects were virtually absent, political democracies crumbled in most countries, and finally, 'the most dramatic backlash occurred in Iran, where an oppressive modernizing autocracy was replaced by a traditional theocracy coupled with mob rule' (p. 215). As a result of these, the orthodox economic view of 'development equals growth' has waned, and alternative views have emerged.

### Alternative Concepts of Development

Although concepts of development proliferate, it is useful to focus on four major views of what constitutes development:

(1) Development is economic growth measured by increase in *per capita* GNP ('Growth Only' view).

(2) Development is economic growth, measured as above, coupled with diversification of the economy ('Growth with Diversification' view).

(3) Development is growth with equity, i.e. growth associated with redistribution of economic benefits ('Growth with Equity' view).

(4) Development is a multidimensional concept focusing on basic needs, self-reliance, equity, social values, etc. ('Multidimensional' view).

Since the 1970s the growth-based views (1, 2, and to some extent 3 above) have been losing ground to the multidimensional view (Nugent and Yotopoulos, 1979). As Hettne and Wallensteen (1978) point out:

> increase in GNP *per capita* is . . . a very practical definition: it is relatively easy to measure . . . It says, however, very little about what is actually going on in a society or the fate of its inhabitants . . . Multidimensional definitions are . . . cumbersome . . . [but say] more about a given society and the changes therein than unidimensional ones. (p. 54)

There are two versions of the multidimensional development view. The 'soft' variant calls for local self-reliance (Rist, 1980), soft technological choices (Abdalla, 1980; Illich, 1973a; Lovins, 1977), reaffirming of cultural values (Henry, 1981; Rist, 1980), etc. In contrast, there is a 'hard' variant of the multidimensional view of development, favored by economists, which emphasizes growth along with equity and open policy (Adelman, 1980), allocative efficiency, stability and equity (Bell, 1980), basic-needs satisfaction, equity and employment (Seers, 1969). Naturally, these positions are not exclusive. There are, however, strong antagonistic elements particularly between the growth-emphasizing and growth-de-emphasizing views. These have led to a variety of development strategies such as basic-needs strategy (Burki and Haq, 1981; Singh, 1979), export-led growth (Cline, 1982; Wynn, 1982), autarchy (Amin, 1979; Senghaas, 1980), decentralized or 'alternative' development (Rist, 1980), development championed by state enterprises (Gillis, 1980), balanced growth (Taylor, 1982), etc.

## Marketing and the Views of Development

Philosophically, the multidimensional view, especially the 'soft' variant, is very compatible with the marketing concept − it focuses on the 'consumers' of the development programs, their aspirations and needs. Such a view emphasizes the importance of local self-reliance at the level of a community (Rist, 1980), and emphasizes 'a style of development that . . . calls for specific solutions to the particular problems of [a] region in the light of cultural as well as ecological data and long-term as well as immediate needs' (Hettne and Wallensteen, 1978, p. 65). The needs are also viewed broadly. Besides *welfare* (measured in economic terms), the community's needs for *security, identity* and *freedom* have to be met (Hettne and Wallensteen, 1978, p. 61).

The implications for the alternative views of development for marketing are explored in Table 4.2. As the table shows, the contrast is the greatest between the 'Growth Only' view of development and the 'soft' variant of the multidimensional view of development. The latter's emphasis is on aesthetic, life-enriching consumer values achieved by the use of diffused, localized, informal institutions sharing power equitably with consumers.

It should be pointed out that many of the conventional theories linking marketing and development (see, for example, Drucker, 1958; Layton, 1982) hold that growth, by itself, would have the marketing impact associated with 'Growth with Equity' view and, conversely, marketing innovations would, by themselves, lead to equitable growth. This is a misconception which arises from the ignoring of external (foreign) linkages which transmit the benefits of growth in the Third World, especially marketing-led growth, to foreign metropolitan economies (Sunkel, 1979). These inadequacies in the marketing literature are the result of neglecting: (a) theories that deal with development as a process, and (b) the role of alternative 'agents' of development, viz. private enterprise, the state, and community-based movements. The next two major sections address these issues.

## Theories of Development

Theories about the process of development vary, depending on what is meant by development (growth, redistribution, multidimensional concept, etc.) and what process is being examined (external linkages, internal-resource mobilization, social and cultural change, etc.). From the standpoint of marketing, it is useful to consider three types of development theories, those dealing with:

Table 4.2: Relationships Among Views of Development and Selected Aspects of Marketing

| Views of development | Overall market size | Marketing costs, GNP share | Competitive structure | Product diversity | Channel structure | Channel control | Consumer values | Consumer power |
|---|---|---|---|---|---|---|---|---|
| | | | | | Aspects of marketing | | | |
| Growth only | Usually stagnant market, rising exports | Increasing | Concentrated, usually foreign dominated | Medium to high | Rising vertical integration | By 'marketer' | Consumptionist, elitist | Usually low, declining |
| Growth with diversification | Diversified but slow growing | Increasing | Concentrated, national firms or capitalists | High | Rising vertical integration | 'Marketer' | Consumptionist, elitist | Usually low, declining |
| Growth with equity | Expanding domestic market | Increasing but controls introduced | Concentrated in lead sectors, equitable elsewhere | Medium, focus on basic goods | Vertical with state inroads | 'Marketer' with state interventions | Consumptionist | Low but consolidating |
| Multidimensional development — hard variant | Expanding domestic market | Attempt to make markets more cost-efficient | Attempt to diffuse concentrated structure | High priority to basic needs | Attempt to reduce concentration | 'Marketer' | Consumptionist | Low but consolidating, strong consumer protection moves |
| Multidimensional development — soft variant | Controlled, need-based market expansion | Controlled at low level | Diffused, localized, human-scale | Low: held to 'adequate' level, focus on balanced needs | Short, informal channels | Producers and consumers | Aesthetic, life-enriching | Convergence of interest with producers, equitable power |

(1) growth and equity
(2) underdevelopment and dependency
(3) alternative forms of development

*Growth and Equity*

The idea that growth will solve various developmental problems such as poor resource mobilization and allocation, global disparity, and internal inequity is still championed by its adherents (Rostow, 1978). The reality of development experience is negating most of the tenets of growth-based theories (Hobsbawm 1979; Nugent and Yotopoulos, 1979). In fact, inequity (rather than equity) seems to be the major result of *laissez-faire* growth. This is true for Third World countries of today as well as for the Organisation for Economic Cooperation and Development (OECD) countries during their industrializing periods. According to Adelman (1980):

> Systematic statistical investigations indicate that, in most developing countries, there occurred a long process of decline in the relative incomes of the poorest as a direct consequence of accelerated economic development . . . In most of the developed European countries, the Industrial Revolution initiated a U-shaped time path in the absolute and relative incomes of the poorest . . . On the average, one to two generations elapsed before the absolute incomes of the poorest regained the same levels as they had before the Industrial Revolution began. (p. 216)

In the contemporary world, such immiserating growth is morally and politically unacceptable. In fact, most of the development success stories of this century – USSR, Japan, China, Taiwan, Korea, Israel, Singapore, Yugoslavia, etc. – have reversed the European formula of 'growth before redistribution' and instituted policies of 'redistribution before growth'. In pointing to this fact, Adelman (1980) notes that this process of development has worked irrespective of political ideology. The implications of this for marketing are:

(1) The view of marketing merely as an engine of growth is not very useful.
(2) In those countries where redistribution policies are part of development planning, the control of marketing institutions is an important issue.

*Structural Theories: Underdevelopment and Dependence*

An implicit assumption of conventional development economies is that the Third World countries benefit from integration into the world market. Under this assumption, engaging in international trade and permitting inflows of foreign capital have positive development effects in the Third World.

The dependency theories, articulated primarily by Latin American economists, challenge the supposedly positive effects of international integration. With intellectual antecedents in the classical theories of imperialism (Hobson, Lenin), and the structuralist views about unfavorable trade terms for the Third World (Myrdal, Prebish, Singer), the 'dependistas' have argued that:

'Center' and 'periphery' exist among and within nations. The central countries in the world economy are the industrialized capitalist nations and the peripheral countries are those of the Third World. Within each Third World country, however, there exists a central, metropolitan, prosperous sector and a peripheral, impoverished, rural sector.
· There is a disharmony of interests between center and periphery.
· The metropolitan countries – those at the center – exercise their influence on the peripheral countries through an internationalized elite. A situation of dependency develops.
· In general, dependency and growth are negatively related. Whatever growth occurs, its fruits are shared by the center and the Third World elite, resulting in the marginalization of the periphery.

These relationships are shown in Figure 4.1, based on Galtung's structural view of imperialism (Galtung. 1980). As we can see, there is a *harmony of interest* only between the center of the 'central nation', (e.g. USA) and center of the 'peripheral nation' (e.g. Bolivia). However, there is *disharmony of interest*, both within the 'central nation' and within the 'peripheral nation', as well as between the periphery of the two nations (e.g. the textile workers in the USA complaining about unfair competition from textile workers in South East Asia).

Given these structural relations, the center of the 'central nation' establishes a bridgehead – often by means of a transnational company – in the center of the 'peripheral nation'. This bridgehead helps the *transmission of (economic) value* from the periphery of the 'peripheral nation' to the center of the 'central nation', with the center of the 'peripheral nation' (i.e. the Third World elite) sharing in the benefits. To the extent marketing systems are such transmitters of value, they would detract from the development of the periphery. Hence, an important distinction

Figure 4.1: A Structural View of Imperialism

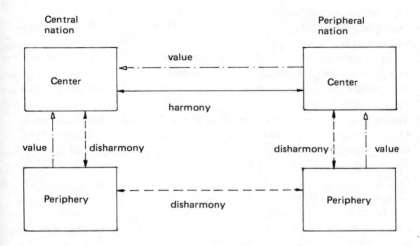

Source: Based on Galtung (1980).
needs to be made between marketing institutions and processes which facilitate development and marketing institutions and process that detract from development.

## Alternative Development: Search for a Theory

In recent years the disappointment with major development theories and models — conventional as well as dependency-type — has spurred the search for alternative models. The quest for alternative actually starts at the grass roots. Community-based groups and activists, frustrated with so-called development efforts or lack thereof, initiate an alternative *practice* of development. These alternative-development models are localized experiments in which people take the task of development into their own hands, and start shaping appropriate structures and initiating appropriate processes. Interestingly, the quest for alternative-development models is global — the industrialized Western nations are searching for alternatives (Galtung, 1980a; Irvine, 1980) just as the Third World countries are (Abdalla, 1980; Illich, 1973b; Rist, 1980). Although there are many alternative development 'models', the essential features of such experiments are:

- localized, community-based efforts
- collective self-reliance
- appropriate technology
- focus on human needs
- respect for culture
- preservation of eco-system
- participation
- non-alienating organization of production
- mutual help and cooperation

There is, as yet, no viable *theory* of alternative development. In fact, Utopian communities have existed at various times and places in history. Both conventional and Marxian social scientists berate Utopias because these are atheoretical — there is no viable theory that either predicts or can guide a Utopia. The difference between present-day alternative-development efforts and Utopias is that today's movements span the globe and *are developing a linking infrastructure* (see *IFDA Dossier*). The emerging nexus of alternative-development efforts and intellectual interest in these indicate that a *pre-theory* in alternative development already exists. It is only a matter of time before a viable theory emerges. There is very little research on the role of marketing under alternative forms of development, but it is clear that marketing systems face a great challenge in adapting to alternative-consumption styles (Shama, 1980). There is, indeed, an emerging recognition that a 'revisioning' of the marketing management paradigm is needed as the alternative-development styles proliferate (Rosenberg, 1983).

*Marketing and Theories of Development*

The three types of development theories have several implications for marketing. Marketing models based on the 'stages of growth' view (see, for example, Preston, 1968; Slater, 1976) need seriously to reconsider the growth-equity links. Apart from being misguided in visualizing these links, conventional economic-growth theories have been disproved by the reality of the development experience on several other counts (see Table 4.3). If idealized reconstructions of industrialized countries' experiences are irrelevant for the Third World, if definitive and meliorating stages of growth do not exist, then marketing policies based on such views are likely to be counterproductive. This challenge to the theoretical relationship between marketing and development is occasionally recognized (Hilger, 1977), but the next logical step of exploring alternative theories of development is not undertaken.

Table 4.3: Some Contradictions of Conventional Economic-growth
Theories

| Concepts provided by conventional economic-growth theories | Realities of recent development experience |
| --- | --- |
| 1. Growth will bring about equity trickle-down effects | High-growth countries have experienced trickle-up and marginalization effects |
| 2. Keynesian demand-stimulation policies should minimize the problem of unemployment | High unemployment levels have persisted in the Third World |
| 3. Rural-urban disparities will disappear with marginal rural workers migrating to cities and the productivity of agriculture increasing | Skilled and capable rural workers have migrated, displacing inefficient urban workers, creating 'lumpen proletariat'. Agricultural productivity remains low |
| 4. Because of pool of available technology, Third World countries can quickly bridge the technology gap | While the opportunities exist, in reality highly capital and energy-intensive technologies have been chosen |
| 5. International trade will even out benefits and factor disparities. | Multinationals have been able to manipulate factor advantages to their gain, not to the benefit of Third World countries |

Source: Based on Nugent and Yotopoulos (1979).

The structural theories of imperialism and dependency are extremely relevant for marketing. As Figure 4.1 shows, the ultimate result of dependency is the transmission of economic value from the poor, peripheral sectors of the Third World to the dynamic central sectors of the advanced countries (Chilcote, 1980). Marketing institutions and processes play an essential role in this transmission of economic value. There are a variety of ways in which value can be transferred from the periphery to the center, including:

· exports to Third World of luxury consumer goods or overpriced capital goods
· imports from Third World of underpriced raw materials or labor-intensive goods
· fees and royalties from the sale of technology, especially technology with very low marginal cost of transference
· investing in Third World companies to cater to local markets, followed by repatriation of profits
· disinvesting and repatriating capital accumulated through operations in the Third World
· importing human capital from the Third World

• attracting bank deposits and equity capital from Third World investors
• variety of transfer pricing methods among subsidiaries of transnational corporations
• orienting 'development' projects financed by aid to the economy of the donor country

In all these mechanisms, marketing decisions, institutions, and activities play a role in the transferral of value. It is important to understand how marketing processes like:

• creation and expansion of markets
• proliferation of consumption values and patterns
• pricing and sales-terms determination
• market segmentation and product positioning
• evolution and integration of channels
• adaptation and adoption of products
• differentiation and proliferation of brands
• generation and control of market information
• evolution of global marketing organizations and interorganizational marketing systems
• emulation and adaptation of marketing communication media and messages
• emulation and adaptation of marketing management styles, etc.

contribute to: (a) creating and strengthening dependency structures, (b) transmitting value from periphery to center, given existing dependency structures. Furthermore, it needs to be understood what the *developmental impact* of such value transferral is. Specifically, does the process of transfer of value lead to:

(1) stagnation and underdevelopment, or
(2) dependent forms of development, or
(3) coequal and interdependent forms of development?

The marketing literature has yet to address these issues. However, the impact of marketing on transfer of value needs to be investigated and assessed.

The implications of alternative development models for marketing are drastic. As currently construed, marketing is almost antithetical to alternative development. Marketing calls for increased division of labor, expanding markets, finer segments, more centralized information, greater corporate concentration, and alienating strategies (for elaboration of some of these, see Sorensen, 1982). To the extent alternative development efforts succeed, marketing in its conventional form will decline in importance. There would, however, emerge the need for newer marketing concepts and techniques that help in:

* need-assessment
* enriching consumption and life patterns
* selecting appropriate technologies
* designing need-based consumption packages
* improving inter-community communications
* improving alternatives for creative human activity
* analyzing ecological impact of consumption
* socializing people for alternative life-styles

The challenge lies for marketing to develop concepts and techniques that will be responsive to the needs of alternative development models.

## Agents of Development

Development is an intricate, multifaceted and long-drawn out task. For Third World countries, it is the premier societal task. Naturally, the question of which agency shoulders the responsibility of development is very important. In traditional development thinking two agents of development are considered: the private sector and the state. The alternative development models just described have added a third possibility: the community, often represented by a voluntary agency or movement. When it assumes primacy, each development agent — the private sector, the state and the community — represents a particular regime of development. The first represents a private capitalist regime, the second represents a statist regime (which, in practice, has turned out to be a state capitalist regime in most cases — see Amin, 1978), and the third represents a decentralized regime.

### Marketing and Agents of Development

For the most part, marketing literature has focused on the role of the private sector in economic development (see, for example, Moyer and Hollander, 1968; Preston, 1968; Slater, 1968). Some of the recent marketing literature shows an awareness of the growing role of the state (see, for example, Dholakia and Khurana, 1979; Hilger, 1977; Sorensen, 1978). The development literature is increasingly recognizing the active role of the state and its organs in the process of development (see, for example, Burki and Haq, 1981; Gillis, 1980; Leibenstein, 1980). The third possible development agent — the community — has received some attention in the development literature, but has not yet been recognized in the marketing literature. This is an obvious gap that needs to be filled.

The marketing implications of each development regime need to be explored in detail. It should be noted that the community-based decentralized regime is very different from the other two; the societal, sectoral and channel aspects of marketing are only minimally important, and the focus is on the community of producer-consumers.

## Concluding Observations

In the years to come, development is likely to become the top item on the global agenda. This is not because of the Malthusian spectre of hungry teeming millions as was once widely believed, but because of the realization that the problems of development — stagnation, poverty, environmental destruction, alienation, cultural homogenization, inequity, unresponsive institutions, etc. — are not just problems of the Third World alone. As developmental concerns intensify, so will the search for developmental alternatives. The discipline of marketing, if it is to remain relevant, will have to work out designs of marketing to meet the challenges of development. This calls for multipronged efforts. Not only must marketing people recognize the alternative notions and theories of development, they must evolve alternative marketing concepts suitable for the variety of development trajectories found in the contemporary world.

## Note

1. Parts of this chapter were presented earlier at the Marketing and Economic Development Session of The American Marketing Association Annual Fall Conference, Chicago 1982.

# References

Abdalla, Ismail-Sabri 'What Development? A Third World Viewpoint', *International Development Review, 22*, 2-3, 1980, 13-16

Adelman, Irma 'Economic Development and Political Change in Developing Countries', *Social Research, 47*, Summer 1980, 213-34

Amin, Samir 'Development Theory and the Crisis in Development', in B. Hettne and P. Wallensteen (eds), *Emerging Trends in Development Theory*, Swedish Agency for Research Cooperation with Developing Countries, Stockholm, 1978, pp. 13-21

—— 'Toward an Alternative Strategy of Auto-Centered Development', in G. Modelski (ed.), *Transnational Corporations and World Order*, W.H. Freeman, San Francisco, 1979, pp. 404-13

Bell, Philip W. 'Economic Theory and Development Economics: Where Do We Stand?' *Social Research, 47*, Summer 1980, 235-47

Burki, Javed and Haq Mahbub ul 'Meeting Basic Needs: An Overview', *World Development, 9*, February 1981, 167-82

Chilcote, Ronald H. 'Theories of Dependency: The View from the Periphery', in I. Vogeler and A.R. de Souza (eds), *Dialectics of Third World Development*, Allanheld, Osmun, Montclair, NJ, 1980, pp. 299-309

Cline, William R. 'Can the East Asian Model of Development Be Generalised?' *World Development, 10*, 2, 1982, 81-90

Cox, R., Goodman, C. and Fichandler, T.C. *Distribution in a High Level Economy*, Prentice-Hall, Englewood Cliffs, NJ, 1965

Dholakia, Nichilesh and Khurana, Rakesh *Public Distribution Systems: Evolution, Evaluation, and Prospects*, Oxford and IBH, New Delhi, 1979

Drucker, Peter F. 'Marketing and Economic Development', *Journal of Marketing, 22*, January 1958, 252-9

Fisk, George 'Taxonomic Classification of Macromarketing Theory', in C.W. Lamb and P.M. Dunne (eds), *Theoretical Developments in Marketing*, American Marketing Association, Chicago, Il., 1980, pp. 146-9

Galtung, Johan 'A Structural Theory of Imperialism', in *Dialectics of Third World Development*, Allanheld, Osmun, Montclair, NJ, 1980, pp. 261-98

—— 'Crisis in the West', *International Development Review, 22*, 2-3, 1980a, 51-5

Gillis, Malcolm 'The Role of State Enterprises in Economic Development', *Social Research, 47*, Summer 1980, 248-89

Henry, Paul-Marc 'Economic Development, Progress and Culture', *Development: Seeds of Change, 3*, 4, 1981, 17-25

Hettne, Bjorn and Wallensteen, Peter 'Concluding Observations', in B. Hettne and P. Wallensteen (eds), *Emerging Trends in Development Theory*, Swedish Agency for Research Cooperation with Developing Countries, Stockholm, 1978

Hilger, Marye Tharpe 'Theories of the Relationship Between Marketing and Economic Development: Public Policy Implications', in C.C. Slater and P.D. White (eds), *Macromarketing: Distributive Processes from a Societal Perspective: An Elaboration of Issues*, University of Colorado, Business Research Division, Boulder, Co., 1977, pp. 335-50

Hobsbawm, E.J. 'The Development of the World Economy', *Cambridge Journal of Economics, 3*, September 1979, 305-18

Hunt, Shelby D. 'The Nature and Scope of Marketing', *Journal of Macromarketing, 40*, July 1976, 17-27

IFDA *Dossier* (journal) International Foundation for Development Alternatives, Nyon, Switzerland

Illich, Ivan *Tools for Conviviality*, Harper and Row, New York, 1973a
—— 'Outwitting the "Developed Countries" ', in C.K. Wilber (ed.), *The Political Economy of Development and Underdevelopment*, Random House, New York, 1973b, pp. 401–9

Irvine, John 'The Choice of Ways of Life in the North', *International Development Review, 22*, 2–3, 1980, 55–67

Kotler, Philip *Principles of Marketing*, Prentice-Hall, Englewood Cliffs, NJ, 1981

Layton, R.A. 'A Theory of the Role of Marketing Systems in Economic Growth', American Marketing Association Annual Educators' Conference, Chicago, August 1982

Leibenstein, Harvey 'Issues in Development: An Introduction', *Social Research, 47*, Summer 1980, 204–12

Lovins, Amory B. *Soft Energy Paths*, Harper and Row, New York, 1977

Markin, Rom J. and Duncan, Calvin P. 'The Transformation of Retailing Institutions: Beyond the Wheel of Retailing and Life Cycle Theories', *Journal of Macromarketing, 1*, Spring 1981, 58–66

Moyer, Reed and Hollander, Stanley C. (eds) *Markets and Marketing in Developing Economies*, R.D. Irwin, Homewood, Il., 1968

Nugent, Jeffrey B. and Yotopoulos, Pan A. 'What Has Orthodox Development Economics Learned from Recent Experience?' *World Development, 7*, June 1979, 541–54

Preston, Lee F. 'The Commercial Sector and Economic Development', in R. Moyer and S.C. Hollander (eds), *Markets and Marketing in Developing Economies*, R.D. Irwin, Homewood, Il., 1968, pp. 9–23

Rist, Gilbert 'Alternative Strategies to Development', *International Development Review, 22*, 2–3, 1980, 102–15

Rosenberg, Larry J. 'Re-Visioning Market Management as the Paradigm Shifts', Workshop on Alternative Paradigms in Marketing, University of Rhode Island, May 1983

Rostow, W.W. *The World Economy: History and Prospect*, University of Texas Press, Austin, Tx, 1978

Seers, Dudley 'The Meaning of Development', *International Development Review, 11*, 4, December 1969, 2–6

Senghaas, Dieter 'The Case for Autarchy', *International Development Review, 22*, 1, 1980, 3–10

Shama, Avraham *Marketing in a Slow-Growth Economy*, Praeger Publishing Company, New York, 1980

Singh, Ajit 'The "Basic Needs" Approach to Development vs. The New International Economic Order: The Significance of Third World Industrialisation', *World Development, 7*, June 1979, 585–606

Slater, Charles C. 'Marketing Processes in Developing Latin American Countries', *Journal of Marketing, 32*, July 1968, 50–5
—— 'A Theory of Market Processes', in C.C. Slater (ed.), *Macromarketing: Distributive Processes from a Societal Perspective*, University of Colorado, Business Research Division, Boulder, Co., 1976

Sorensen, Olav Jull 'A Conceptual Framework for Analysis of Government Intervention in the Distributive Trade in Ghana', Working Paper Series, 78–4, School of Administration, University of Ghana, February 1978
—— 'Marketing and Economic Development – The Case of Division of Labor', Seventh Annual Macromarketing Seminar, University of Colorado, August 1982

Sunkel, Osvaldo 'Big Business and "Dependencia" ', in G. Modelski (ed.), *Transnational Corporations and World Order*, W.H. Freeman, San Francisco, 1979, pp. 216–25

Taylor, Lance 'Back to Basics: Theory for the Rhetoric in the North-South Round', *World Development, 10*, 4, 1982, 327–35

Wynn, Sam 'The Taiwanese "Economic Miracle" ', *Monthly Review, 33*, April 1982, 30–40

# 5 MARKETING PROBLEMS IN LDCs: THE CASE OF EGYPT

Essam Mahmoud and Gillian Rice

## Introduction

International marketing strategy is essentially derived from the inter-action between the firm and its external environment, where the environmental variable can be reduced to several subvariables such as the economic, social, political and technological. International market-ing strategy includes the entry decision and marketing-mix decisions concerning products, promotion, distribution and pricing.

Market size and growth are widely associated with marketing and investment patterns such that the importance of a market will offset environmental variables to a certain extent (Kobrin, 1976; Davidson, 1980; Rice, 1982). Nevertheless, many international marketing decisions have a long time-horizon, and so are particularly vulnerable to environmental change. Pearson (1980) argues that developed countries, by definition, are going through a profound, and as yet unfinished, social transformation. This means that there is a high likelihood that the long-term political, economic and social conditions in a country such as Egypt will be considerably different from present conditions. With reference to the problems of implementing marketing strategy, the present conditions in developing countries include the paucity of marketing information, the duality of the economy, a poor infra-structure, often unstable political conditions, and inadequate admini-strative and technical skills.

This chapter deals with the problems of marketing in one develop-ing country, Egypt. The following analysis evaluates the Egyptian environment for marketing. While Egypt is typical of many developing countries and is therefore usefully employed as an example, the analysis will indicate the idiosyncrasies in its environment of particular interest to marketers. The discussion focuses upon selected environmental issues such as economic conditions, bureaucratic problems, demographic characteristics, the infrastructure, and the socio-cultural context. Finally, a summary of marketing problems in Egypt and their implica-tions for strategy is presented.

**The Egyptian Economy and Related Marketing Problems**

Egypt enjoyed overall economic growth during the years 1977–82 — the latest period for which information is available. Due largely to petroleum exports, remittances, tourism and Suez Canal revenues, the country maintained annual real gross national product growth-rates ranging from 8 percent to 10 percent (*Business America*, 1982a). According to the *Business America* report, the outlook for these key activities remains good. *Per capita* income in Egypt is US $520 (*Middle East and African Economist*, 1982a) which puts Egypt in the middle range of the developing countries. This figure reflects Egypt's large population (see Table 5.1), but living standards are admittedly poor for the majority of the country's people.

*The Dual Economy Problem*

*Per capita* income and growth are important, but it is the spread of wealth and the general level of discretionary income which influences major shifts in the demand from different groups of consumers for products and services (Michell, 1979). With the rise in world trade, a dual society tends to emerge in developing countries; an elitist segment demands the products of the industrialized economy, while the vast majority continue their present subsistence economy. From a marketing perspective, the presence of economic dualism (the coexistence of modern and traditional sectors within the economy) may be problematic. It may be necessary to conduct market assessments for each sector. Most international marketing textbooks discuss the marketing implications of economic dualism (for example, see Cateora, 1983); such a discussion is not repeated here. Rather, evidence relating to the existence of a dual economy in Egypt is examined.

In order to detect economic dualism, it seems reasonable to investigate income and consumption patterns. No single data source can be relied upon to estimate income distribution in Egypt. Ikram (1980) suggests that the most consistent numbers come from a series of three consumer-budget surveys undertaken by the Central Agency for Public Mobilization and Statistics and predecessor agencies in 1958-9, 1964-5 and 1974-5. In general, the surveys and other sources seem to indicate that the Egyptian income distribution is fairly egalitarian[1] by the standards of developing countries. This conclusion, of course, depends on the overall quality of the expenditure-survey data. A *Business International* (1980) survey reports a sharp widening in the disparities in both rural and urban income distribution since 1974. For example, in rural areas the top 10 percent take approximately 25 percent of available income and the lowest 40 percent take about 20 percent of that income, with the disparity slightly greater in urban areas.

With respect to consumption behavior, Egypt does not differ greatly from most developing countries in having relatively low spending levels in the countryside. The Household Expenditure Survey of 1974-5 cited in Ikram (1980), reported an average annual expenditure of 375.42 Egyptian pounds for rural families and an average annual expenditure of 556.75 Egyptian pounds for urban families. The lower spending by rural families is usually explained by incomplete monetization of the rural economy and lower markups on food. As in most poor countries, the budget share devoted to food consumption is high: more than 50 percent of the budget for all consumer groups except the very richest (Ikram, 1980). Among non-food items there is a sharp increase in expenditures on transport and communications (especially on automobiles in the top income groups) and on categories such as culture and entertainment. These increases simply reflect growing diversity in the consumption basket as income goes up. In addition, a considerable part of the income of the richer class in Egypt appears to be spent on imported luxury items.

The multinational marketing manager would be unwise to ignore the effects of the dual-economy problem upon the size of the market for certain goods in Egypt. The real opportunities for marketers frequently lie in regional and cultural segments rather than in thinking about a broad, national-market opportunity. For example, the market for most consumer and durable goods is concentrated in Cairo and Alexandria, where a large demand for foreign goods exists. Market opportunities also extend to Port Said and other cities around the Suez Canal.

In the last ten years, however, the government has been attempting to decentralize governmental authority in order to weaken this market concentration and develop the more rural areas of Egypt (Mahmoud 1973; *Business International*, 1980).

## Government Trade and Economic Policies

Government action to limit the freedom of marketing decision-making is a potential problem area. It is, however, reassuring for the multinational enterprise that Egypt is moving slowly towards a more liberal trade policy. The broad framework of a fundamental change toward a more open and market-oriented economy was enunciated a decade ago in April 1974 by the late President Anwar El-Sadat in his annual report on the Egyptian economy — the October *Working Paper*. The 'open-door' investment policy of 'El-Infitah' (the opening) was implemented with the passing of Law 43 in 1974, and later amended in 1977. This policy sets out broad guidelines and incentives for the entry of foreign capital. Its original intention was to create a secure investment climate for domestic, Arab and other foreign investment. The development of the Egyptian market through foreign investment is welcome in the form of joint ventures with the private and/or public sector. Priority is given to those projects designed to generate exports, encourage tourism, or reduce the need to import basic commodities, as well as to projects which require advanced technical expertise or make use of patents or trademarks.

The problems for the multinational enterprise, with respect to Egypt's trade policy, lie in the risk of policy reversals. They may occur for a variety of reasons, and some may be the result of the liberalization process itself. Unless carefully and gradually implemented, liberalization often creates social and political tensions that can force a government to abandon or change drastically the policy. For example, early in 1982 the Egyptian government placed a high priority on intermediate and capital goods rather than luxury non-essential imports (*Middle East and African Economist*, 1982c). This new emphasis on the productive sector rather than on the consumer sector resulted both from the decrease in available foreign exchange and President Hosni Mubarak's desire for a more equitable distribution of Egypt's financial resources.

Egypt's dependence on imports — it currently imports over 70 percent of its wheat and flour needs, for example (*Business International*, 1980) — makes it dangerously prone to inflationary pressures from abroad. The trade deficit in 1982 was estimated to be in the range of $1.5 billion (US) (*Business America*, 1982a). Negative results on the trading account continue to exert downward pressures on the value of the Egyptian pound, leading to a higher cost of imports. At the time of writing the policy of the government is to insulate the majority of consumers from the pressures of world inflation through its subsidy program. Price controls are also implemented by the Egyptian government on most goods, limiting the manager's freedom to control his marketing-decision variables. Inflation as measured by the official Consumer Price Index dropped from 18.7 percent in 1980 to 9.6 percent in 1981 (*Middle East and African Economist*, 1982c).[2] But consumers whose market baskets included more non-subsidized and especially imported goods faced higher rates of inflation — 20 percent to 30 percent, reflecting world prices. Luxury commodities, in addition, tend to attract indirect taxes, sometimes referred to in Egypt as 'price differences' (Ikram, 1980). President Mubarak has declared: 'any projects we will approve have to be those that produce the basic needs of the struggling classes, not luxury goods whose use is restricted to a minority who can afford them'. (*Middle East and African Economist*, 1981).

## Government Economic Planning

In assessing and forecasting the economic environment, the international marketer must become familiar with the planning activities and the resulting plans of the host government. It is also important to appraise the degree of commitment to planning and to the plans that actually exist. The problem for the multinational enterprise is that its own sales forecasts and strategic plans may depend to a certain degree on the government's economic plans, and in many countries, for a variety of reasons, government actions may not follow published plans. For example, in Egypt ministerial changes cause instability in planning, and this affects the continuity of existing projects. The construction project to build the 'Cairo International Market' (where the annual Cairo fair is held) took almost twelve years to complete due to the changing policies and priorities of the different ministers in office (Mahmoud, 1973). Ikram (1980) gives an indication of the frequency of changes in high-level Egyptian government personnel. From 1974 to 1978 there were five different ministers of planning, five different finance ministers and three different ministers of economy. Problems of government planning associated with personnel changes are exacerbated because, contrary to Western organizations which tend to have comparatively stable goals, organizational goals in Moslem organizations (as in Egypt) seem to shift with the changeover of organization heads. This stems from a belief on the part of Islamic managers that corporate entities need strong leaders who are willing to force their wills on their organizations (Wright, 1981).

The current problems with the actual applications of the 'open-door' investment policy, and therefore the problems in this regard for multinational enterprises, are primarily bureaucratic. Such issues are elaborated upon in the following section.

## Bureaucratic Problems in Egypt

Ayubi (1982) noted that, for a variety of organizational and political reasons, the performance of the Egyptian bureaucracy is declining sharply in quality, when the desire to encourage foreign investment is actually calling for a more innovative, flexible and efficient bureaucracy.

An ex-minister for Administrative Development, who had been in charge of administrative reform for a number of years himself complained of the Egyptian bureaucracy in the following words:

> What would you say of a government machine that adopts the open-door policy and is (expected) to present legislation indicating privileges and exemptions aimed at the encouraging of investors, local and foreign, and the attracting of investment for financing development projects in the country; and which then simultaneously sows hundreds of handicaps and problems in the path of these investors? (Ali al-Salmi, quoted by Al-Musawwar, 1979)

The principal criticism made by investors is the lack of coordination between various government agencies and their apparent inability to honor important undertakings (*Business International*, 1980). For example, a customs exemption from the investment authority (the General Authority for Investment and Free Zones, or GAIFZ) does not automatically mean the customs service will abide by it.

It has been said that Egyptian customs officials are a law unto themselves. Some foreign suppliers have had particularly bad experiences. A *Business International* (1980) survey reported that one import contract for telescopic cranes required 39 signatures. The supplier risked losing a big oil company account and eventually pulled out of Egypt. It normally takes three or four days to clear customs in Alexandria. For complaints, the supplier must pay first and then lodge a complaint with the customs research center, which often takes months to resolve the problem.

Administrative difficulties are also faced by international marketers seeking to finalize their contracts and obtain payment for their goods. Normally a letter of credit is opened and cleared within a few days. With the public sector,[3] however, this is a difficult and lengthy process taking anywhere from three to six months. The award must be approved initially by the Central Bank, which acts as the agent for the Ministry of Finance. Every Tuesday, a special committee of the Central

Bank meets in order to allocate funds on a priority basis. If the credit is not opened on one Tuesday, it has to wait until the next. There are also problems if the order is, for example, in Norweigian kroner or even sterling, as the vast majority of Egypt's trade is conducted in dollars. Other problems can arise because of the delay, such as price rises and renegotiation of terms, or finding a ship sailing for Alexandria, when the letter of credit finally comes through.

In response to international marketers' complaints that they have been deterred by bureaucratic obstacles, (*Middle East and African Economist*, 1982b), Egypt is making efforts to clarify the investment situation and to speed up and centralize the investment approval process so as to attract new investors into priority sectors. For example, according to the *Business International* (1980) survey, GAIFZ is improving its promotion effort through trade missions abroad and through it own promotions department in Cairo, where it has set up a special information center.

**Demographic Characteristics of Egypt and Associated Marketing Problems**

The demographic characteristics of Egypt are typical of most developing countries. Selected indicators are listed in Table 5.1; and two marketing problems associated with Egypt's demographic characteristics are discussed here. First, Egypt has a relatively low literacy rate despite increased government emphasis on education which admittedly led to an improvement in the literacy rate from 26 percent in the 1960s to 54.3 percent in 1980. Illiteracy remains high, particularly among older people, and this is of some significance for marketing because these people are responsible for most buying decisions (Leff and Farley, 1980). The low literacy rate combined with low radio and television ownership,[4] has clear implications for communications with customers. Marketers must use appropriate media such as billboards, which are available and provide a useful medium of communication.

The second problem applies to multinational companies which manufacture in Egypt, using Egyptian labor. The emigration of Egyptians abroad is of some demographic importance, particularly for the quality of the labor force. Loss of manpower through migration to oil-rich Arab countries has badly hit middle management and the skilled labor of the public sector. The shortage of skilled craftsmen in the construction industry, for example, is a severe constraint on

Table 5.1: Selected Demographic Indicators

| |
|---|
| Population (1980): 41.99 million |
| Population growth-rate (1975–80): 2.6% per annum |
| Life expectancy at birth (1979): 57 years |
| Percentage of population under 15 years of age (1970): 40 |
| Rural population (1980): 54.6% |
| Literacy rate (1980): 54.3% |

Sources: *Statistical Digest 1981*, Paris, UNESCO, 1981; *United Nations Statistical Yearbook 1979/80*, New York, United Nations, 1981. Ikram, K., *Egypt Economic Management in a Period of Transition*, Baltimore, Maryland, The Johns Hopkins University Press, 1980.

production. In most fields the foreign investor should expect and is expected to train his workforce as a major part of his contribution for being in Egypt.[5] A related problem here is the language barrier when training workers. In the last few years, however, the government has emphasized the learning of more than one language. Engineers are now trained in both Arabic and English. The labor-shortage and labor-quality problems may affect the costs of a manufacturing and marketing operation in Egypt. While the price of labor is relatively cheap, hiring professionals is expensive. An additional problem is the very low productivity in all economic sectors (Mahmoud, 1973; *Middle East Reporter*, 1982b).

## Marketing Infrastructure Problems

In their discussion of marketing infrastructure, Douglas and Craig (1982) identify 'integrative networks' which affect the feasibility or desirability of utilizing specific types of marketing programs and strategies. Integrative networks include a variety of factors, such as the availability of television advertising and supermarkets, the development of the transportation network and the communication system (the physical infrastructure) and the existence of market-research organizations. This section provides a brief discussion of the typical problems faced by multinational companies because of the nature of Egypt's integrative networks or infrastructure.

### Physical Infrastructure Problems

The pervasive impression is that the physical infrastructure in Egypt is seriously underdeveloped. Despite the acceleration in investment since

1973, the capacity of port facilities, railways, the inland water transport system, and telecommunication is seriously limited. The road-transport system is not seriously deficient, however, and has experienced rapid growth since 1965 (Ikram, 1980).

In a dicussion of similar problems in India, Sarma and Rao (1972) concluded that 'deficiency in communications will limit the range of physical distribution and thus the extent of the market, confining the sales to nearby consumers, preventing the growth of specialized marketing agencies and specialized production patterns.' Perhaps this problem is of somewhat lesser significance in Egypt than in India because the Egyptian population has always been concentrated in less than 4 percent of the total land area. Nevertheless, although the habitable area has many attractions for industries that wish to supply the growing domestic and regional markets, inadequacies in integrative networks remain obstacles to multinational enterprises. A comprehensive communications system is a prerequisite to breaking down the traditional high-cost market structure in less developed areas (Michell, 1979).

The telecommunications network in Egypt has become totally inadequate to the needs of the economy. Egypt's density of 1.34 telephones per 100 population is significantly lower than that of other Middle Eastern countries (Iran, 2.00; Turkey, 2.52; Syria, 2.30; Iraq, 1.69). The telephone density in Cairo is about 5.0 and in Alexandria 3.4, compared with Algiers, 9.5; Teheran, 8.2; and Manila, 23.2. As many as 1,000 villages in Egypt do not have even primary access to the telephone service, for example, a public call office (Ikram, 1980). Cairo's telephone system is now part of the business world's folklore. An article in *World Business Weekly* (1981) estimated that in Cairo, 50 percent of the telephone lines can be out of service at the same time, and 75 percent of all dialled calls fail to get through on the first attempt. Perhaps in no other sphere, however, has there been such a marked improvement in services as in telecommunications over the last six or seven years. The long-term goal of Areto (the telephone organization) is to provide a fully comprehensive system by the turn of the century. But many logistical problems remain. Obtaining a new telephone line is still a major achievement involving influence in high places. Waiting time runs from months to two years. There is a three to six-month waiting list for telex facilities, although the telephone authority now allows foreign companies to import telexes. The telephone directory is available in Arabic only, except in various embassies. For those with telephones (and having a line is often an essential prerequisite to renting accommodation), the service has improved dramatically since a major overhaul of the system in central Cairo in 1979. International communications have also improved considerably, and it is now possible to dial direct from Egypt to the outside world. This facility is still limited to special subscribers spending a certain minimum amount per month.

## Marketing-control Problems

The organization of the retail trade in Egypt may cause marketing control problems for the multinational. Egypt's retail trade is dominated by a large number of small, privately owned shops and vendors. The wholesale and distribution operations tend to be carried out by vertically integrated merchants or public-sector trading companies. The generally small size of firms and limited market opportunities (for example, because of low levels of consumer expenditure) often lead to local competition and long channels of distribution. The latter effect gives the distributor a predominant role (Hibbert, 1979).

Regardless of the method of entry into the Egyptian market (for example, direct exporting, sales subsidiary, manufacturing subsidiary), and despite a possible reduction of central marketing control, it is advisable to deal with an Egyptian partner. Dunn (1979) noted that, because of market and legal factors, even multinational companies which usually sell direct in other overseas markets find local partners indispensable in the Middle East. Knowledge of local trading practices and customs is often essential in making a sale. Also, concluding a transaction or bidding on a project often takes a long time – too long for an official of the home office to spend in the area. The government is frequently the ultimate customer in Egypt. Knowledge of government buying procedures is therefore critical to sellers. This knowledge, however, is difficult to obtain without local partners. Finally, there may be continuing problems with quotations, financing, import regulations, and collections that are best solved by a local representative.

## Marketing-research Problems

Egypt has a fairly well-developed statistical system that generates a considerable body of data. The problems, however, are that these are not always conceptually useful for marketing problems; they often are not available at the appropriate time (Ikram, 1980); they are published in Arabic; and they may be unrealistic indicators (Brasch, 1978). As Keegan (1980) points out, these difficulties may not be of prime significance as it is the nature of marketing research everywhere that only a small amount of data in the typical study is obtained from public sources. Companies capable of doing marketing research exist in Egypt (US Department of Commerce, 1981), but the familiar problems of undertaking marketing research in developing countries remain. These are problems of infrastructure, such as an absence of telephones; and of culture, for example, a greater reluctance on the part of people to talk to strangers, and when people do respond, the existence of 'courtesy bias' (Kaynak, 1978; Yavas and Kaynak, 1980). Professor Kaynak develops these points further in Chapter 14 of this book.

*Advertising Problems*

Opportunity for advertising in Egypt are improving. Commercial advertising can be placed in newspapers and magazines and on radio, television, cinema and posters through the government-owned advertising agency. Nevertheless, even in the advanced sector of developing countries such as Egypt, modern advertising is relatively new. Consequently, the advertising techniques and the associated returns may appear highly uncertain to local business partners (Leff and Farley, 1980). The problems that do exist therefore concern the appropriate amounts of advertising expenditure (see Leff and Farley, 1980 for a detailed discussion) in addition to cultural adaptation of messages, brand names and packaging (for example, see *Business America*, 1979) and media selection, which is constrained by factors such as the reach of media vehicles and literacy-rates.[6] Selected examples of the cultural implications for advertising are included in the following section.

## The Socio-economic Environment in Egypt and Related Marketing Problems

Cultural and social considerations are probably the most constraining uncontrollable variables when marketing in any foreign country. The marketing implications of cultural differences may be seen in terms of a number of activities within the overall marketing function such as marketing research, the understanding of consumer behavior, organizational behavior and salesman activity, and marketing-strategy formulation (Redding, 1982). For example, the consumer base in a Middle Eastern nation cannot be understood by reference to Western models. Selected cultural aspects of Egyptian society which may be problematic from the standpoint of marketing strategy and marketing organization are discussed below.

Egypt is a predominantly Moslem country; 92 percent of the population follows the Islamic faith. An important feature of the socio-cultural environment, which may have implication for the success of Western-oriented products and advertising, is Islamic revivalism. People unhappy with rapid social change and the spread of Western values are finding solace in Islamic fundamentalism. Some observers believe that social conservatism has grown in Egypt as a social consequence of increasing contact with the oil-exporting states (Ikram, 1980).

Reliance on purely economic or demographic indicators can foster misconceptions regarding the size of a market and consumer behavior if an in-depth understanding of Egyptian culture is missing. This can be illustrated by an examination of consumer decision-making.

Because of prevailing natality and mortality conditions, the populations of developing countries are relatively young (see Table 5.1). Consequently, much of the potential market, even for established products, consists of new buyers without firm preferences for specific brands or products (Leff and Farley, 1980). This does not fully account for the family structure in Egypt, however, which is heavily influenced by Islam. Consumer decision-making depends partly on the fact that the father, who according to Islam, protects and provides for the entire family. The family members, in return, are to respect all the father's wishes and remain psychologically and physically under his domain. Obligations towards parents are sacred. From a marketing standpoint questions may be raised as to the amount of a teenager's discretionary income. The tradition of deference to parental wishes is likely to affect buying patterns in clothing and leisure expenditure, especially in view of the fact that it is normal to live at home until marriage. According to Luqmani, Quraeshi and Delene, (1980), the image of functional products could be enhanced with advertisements that stress parental advice or approval; even with children's products, there should be less emphasis on children as decision-makers. In addition, advertising appeals based on Western values of youthful looks and energy are likely to be less successful in Egypt, where the older generation, in general, is much more respected. Signs of old age may be helpful; grey hair, for example, can represent wisdom through experience (Pezeshkpur, 1978).

The position of women in Egypt can only be understood in the religious context of Egyptian society, which has emphasized the seclusion of women and their domestic roles. Improved educational opportunities have increased their social and occupational mobility in recent years, but although women constitute about a third of total enrollment in universities, in the field of education as in other areas of Egyptian society, female emancipation is still in its early stages. The Islamic influence includes an obligation to conform to codes of sexual conduct and social interaction which includes modest dress for women in public. More colorful clothing and accessories are worn by women at home, however, so promotion of products for use in private homes should be more intimate — such audiences could be reached effectively through women's magazines (Luqmani *et al.*, 1980). The use of magazines as a communications medium would necessarily be confined to educated women. A further implication of the Islamic moral code is that communications with customers should avoid use of immodest exposure and sexual connotations in public settings.

Marketing control, the reporting structure, training and recruitment, and operating practices used in the marketing or selling function must be adpated to the local culture if they are to succeed. The Egyptian culture is characterized by a much slower pace of life. What takes one day to accomplish in North America or Europe may take a week in Egypt. Attitudes towards doing business emphasize the importance of personal relationships (Fleming, 1981). Arbose (1982) attributed the success of Japanese salesmen in Egypt to their appreciation of the local attitudes towards doing business. For example, the Japanese are more polite, patient, efficient, flexible, alert, neat and generous than their Western counterparts. The Japanese salesman wait patiently and know the different attitudes Middle Easterners have towards time. They are prepared to talk for one or two hours before mentioning business. An article in *Business America* (1982b) advises that such a patient style of market development usually leads to successful business dealings in Egypt. Furthermore, the fundamental Islamic concept of worship (five times a day, while the timing of prayers varies) means that the foreign marketer has to take into account the variability and shift in prayer timings in planning sales calls, work schedules, business hours, customer traffic, and so forth (Luqmani *et al.*, 1980).

Perception and decision perspectives are different for the Moslem manager, who believes decisions should be made while perceiving inter-relationships between worldly incidents as well as metaphysical events. Wright (1981) explains that while an American superior may be hesitant to terminate the services of an elderly employee because it may be bad for organizational morale and that it would be 'a shame' to discharge a person with long years of service, the Moslem manager would share the feelings of hesitancy, but because it would be a 'sin' to treat an older person in such a way. These perspectives are, of course, very divergent, and may result in serious misunderstandings when individuals from the two different cultures have to work together.

## Marketing Problems in Egypt: A Summary

In order to summarize the problems faced by marketers in Egypt, a comprehensive classification of marketing problems according to the particular environmental variables from which they result is given in Table 5.2. Examples of possible solutions or methods of coping with the problems are also offered. Specific marketing-mix implications will, of course, depend on industry, product and firm characteristics, and cultural considerations. Wright (1981) illustrates the latter point with an example which is useful to repeat here as it demonstrates problems which can occur when operating within the Egyptian cultural environment:

> An Egyptian employee told her American boss who had just fired her: 'Look what you have done to me will bring a curse on you. Don't you think you will be staying here for much longer!' Soon afterwards, the manager became very sick with intestinal disorders. The company flew him back to the U.S. for treatment. When he became well, he was sent back to Egypt. However, the same disease struck again and the American manager finally had to be transferred out of Egypt. The Egyptian marketing manager's reaction to the event was, 'Well, it is possible that the curse had its effect.' Conversely, the American financial manager in the same firm argued: 'Baloney! What's all this about a curse? We all know Egypt has hygiene problems and so our general manager was a victim of the poor hygiene in this country.'

In this example it is evident that the Egyptian manager had perceived an interrelation between worldly and detail phenomena, while the US executive had viewed the same situation from the perspective of worldly phenomena. As also discussed by Pezeshkpur (1978), these perspectives are, of course, very divergent, and may result in serious misunderstandings when individuals from the two cultures have to work together.

## Conclusion

This chapter has conducted an assessment of the marketing problems faced by multinational enterprises in Egypt. The most common problems are caused by the following: the existence of a dual economy;

Table 5.2: Marketing Problems in Egypt: A Summary According to Source

| Source of marketing problem in the business environment | Example of marketing problem | Possible solution |
|---|---|---|
| Dual economy: co-existence of modern and traditional sectors | Affects the market size for certain goods | Market assessments and different products for each sector (see Cateora, 1983) |
| Economic performance: trade deficit; inflation; weak currency | Import restrictions on many consumer goods | Market products which satisfy government demands as well as the needs of customers |
| Government-controlled prices | Limited managerial control over prices | Use of other marketing mis-variables to attract customers |
| Public-sector control of the economy | Bureaucratic delays | The use of agents with influence in high places can speed up the process, e.g. Arab Contractors Company |
| Frequent ministerial changes | Planning uncertainty | Maintain a good marketing information system |
| Relatively low literacy rates | Limits choice of advertising copy and media | Use poster advertising with pictures; use a local or international advertizing agency or develop in-house creative skills |
| Emigration of labor to oil-rich countries | Lack of skilled labor resources | It is necessary to train labor which may be required for certain marketing production activities |
| Underdeveloped physical infrastructure | It is difficult and costly to exploit market opportunities in rural areas | Concentrate on markets in urban centers, e.g. Cairo, Alexandria |
| Inadequate telephone system | Poor communications within Egypt and with the outside world | The company can import its own telex facility |
| Lengthy distribution channels; small distribution units | Unfamiliarity with local trading practices; loss of marketing control | Obtain a trustworthy and experienced Egyptian partner |
| Published data on economic, social and demographic variables | Data are out of date or not conceptually useful for marketing | Concentrate on marketing research using primary rather than secondary data |
| Physical infrastructure; socio-cultural factors | Locating respondents and obtaining unbiased information when conducting marketing research (see Kaynak, 1978) | It is advisable to deal with an Egyptian marketing research agency, preferably one employing consultants who also have experience in the West to facilitate |

*Table 5.2 contd.*

| | | language and cultural trans-<br>lation of research instru-<br>ments |
|---|---|---|
| Low TV and radio<br>ownership | Limits media oppor-<br>tunities for advertising | Utilize the opportunities<br>that are available, e.g.<br>billboards, cinema |
| Social trends: Islamic<br>revivalism | Future growth could<br>limit market for con-<br>sumer/Western goods | Cultural adaptation of<br>product |
| Islamic impact upon<br>family structure and<br>decision-making | The 'teenage market' is<br>very limited despite the<br>fact that demographically,<br>it comprises a sizeable<br>proportion of the<br>population | Products and promotional<br>messages must be designed<br>recognizing the authority<br>of the father with respect<br>to most family purchases |
| Middle Eastern and<br>Islamic cultural traits,<br>e.g. respect for the<br>older generation | Western-style promotional<br>messages emphasizing<br>youthful ideals may fail | Promotional messages<br>should emphasize respect<br>for the older generation and<br>experience and wisdom |
| Islamic code of moral<br>behavior | Western-style advertising<br>using scantily-clothed<br>models or sexual<br>connotations may be<br>offensive to target market | Communications strategy<br>should avoid use of im-<br>modest exposure and<br>sexual connotations in<br>public settings |
| Egyptian attitudes<br>towards doing busi-<br>ness: the slow pace;<br>the importance of<br>personal relationships;<br>the influence of Islamic<br>beliefs on the business | Unfamiliar operating<br>practices in the market-<br>ing function | Appreciate the need to<br>develop an understanding<br>of the Egyptian business<br>culture and act accordingly |

government trade and economic policies and the risks of policy reversals; dealing with the Egyptian bureaucracy; demographic characteristics such as illiteracy and labor emigration; an underdeveloped and unfamiliar marketing infrastructure; and a socio-cultural environment strongly influenced by the Islamic tradition. Every aspect of the marketing function is affected; from market assessment, marketing research and market entry, to the marketing-mix variables, marketing organization and control. The problems are probably typical of those encountered in all developing countries although the importance of the different aspects of a company's external environment (social, economic, technological and so on) will vary according to different national markets. The implication for the multinational marketing manager is that he should develop an awareness of or sensitivity to local conditions. The difficulty of marketing in developing countries such as

Egypt is in recognizing the problems; dealing with the problems is an easier task. Therefore, the success of the multinational marketer will be measured by his abilities to appreciate environmental differences and to adopt geocentric attitudes.

## Notes

1. Precise figures are not available to the authors.
2. This one-year effect may be artificial, and is likely to be politically motivated. Hence, it is important for managers to recognize the political process behind economic-policy decisions. More specifically, Poynter (1982) discussed 'government intervention risks' as 'the probability that a political decision will be made which will force change in the operations, policies and strategies of the foreign investor.'
3. The public sector accounts for 80 percent of industrial output and will continue to be a dominant force in the Egyptian economy. The demise of the public sector is not politically feasible, nor is it an objective of government policy.
4. Ownership of radio receivers in 1979 was 132 per 1,000 inhabitants; ownership of TV receivers in 1979 was 32 per 1,000 inhabitants (*United Nations Statistical Yearbook*, 1979/80).
5. Normally, when foreign technicians are imported, provision must be made for training Egyptians eventually to assume the foreigners' jobs.
6. See above, the section 'Demographic Characteristics of Egypt and Associated Marketing Problems'.

## References

Al-Musawwar, 'Al al-Salmi 'Al-biruqratiyya al-hukumiyya . . .' [Government Bureaucracy as a constraint to New Construction] no. 2849, 19 May 1979, p. 16
Arbose, Jules 'Wise Men from the East Bearing Gifts', *International Management*, May 1982, 67–8
Arubi, Nazih N.M. 'Bureaucratic Inflation and Administration Inefficiency: The Deadlock in Egyptian Administration', *Middle Eastern Studies*, vol. 18, no. 3, 1982, 186–299
Brasch, John J. 'Sales Forecasting Difficulties in a Developing Country', *Industrial Marketing Management*, vol. 7, 1978, 354–60
*Business America* 'Adapting Export Packaging', 3 December 1979, 1–7
—— 'Strong U.S. Interest Sustains Our Share of Import Market', 9 August 1982a, 31–2
—— 'Egypt Adequate Market Research and Financial Support Should Result In Successful Ventures for U.S. Firms', 15 November 1982b, 28–30
*Business International* 'Egypt Opportunities for Suppliers and Investors', July 1980
Cateora, Philip R. *International Marketing*, fifth edition, Richard D. Irwin, Inc., Homewood, Ill., 1983
Davidson, William H. 'The Location of Foreign Direct Investment Activity: Country Characteristics and Experience Effects', *Journal of International Business Studies*, vol. XI, no. 2, Fall 1980, 9–18

Douglas, Susan P. and Craig, Samuel C. 'Marketing Research in the International Environment', in Ingo Walter (ed.), *Handbook of International Business*, John Wiley and Sons, Inc., New York, 1982
Dunn, Dan T. Jr. 'Agents and Distributors in the Middle East', *Business Horizons*, vol. 22, October 1979, 69–78
Fleming, Quentin W. *A Guide to Doing Business on the Arabian Peninsula*, AMACOM, New York, 1981
Hibbert, E.P. 'The Cultural Dimension of Marketing and the Impact of Industrialisation', *European Research*, January 1979, 41–7
Ikram, Khalid *Egypt Economic Management in a Period of Transition*, The Johns Hopkins University Press, Baltimore, Maryland, 1980
Kaynak, Erdener 'Difficulties of Undertaking Marketing Research in the Developing Countries', *European Research*, vol. 6, no. 6, November 1978, 251–9
Keegan, Warren J. *Multinational Marketing Management*, second edition, Prentice-Hall Inc., Englewood-Cliffs, New Jersey, 1980
Kobrin, Stephen J. 'The Environmental Determinants of Foreign Direct Manufacturing Investment: An Ex Post Empirical Analysis', *Journal of International Business Studies*, vol. 7, Fall/Winter 1976, 29–42
Leff, Nathaniel H. and Farley, John U. 'Advertising Expenditures in the Developing World', *Journal of International Business Studies*, vol. XI, no. 2, Fall 1980, 64–79
Luqmani, Mushtaw, Quareshi, Zahir A. and Delene, Linda 'Marketing in Islamic Countries: A Viewpoint', *MSU Business Topics*, vol. 28, Summer 1980, 17–25
Mahmoud, Essam 'The Development of Labour Productivity in the Construction Industry', unpublished MBA thesis, Ain Shams University, Cairo, 1973
Michell, Paul 'Infrastructures and International Marketing Effectiveness', *Columbia Journal of World Business*, Spring 1979, 91–101
*Middle East and African Economist* vol. XXXV, no. 11, November 1981, 80
—— vol. XXXVI, no. 4, April 1982a, 27
—— vol. XXXVI, no. 5, May 1982b, 35
—— vol. XXXVI, no. 7/8, July/August 1982c, 43
—— vol. XXVIII, no. 256, 17 April 1982b, 18–20
Pearson, Conrad E. 'An Expert Panel Model for Assessing Political Risk', in T.H. Inmoran (ed.), *International Political Risk Assessment: The State of the Art*, Landegger Papers in International Business and Public Policy, School of Foreign Service, Georgetown University, 1980, 14–30
Pezeshkpur, Changiz 'Challenges to Management in the Arab World', *Business Horizons*, August 1978, 47–55
Poynter, Thomas A. 'Government Intervention in Less Developed Countries: The Experience of Multinational Companies', *Journal of International Business Studies*, Spring/Summer 1982, 9–25
Redding, S.G. 'Cultural Effects on the Marketing Process in Southeast Asia', *Journal of the Market Research Society*, vol. 24, no. 2, April 1982, 98–115
Rice, Gillian 'The Effects of Political Uncertainty on International Marketing Strategy', unpublished PhD thesis, University of Bradford, 1982
Sarma, M.T.R. and Rao, T.R. 'Problems of Rural Marketing in India', *New Perspectives in Marketing*, Indian National Council of Applied Economic Research, 1982, 1–15
*Statistical Digest* 1981, UNESCO, Paris, 1981
US Department of Commerce 'Marketing in Egypt', *Overseas Business Report*, December 1981
*United Nations Statistical Yearbook* 1979/80, United Nations, New York, 1981
*World Business Weekly* 'Cairo Telephone System Improves', February 1981, 19
Wright, P. 'Organisational Behavior in Islamic Firms', *Management International*

*Review*, vol. 21, no. 2, 1981, 86–94

Yavas, Ugur and Kaynak, Erdener 'Current Status of Marketing Research in Developing Countries: Problems and Opportunities', *Journal of International Marketing and Marketing Research*, 1980, 79–89

# 6 ECONOMIC AND MARKET ENVIRONMENT: THE CASE OF HONG KONG

C.L. Hung

## Introduction

Hong Kong is an interesting case for international marketing studies. It provides a fascinating example of how history, geography, topography, demography, government policies and political conditions interact to shape the economy and the market environment.

The purpose of this paper is to examine these interacting forces and to review some of the distinctive features of the economy and the market. An understanding of these features is essential for successful marketing in Hong Kong. This paper, however, is not concerned with specific recommendations on marketing strategy as no single strategy can be appropriate for all cases. The best marketing mix for any marketer has to be individually tailored to take into consideration the type of product, the target consumers, the market objectives and the competition.

The first section of this paper provides a brief historical account of the Hong Kong economy and its industrialization in the post war years. This is followed by an examination of the present industrial structure. The last part is a survey of the marketing-related perceptions of foreign manufacturers operating in Hong Kong and a discussion of the important market characteristics.

## History of Development

Hong Kong was annexed by the British to serve as their trading post in the Far East. It comprises Victoria Island and the adjacent Kowloon Peninsula — ceded in perpetuity after the two Anglo-Chinese Wars (1840-2 and 1856-8) — and the contiguous mainland and islands known as the New Territories leased for ninety-nine years in 1898. The land area is around 1,060 square kilometers (459 square miles), 90 percent of which is in the New Territories.

*The First Hundred Years*

The first hundred years of the development of Hong Kong may be described as a century of growth of an entrepôt economy. Possessing a strategic location in the Asian Pacific and a fine natural harbor, it first served as a distribution, sorting and grading center for the British and Chinese traders. After it became a British colony, the freedom of trade and the security of British rule attracted many more British and Chinese merchants to Hong Kong. Banks, shipping and insurance companies also began to arrive, and soon expanded and diversified the scope of their activities. Some of the larger companies even acted as management agencies, and arranged syndicated loans for the construction of roads, railways, port facilities and other capital projects throughout southern China. By the 1930s Hong Kong was already a very busy trading port in the Far East.

During these years the industries that existed in Hong Kong were extremely rudimentary, and were mostly linked to its port and trading activities. The industries which could be regarded as having some importance were shipbuilding and repairing, plus related operations such as the manufacture of ropes, nets, hinges and wire. Local demand for basic necessities also brought forth the manufacture of wearing apparel and food products. These activities, however, were limited in scope, and were confined almost exclusively to cottage-industry-type operations.

In the interwar years the growth in population and the Commonwealth preference scheme under the Ottawa Agreement of 1932 could have given Hong Kong manufacturers some inducement to expand production and to export to nearby Commonwealth countries; but World War II soon broke out and Hong Kong was occupied by the Japanese in 1941. This brought local industries as well as its entrepôt trade with China to a halt.

*The Postwar Years*

When the war ended, Hong Kong was in shambles. But even before reconstruction plans were finalized, there came two external shocks, either of which could have been disastrous to the fragile economy. However, both shocks eventually turned out to be blessings in disguise because they forced Hong Kong to embark upon a process of industralization. The result was a spectacular transformation of the Hong Kong economy from an entrepôt port to an industrial city, with achievements that impressed as well as surprised the whole world.

The first shock was the population explosion. When the Japanese surrendered in August 1945, Hong Kong had a population of less than 600,000. With the return of peace, many former residents who had fled to the Chinese mainland during the war returned to Hong Kong. The population more than doubled in one year to 1.5 million in mid-1946. The second shock resulted from the civil war between the Nationalists and the Communists in China, and Hong Kong had another influx, this time of refugees. Around three-quarters of a million Chinese sought refuge in Hong Kong during the civil-war years, and this brought the population to over 2.3 million in 1950. This quadruple increase in population in half a decade exerted tremendous pressure upon the economy. Although entrepôt trade with China revived quite satisfactorily during the late 1940s, it could not provide enough employment for the people, nor could it generate sufficient incomes and government revenues to cater to their most basic needs.

When the Communists took over control of the Chinese mainland and the Korean War broke out, Hong Kong's entrepôt business, which was by then still its most important source of income, was dealt a mortal blow. For political and ideological reasons the new Communist government quickly loosened its economic ties with the West and turned instead to Soviet Russia and Eastern Europe. Consequently, Hong Kong lost its traditional importance as an entrepôt port for China's foreign trade. Making a bad situation even worse, the US government in December 1950 imposed a ban on all trade with Communist China because of the latter's participation in the Korean War. This was followed by the United Nations' embargo in May 1951, placing restrictions on its member countries in exporting strategic goods to the Chinese mainland. As a result of these decisions Hong Kong's exports to China — 36.2 percent of its total exports in 1951 — tumbled from C$280 million in that year to only C$90 million in 1952 and C$30 million in 1955.

With its most important source of income almost completely shut down, Hong Kong turned to manufacturing. The first stage of industrialization came with the arrival of refugees from Shanghai. Among these refugees were many entrepreneurs with long business experience in operating cotton spinning and weaving mills. Some of them also brought their machines and capital and re-established their textile factories in Hong Kong. Their manufacturing operations received strong and instant support from the readily available workforce searching for employment, from the local banks looking for alternative investment outlets, and from the established British and Chinese merchant houses able to provide the export channels. Their success was quick, and immediately inspired the local Chinese (who were mainly Cantonese) to set up their own factories. They were soon joined by the overseas Chinese who were seeking a safe and familiar harbor for their capital while political conditions in Indo-China were becoming dubious and chaotic. Industries in Hong Kong began to flourish. They rapidly expanded and diversified — from cotton spinning and weaving to woolen and synthetic fibers, clothing and garments, footwear, toys, artificial flowers, handbags, wigs, furniture, plastic goods, wood and metal products, and more recently into consumer durable goods such as radios and recorders, optical and photographic equipment, electrical appliances and electronics. Heavier industries also emerged, such as metal rolling and the manufacture of chemicals and machine tools, which catered to the needs of local light industries. These developments in turn stimulated the growth of ancillary activities such as the construction of factories, warehouses and office buildings, and of auxiliary services such as banking, insurance, transportation, advertising, legal and management consultancies. By mid-1960 Hong Kong was not only a world famous industrial city, it was also well known as a financial, insurance and shipping center with a business volume second only to Tokyo in the Asian Pacific region.

The process of industrial transformation in Hong Kong could be regarded as completed in 1959 when, for the first time in its history, domestic exports, based entirely on its manufacturing industries, surpassed re-exports by a margin of more than two to one (C$400 million vs C$175 million). Full employment was achieved by 1960 and has been maintained ever since.[1]

The growth of the Hong Kong economy is reflected in the following statistics. In the quarter-century from 1957 to 1981, the number of manufacturing establishments increased more than fourteen times from 3,200 to 46,700; industrial employment almost seven-fold from 148,000 to 990,000; and domestic exports more than sixty times from C$210 million to C$14 billion (US). In the decade 1972 to 1981, gross domestic product in real terms grew on average at 10.2 percent per annum. In 1980 total expenditure on gross domestic product amounted to C$26 billion (US), yielding a *per capita* gross domestic produce of C$5,160, which was the second highest in the Asian Pacific region.[2]

**Industrial Structure**

Hong Kong's industrial economy displays a number of distinctive features.

In Hong Kong the shortage of land, the lack of mineral resources and the mountainous topography have prevented any substantial development of primary production or heavy industries. This is clearly reflected in the employment statistics. Only 2 percent of Hong Kong's industrial workforce are now engaged in primary-production activities — farming, fishing, mining and quarrying, and these activities generate only 1 percent of the gross domestic product. In the manufacturing sector, the only industries which may be considered as heavy are ship-building and repairing, aircraft maintenance and the manufacture of machine tools. These industries account for less than 2 percent of total employment in manufacturing.

As a result of the small primary sector and the absence of heavy industries, Hong Kong has to import practically all its food to feed the 5.2 million inhabitants, and all the industrial raw materials and machines for the needs of its industries. In 1981 Hong Kong's imports totalled C$29.6 billion (US). Of this amount, raw materials and semi-finished manufactured goods comprised 40 percent, equipment and machines 15 percent and foodstuffs 11 percent. The major import sources were Japan, China, the US, Taiwan and Singapore. These five countries supplied more than 70 percent of Hong Kong's imports in 1981.

The light consumer-goods industries have remained the backbone of the Hong Kong economy. They provide employment to over 40 percent of the total workforce, account for almost all of the domestic exports, and generate more than one-quarter of gross domestic income. In descending order of importance, the leading light industries are textiles and clothing, electronics, plastics (the bulk of which are plastic toys) and watches, clocks and accessories. These four industries combined provide around 65 percent of total employment in the manufacturing sector and 70 percent of Hong Kong's exports of manufactured goods. Other important light industries are sporting and travel goods, handbags, footwear, leather goods, metal products, artificial jewellery and electrical appliances.

Hong Kong's manufacturing industries are highly export-oriented. About 80 percent of locally manufactured products are exported directly to overseas markets. Another 5 to 10 percent are fed to local industries as component parts for the final products which are then exported. All of the four leading industries — textiles and clothing, electronics, plastics and watches, clocks and accessories have an export-output ratio of 85 percent or more. Hong Kong's leading export markets are the US and the European Economic Community — which together absorb more than 60 percent of Hong Kong's exports. Other major foreign markets are Japan, China, Australia, Canada and Singapore.

The overwhelming majority of manufacturing firms in Hong Kong are small firms, established and run by small entrepreneurs, many with the help of family members. Of the 46,700 manufacturing firms registered with the government at the end of 1981, 30,500 employed less than 10 workers and 12,500 employed 10 to 49 workers. In other words, over 90 per cent of the manufacturing firms can be classified as small firms.[3]

The majority of the industrial workforce in Hong Kong is unskilled. Skilled workers, defined as those having obtained a general education standard of mid-secondary school level plus three years' specialized training, comprise only around 15 percent of the total industrial workforce. The low level of industrial skill may be a drag on productivity; but it has also had a beneficial effect. The unskilled workers, like the small entrepreneurs, are capable of easily adapting to new industries, and of moving from one firm to another in accordance with the good or bad economic turn of events at home and overseas. This is an important attribute in Hong Kong's well-known industrial resilience, and partially explains why it has experienced relatively little hardship in its industrial diversification in the past years.

The high labor mobility is, however, sometimes a nightmare to the manufacturers. Due to the strong labor demand from industries, manufacturers are often forced to compete for workers with higher wages. As a result, industrial wages in Hong Kong though still low by Western standards, are no longer cheap when compared to those of neighboring countries. They are now the second highest in the Asian Pacific region, next to Japan.[4] Consequently, many of Hong Kong's manufacturing products can no longer compete on a cost basis with those from China, South Korea and Taiwan.

## Environment and Market Characteristics

A number of natural, demographic and socio-political factors contributed to the dramatic economic growth of Hong Kong in the past. They have also shaped Hong Kong's industrial structure and market environment at the present.

*Natural Environment*

There are two major components in Hong Kong's natural environment which have a significant impact upon its economy and the market — geographical location and topography.

The geographical location of Hong Kong has often been described as 'strategic', and has frequently appeared in accounts of Hong Kong's economic growth. Hong Kong is situated at a cross-roads of major trading routes between the East and the West. It also has a fine natural harbor which is sheltered and is deep enough to accommodate the largest ocean-going vessels. This is crucial to Hong Kong's emergence as an entrepôt center in the Far East. The entrepôt heritage in turn contributed to Hong Kong's transformation in the postwar years by providing its new industries with established overseas links.

Geographical location has also been an important factor behind Hong Kong's prominence as a commercial center. At present, close to 20 percent of the labor force is engaged in wholesaling, retailing and import-export businesses. These businesses together form the second largest sector in the economy next to manufacturing. In its contact with the outside world, Hong Kong is now served by the world's third-largest container terminal (after Rotterdam and New York), a merchant shipping fleet greater in tonnage than that of Greece, an electrified and double-tracked railway system to the Chinese border, and thirty-one airlines operating around 1,000 scheduled passenger and cargo flights each week. Internally, there are hundreds of advertising agencies and legal, accounting and management-consultancy firms. For mass promotion, there are two commercial television stations each with a Chinese and an English channel, 55 Chinese-language and six English-language newspapers and over 400 international and local periodicals. All these ancillary facilities provide excellent marketing support for both the home and export markets.

However, the importance of geographic location to Hong Kong's manufacturing industries should not be overemphasized because it is not particularly favorable to the industries' needs. Hong Kong is not located in an area which is endowed with mineral resources. Its hinterland, China, is an underdeveloped country and has never been a good market for Hong Kong's manufactured goods nor a good source of material supplies.[5] Instead, Hong Kong has to rely on the US, Western Europe and Japan for markets and for material supplies, and these countries are thousands of miles away. The high transportation costs are a heavy burden for Hong Kong's manufacturing industries.

The topography, in contrast to geographical location, has unquestionably been a handicap. Hong Kong is mountainous and is strictly limited in flat lands for industrial or residential purposes. Most of the factory premises in Hong Kong are now actually situated on lands obtained from reclamation or leveling of hills. The high cost of producing these lands and the keen competition for their use have raised land prices in Hong Kong to among the highest in the world. In 1981 office space in central business districts rented for about C$50 per square meter ($42 per square yard) per month. For industrial premises, the monthly rental ranged from C$15 per square meter ($13 per square yard) in upper floors to C$35 ($29 per square yard) for near-ground floors. The shortage of land and the subsequent high cost of office and factory space is something which all marketers have to be aware of in designing their marketing strategies.

## Demographic Pattern

Based upon a projection from the population census taken in March 1981, the total estimated population of Hong Kong in 1982 was around 5.2 million. This represents an overall population density of 4,760 per square kilometer (12,000 per square mile), which is the highest in the world. Furthermore, there are wide variations in density between individual areas. In several metropolitan districts in Victoria Island and Kowloon the population density is as high as 150,000 per square kilometer (388,000 per square mile). The 'compactness' of the city is ideal for intensive distribution, extensive market exposure and mass promotion.

Hong Kong is basically a Chinese community. More than 97 percent of the population are of Chinese origin. Most of them speak Cantonese, but Mandarin and the Shanghai dialects are also used by many. Both English and Chinese are acknowledged official languages, but English is more commonly used in business and legal correspondence. Over 90 percent of the population are literate, and the majority of them are bilingual. In fact, student enrollments in English-language schools outnumber those in Chinese-language schools by a margin of about eight to one.

According to the 1981 census, only 57.2 percent of the population were born in Hong Kong. This is a consequence and a reflection of the influx of refugees in the late 1940s, and of the large number of legal and illegal immigrants from China since 1950. The presence of these refugees and new immigrants has put tremendous strain upon the community in providing them with housing, education and medical care. At the same time, however, it has enlarged the pool of industrial labor and has thus helped to keep local wages from rising too rapidly. Furthermore, and fortunately for Hong Kong, it has not created the serious social conflicts common in many other countries with a refugee problem. This is because the great majority of the refugees and new immigrants are from Guangdong, the same home province as the residents of Hong Kong. They speak the same dialect and share the same customs. Most of them actually have close relatives in Hong Kong, and are thus quickly accepted as members of the indigenous population.

The non-Chinese expatriate community of around 140,000 is a sizeable one in absolute terms, even though it only represents 2.7 percent of the total population. Expatriates of British, European and North American descent comprize about half of this community. Almost all workers in this community are white-collar professionals and occupy senior positions in business and government. They often command a higher salary than their local counterparts and are normally provided with living quarters and other expatriate benefits. This Western community is an identifiable segment in the market which should not be ignored.

The census of 1981 has also produced other useful social statistics for marketers. One such statistic is the age distribution. The population of Hong Kong is young; 36.1 percent are below the age of 20, and 24.8 percent are under 15. At the other end, those aged 65 and over comprise 6.6. percent of the total population. However, in the past ten years there has been a continuous decline in the proportion of children and teenagers and a steady growth in that of senior citizens. This is reflected in the median age of the population, which went up to 26 in 1981 from 21.7 a decade ago.

One important result of this demographic change is that the proportion of the working-age population, i.e. those aged 15 to 65, has increased significantly in the past ten years. It reached 68.6 percent at the end of 1981, up from 59.7 percent in 1971. This indicates that there is now a greater potentially productive population available to support the children and the retired. At the end of 1981 Hong Kong's dependency ratio, defined as the number of persons below 15 and over 65 years of age per 1,000 of the population aged between 15 and 65, was 457. This compared favorably with figures for Canada, Japan and Singapore which were 477, 484 and 517 respectively.

Even more significant than the dependency ratio is the labor-force participation rate. According to the 1981 census, 70.9 percent of Hong Kong's labor force (population between ages 15 and 65) was economically active.[6] This percentage was higher than that of Canada (65 percent), Japan (68 percent) and Singapore (64 percent) in the same year. What this means is that there are in Hong Kong proportionately more men and women working for their living, and fewer depending on their support than in Canada, Japan or Singapore. Examined from another angle, the census reveals that the average number of economically active in the Hong Kong nuclear family of four (two parents and two children) is 1.9. In other words, in 95 out of 100 nuclear families there are two income-earners. This has produced very active consumer households.

*Government Policy*

The government's economic policy always has a decisive influence upon a country's pattern of development, its economic structure and its market environment. Hong Kong's case is no exception; but here, the part played by the government is somewhat controversial. The controversy, however, lies not as much in what it has done as in what it could have done.

Hong Kong was founded by the British as a free port, and this policy has been kept unchanged for more than a century. It is the only country in the world which is still practicing *laissez faire*, termed elegantly as 'positive non-intervention' by the government.[7] In Hong Kong there are no market controls, no protective tariffs, no import quotas, no minimum wages and no tax incentives. The government's presence in the economy is minimal, and is confined to the provision of essential governmental services and infrastructure. Even the basic necessities such as electricity and light, gas, telephone service and public transport are provided for by private companies. The government budget is always a balanced one which aims at maintaining fiscal neutrality. Market forces are allowed to shape the economy, to determine all product and factor prices, and to germinate new industries or wipe away the obsolete ones. Taxes are levied only on income arising in or derived from Hong Kong. There is no capital gains tax, no sales tax and no tax on corporate capital. Excise duties are charged on only four product groups — alcoholic beverages, tobacco, certain hydrocarbon oils and methyl alcohol — irrespective of whether they are imported or manufactured locally. The standard tax rate is 15 percent, applicable to property tax, interest tax and profit tax.[8] Salaries are taxed on a progressive scale from 0 per cent to 25 percent; but the maximum salary tax payable is limited to 15 percent of gross income before any deducation of allowances.

One immediate and obvious effect of this policy of non-intervention is that there is open and very keen competition in the market. All businesses are given a free hand to organize and manage themselves, to plan their marketing strategies and to fight their competitors. There are no restrictive marketing regulations apart from those concerned with product safety or public morals, such as the use of violence or sex in advertisements. The low profit taxes also mean that companies have good abilities to use the accumulated wealth to expand and diversify their operations. To survive the competition and to prosper, one often has to get very large or stay very small. Consequently, many industries in Hong Kong are characterized by a large number of very small firms and a few very large firms. This is not only true of manufacturing industries such as textiles, plastics and electronics, but many other types of businesses such as trading, retailing, real estate, and building and construction, display a similar pattern as well.

Salary difference can be extreme even in the same industry. For example, the monthly salary in factories ranges from C$200 for an unskilled worker to C$600 for a skilled worker, and C$1,200 for a supervisor to C$4,000 for a plant manager. In the government, a clerk earns about C$300 a month and a senior official C$4,000. Furthermore, those in high-income brackets often receive an additional package of fringe benefits to which the low-income earners are not entitled. With no progressive taxes to redistribute incomes, such extremes of earnings have also resulted in extremes of personal wealth, life-styles and living conditions. To many critics this is an undesirable social problem which Hong Kong will eventually have to tackle.

The government has been urged by many to enact new legislation and to use fiscal measures to narrow down the extreme inequalities of income, to improve working conditions for the workers, to protect the tenants from the landlords, to provide subsidized factory premises for industries, and to provide a care system for the poor and the elderly. But the government on a number of occasions has reiterated its intention to stick to its existing policy on the justification that 'it has worked in the past'. In the last thirty years Hong Kong has managed to achieve a whole range of economic goals without recourse to government intervention. Thus, in the eyes of some, there appears to be no compelling reason to change a policy that has had positive results.

## Foreign Investment

The government's liberal economic policy is extended to the treatment of foreign investment, making Hong Kong a haven for multinationals.

The outstanding feature of this policy is that it makes no distinction between foreign and local companies, apart from definitional identification for statistical classification. Both are treated alike. They are registered under the same laws, subjected to the same set of business regulations, and taxed at the same rate. Foreigners can invest in any business and own 100 percent equity. There are no restrictive employment legislations apart from the one which is enacted to protect child and female workers, and this legislation applies to all private businesses. There is freedom for the repatriation of capital and remittances of earnings, interest and other fees. There are no exchange controls, and foreign currencies can move freely in and out at any time and in any amount.

Because of the complete lack of restrictions on foreign ownership, all major sectors of the Hong Kong economy have extensive foreign investment, rendering the business community a cosmopolitan one and making market competition international in both dimension and scope. To give some indications of this phenomenon, only about one-third of the licensed commercial banks in Hong Kong are local banks; and even among the local banks, at least half have foreign-ownership interest.[9] In the insurance area, more than half of the firms are representative offices or subsidiaries of overseas companies. In trading and distribution there are more than 1,000 foreign-company offices. In fact, the largest conglomerates which control about one-half of Hong Kong's import and export businesses are foreign owned.[10] Even in retailing, about half of the largest and most modern department stores are foreign owned, or are run on a partnership basis between local and foreign investors. The manufacturing sector is the only major sector in which local investors have a majority share, and even here foreign ownership is significant. At the end of 1981 there were around 450 foreign manufacturing firms in Hong Kong with a combined investment of about C$600 million.

In 1979 the author undertook a study of foreign investment in the manufacturing sector in Hong Kong. As a part of this study a questionnaire survey was conducted to explore the investment motives and operational characteristics of the foreign manufacturers. The result, summarized in Table 6.1 gives some useful indications of the Hong Kong business environment, and suggests that the government's economic policy is welcomed by foreign investors.

In this study twenty investment factors, covering the major environmental elements, were presented to the foreign manufacturers for evaluation. Only one factor — 'cost of office factory space' — received

Table 6.1: Assessment of the Business Environment by 108 Foreign Manufacturers in Hong Kong

| Environmental factors | Unfavorable | | | | | Favorable | | | | | Average score |
|---|---|---|---|---|---|---|---|---|---|---|---|
| | -5 | -4 | -3 | -2 | -1 | +1 | +2 | +3 | +4 | +5 | |
| Exchange controls | 0 | 0 | 0 | 1 | 0 | 6 | 12 | 19 | 19 | 51 | 3.9 |
| Corporate taxes | 0 | 0 | 0 | 1 | 0 | 14 | 13 | 15 | 33 | 32 | 3.5 |
| Trade restrictions on imports and exports | 0 | 0 | 1 | 0 | 2 | 12 | 9 | 19 | 33 | 32 | 3.5 |
| Business laws and regulations | 0 | 0 | 1 | 2 | 2 | 14 | 8 | 34 | 29 | 18 | 3.0 |
| General attitude towards foreigners and foreign corporations | 1 | 1 | 0 | 0 | 1 | 16 | 12 | 29 | 29 | 19 | 3.0 |
| Financial maturity | 0 | 0 | 1 | 0 | 4 | 9 | 17 | 44 | 20 | 13 | 2.9 |
| Political stability | 1 | 1 | 0 | 1 | 2 | 14 | 19 | 40 | 18 | 12 | 2.7 |
| Geographical location | 0 | 1 | 1 | 2 | 5 | 26 | 6 | 25 | 25 | 17 | 2.6 |
| Government policy towards foreign investment | 0 | 1 | 0 | 1 | 4 | 23 | 19 | 34 | 13 | 13 | 2.5 |
| Availability of managerial skill | 5 | 2 | 4 | 4 | 1 | 16 | 12 | 34 | 11 | 19 | 2.2 |
| Labor-management relationship | 0 | 1 | 1 | 1 | 7 | 21 | 33 | 24 | 14 | 6 | 2.1 |
| Education standard of population | 0 | 2 | 1 | 6 | 4 | 23 | 36 | 27 | 5 | 4 | 1.8 |
| Social overhead facilities | 1 | 1 | 1 | 0 | 7 | 48 | 22 | 17 | 8 | 3 | 1.6 |
| Domestic economic stability | 1 | 2 | 5 | 10 | 10 | 27 | 24 | 22 | 7 | 0 | 1.5 |
| Government's integrity and efficiency in administration | 1 | 1 | 9 | 8 | 10 | 13 | 13 | 41 | 8 | 4 | 1.4 |
| Local market potential | 6 | 8 | 2 | 7 | 6 | 25 | 15 | 22 | 6 | 11 | 1.0 |
| Raw-material supplies | 4 | 9 | 3 | 15 | 11 | 11 | 20 | 26 | 7 | 2 | 0.6 |
| Currency stability | 5 | 7 | 6 | 3 | 19 | 39 | 13 | 13 | 3 | 0 | 0.2 |
| Labor supply and cost | 6 | 5 | 8 | 10 | 16 | 27 | 16 | 17 | 3 | 0 | 0.1 |
| Cost of office and factory space | 65 | 10 | 14 | 7 | 5 | 5 | 0 | 1 | 1 | 0 | -3.8 |

an overall negative rating. On a ten-point scale ranging from +5 (which represented the most favorable rating) to −5 (which represented the most unfavorable), the mean of the average scores was 1.815; eleven factors obtained an average score of more than 2.0. Furthermore, the best ratings were received by those factors which were directly related to the government's economic policy − 'exchange controls' (3.9), 'corporate taxes' (3.5), 'trade restrictions on imports and exports' (3.5) and 'business laws and regulations' (3.0).

## Political Condition

No examination of the market environment in Hong Kong can be complete without some reference to its political status and its future.

The political system in Hong Kong may be best described as 'freedom without democracy'. Political freedom and every civil right of the citizen is guaranteed and protected. There is freedom of speech and of political affiliation. Political activities are permitted as long as they do not threaten national security or lead to civil disturbances. The local Chinese can celebrate their national day on October 1 with the Communists, or on October 10 with the Nationalists. The majority, however, are indifferent and uninspired by either.

Despite the political freedom, there is no democratic representation in government. Hong Kong is administered along the lines traditional for a British colony. The local head of the government is the Governor. Appointed by the Queen, he is responsible for every executive act of the government. The main government chambers are the Executive Council, the Legislative Council and the Urban Council. All members of the Executive Council and the Legislative Council are appointed by the Governor. In fact, one-third of the former body and one-half of the latter are official members holding senior positions in government. The Executive Council's function is to advise the government on all matters of policy and its execution. The Legislative Council is responsible for the enactment of legislation and management of government finance. The Urban Council has the same function as that of a municipal government in Canada. It is a body corporate responsible for civil affairs such as the management of civic centers, city halls, museums, libraries, parks, playgrounds and markets. There are no official members in the Urban Council; half of its members are appointed by the Governor and the other half are elected.

In the international community Hong Kong is not considered a sovereign state, and it has no representation in the United Nations. Its internal administration, however, is very much autonomous. It has fiscal independence, its own currency backed by its own reserves, and it conducts its own negotiations with its trading partners, including the UK and China.

The lack of a democratically elected government and a non-entity political status in the international community has not bothered its people or the foreign investors. Instead, apart from the disturbances in 1967 which were caused by the outspread of the Cultural Revolution in China, Hong Kong has enjoyed good political and social stability. This is evident from the 2.7 average score given to 'political stability' by foreign investors in their evaluation. This stability is also a reason why Hong Kong has been receiving large volumes of investment capital from nearby Asian Pacific countries. These capital inflows have kept local finance plentiful and cheap.

Even though the people are obviously satisfied with the present arrangement, there is uncertainty in Hong Kong's political future. Hong Kong is a British colony on Chinese soil. The treaties of its annexation (Treaty of Nanjing in 1942, Treaty of Tienjin in 1958 and Convention of Beijing in 1898) were forced upon the Manchu government. Hence, the Chinese government has always refused to recognize the validity and legitimacy of the treaties which, nevertheless, are the legal basis for British rule in Hong Kong. However, China has not attempted to re-annex Hong Kong even though there had been ample opportunities in the past — in 1945 after the Japanese surrendered, in 1949 when the Communists took over control of the Chinese mainland, and in 1967 during the Cultural Revolution. The reason for non-intervention is economic in nature. In all these years more than half of China's foreign-exchange earnings have come directly from Hong Kong. Furthermore, through Hong Kong, China maintains its contact with the free world and keeps abreast with technological developments in the West.

Unfortunately, the lease for the New Territories will expire in 1997. Without another legal document to extend the legitimacy of its rule, Britain will have to return the New Territories to the Chinese. Although the British government may claim that the Victoria Island and Kowloon Peninsula were actually ceded to Britain and therefore it may legally continue to hold on to these territories, the loss of the New Territories will probably mean the end of the economic miracle of Hong Kong.

This political situation is a delicate one, and poses a dilemma to China. On one hand, the Chinese government cannot continue to let a foreign country have sovereignty and political control over its territories; on the other, the departure of the British may mean the end of present-day Hong Kong and the loss of enormous economic benefits to China.

*The Consumers*

In the past few years it has become more and more apparent that the people's life-style and consumption behavior have been affected by the uncertainty of the future. Increasingly, people realize that they are living in a 'borrowed place on borrowed time', and that time is running short.[11] Thus, there has developed in many people a mentality that is self-centered and short-sighted. There is little inclination to save for the future. They tend to spend money as quickly as it is earned — eating and drinking lavishly and showing little restraint in the purchase of luxury goods. This consumption mentality, even more than the people's income-levels, accounts for the thriving expensive-luxury-goods market in Hong Kong.

There is also a conspicuous preference for foreign imports. This is a behavior attributable as much to the colonial status of Hong Kong and a subconscious lack of self-confidence among the people, as to a desire to imitate foreigners. Many Hong Kong products are recognized as quality products in overseas markets, but a 'made in Hong Kong' label commands little respect from its own people. Hong Kong is the world's number-one exporter of garments; but at the same time, it imports large quantites of expensive garments from Italy, France, the UK and Japan. Hong Kong sells to the outside world more toys than any other country; but in the department stores there are more toys from the US and Japan than its own. Hong Kong has overtaken Switzerland in the export of watches, but it is Switzerland's second largest export market for custom-made watches. Hong Kong produces more radios, tape recorders, cameras and photographic equipment than its people can buy; but those that are found in its people's homes are more often made in Japan, the US or West Germany. In fact, this preference for foreign brands is so strong that some foreign imports are actually made in Hong Kong but sent overseas for 'stamping', and then shipped back to be sold as imported goods. At the same time, many local manufacturers are being forced to abandon the local market because of the people's reluctance to buy local goods. The fact that many local-product designs can only be purchased overseas is well known; this fact is taken to imply that those designs which are sold in the home market are rejects and returns from overseas.

The external trade figures provide a good testimony to this consumer psychology. Hong Kong's leading exports of manufactured goods are 'articles of apparel and clothing accessories', 'miscellaneous manufactured articles' (mostly toys), 'photographic apparatus, equipment and supplies; optical goods and watches, clocks and accessories', 'electrical

Table 6.2: Hong Kong's Foreign Trade, 1981 (amount in C$ million)

| Commodity section/division | Imports | | Domestic exports | |
|---|---|---|---|---|
| | Amount | % of total | Amount | % of total |
| Food and live animals | 2,996 | 10.1 | 218 | 1.3 |
| Beverages and tobacco | 441 | 1.6 | 41 | 0.2 |
| Crude materials, inedible, except fuels | 1,202 | 4.5 | 211 | 1.2 |
| Mineral fuels, lubricants and related materials | 2,348 | 8.7 | 21 | 0.1 |
| Animal and vegetable oils, fats and waxes | 91 | 0.3 | 2 | 0.0 |
| Chemicals and related products | 1,940 | 7.2 | 167 | 1.0 |
| Manufactured goods classified by material | 8,597 | 31.9 | 1,843 | 10.7 |
| Machinery and transport equipment; telecommuncation and sound-recording and reproducting apparatus and equipment | 1,311 | 4.9 | 1,203 | 7.0 |
| Electrical machinery, apparatus and appliances | 2,127 | 7.9 | 1,245 | 7.2 |
| Others | 3,479 | 12.9 | 774 | 4.5 |
| Miscellaneous manufactured articles; articles of apparel and clothing accessories | 1,119 | 4.2 | 6,057 | 35.2 |
| Photographic apparatus, equipment and supplies and optical goods; watches and clocks | 2,035 | 7.6 | 1,735 | 10.1 |
| Miscellaneous manufactured articles | 1,143 | 4.2 | 2,834 | 16.5 |
| Others | 667 | 2.5 | 804 | 4.7 |
| Commodities and transactions not classified | 134 | 0.5 | 72 | 0.4 |
| Total merchandise trade | 29,630 | 100.0 | 17,227 | 100.0 |

Source: Hong Kong Government, *Hong Kong 1982, A Review of 1981*, Appendix 4, Hong Kong, 1982.

machinery, apparatus and appliances' and 'telecommunication and sound-recording and reproducing apparatus and equipment'. In 1981 these five categories of manufactured goods accounted for C$13,074 million or over three-quarters of Hong Kong's domestic exports (Table 6.2). But these same products were also Hong Kong's leading consumer-goods imports. Their combined value C$7,735 million, was more than one-quarter of total imports, or on average, C$1,500 for each Hong Kong resident.

## Summary

Hong Kong's economy and trade have been distinctly shaped by its history, geography, topography, demographic position, governmental economic policy and political conditions. Historical events which were out of its control forced Hong Kong to embark upon a process of industrial transformation. The distinct geography led to its emergence as an entrepôt port, and later as a commercial and financial center. The topography restricted the development of primary and heavy industries, and resulted in a predominance of light consumer-goods industries. Demographic patterns created an energetic workforce, distinctive market segments and active economic households. The government's economic policy was instrumental in fostering private investment by local and foreign investors, in producing a sizable and affluent upper class, and in making market competition keen and international — both in dimension and scope. Finally, whereas political stability in the past contributed to the inflows of investment capital, the uncertainty of the future has turned many people into extravagant consumers.

Hong Kong is officially a 'developing country member' of the Asian Development Bank; however, the Hong Kong market is anything but underdeveloped. There are no primitive rural sectors, no artificial barriers, no economic bottlenecks, no deficiencies in marketing-support facilities and no shortage of competitors. Furthermore, the Hong Kong market is enormous, and the profit potential excellent. With appropriate strategies, a marketer should find the Hong Kong market one of the most rewarding in the world.

# Notes

1. Since 1960 the unemployment rate in Hong Kong has never exceeded 5%.
2. According to the World Bank, the three countries with the highest GNP *per capita* in the Asian Pacific region in 1980 were: Japan (US$8,800), Hong Kong (US$4,000) and Singapore (US$3,820).
3. According to the Working Party on Small Scale Industry of the United Nations' Economic and Social Commission for Asia and the Pacific, a small firm is defined as one which employs less than 50 workers.
4. In 1981 the average industrial wage in the manufacturing sector in Hong Kong was around C$375, as compared to C$150 to C$250 in the Philippines, South Korea and Taiwan. In September 1981 the overall industrial wage index was 250, up from 100 for the base period July 1973 to June 1974. This represented a 150% increase in seven years. During the same period the consumer price index rose by about 100%; thus, the increase in real wages was about 36%.
5. China is Hong Kong's second most important import supplier, next to Japan; but the bulk of the imports are food products, not industrial raw materials.
6. 'Economically active' category includes those who work for others for an income as well as those who are self-employed.
7. The term 'positive non-intervention' is often used on various official occasions, e.g. budget speeches. A detailed discussion of this policy is found in Haddon-Cave (1980).
8. Since 1976 there has been a small surcharge on profits of incorporated businesses. In 1981 the effective profit-tax rate for corporations was 16.5%.
9. A local bank is defined as one which has an original local registration. Hence, even if a bank is now majority owned by foreigners it would still be regarded as a local bank if it was originally registered in Hong Kong.
10. The conglomerates are the offshoots of the merchant houses established by the British in the 19th century. They are so deeply entrenched in Hong Kong that they are more often regarded as local corporations.
11. This is a phrase borrowed from Hughes (1968).

# References

Haddon Cave, 'Introduction: The Making of Some Aspects of Public Policy in D. Lethbridge (ed.), *The Business Environment of Hong Kong*, Oxford University Press, Hong Kong, 1980
Hughes, R. *Hong Kong: Borrowed Place – Borrowed Time*, Andre Deutsch, London, 1968

# Further Reading

Cheng, T.Y. *The Economy of Hong Kong*, Far East Publications, Hong Kong, 1977
Endacott, G.B. *A History of Hong Kong*, Oxford University Press, Hong Kong, 1968
England, J. and Rear, J. *Chinese Labour Under British Rule*, Oxford University Press, Hong Kong, 1975
Geiger, T. and Geiger, F.M. *The Development Progress of Hong Kong and Singapore (Tales of Two City States)*, Macmillan, Hong Kong, 1976

Hong Kong Government *Hong Kong Annual Report*, various issues
—— Census and Statistics Department *Monthly Digest of Statistics*, various issues
Hopkins, K. (ed.) *Hong Kong: The Industrial Economy*, Oxford University Press, London, 1971
Riedel, J. *The Industrialisation of Hong Kong*, Institut for Weltwirtshaft an der Universität Kiel, Tubingen, 1974
Szczepanik, E. *The Economic Growth of Hong Kong*, Oxford University Press, London, 1958

# 7 AFRICAN MARKETING: THE NEXT FRONTIER

Françoise Simon-Miller

## Marketing and Development

Of all the Third World regions, Africa has long been considered the twilight zone of modern marketing. Many socio-historical patterns have contributed to creating and maintaining this perception. Colonial channels of trade limited much of West Africa to France, for instance, and French governments have strived to maintain close economic ties since independence, with the six countries that form the Union Monetaire d'Afrique de l'Ouest (UMAO). A regional customs union, the Communuaté Economique de l'Afrique de l'Ouest (CEAO) was set up 1973 to counter Nigeria's attempts to form a larger West African community. UMAO enjoys certain benefits such as the guaranteed convertibility by the French Government of its unified currency, the CEC franc, at a rate maintained for twenty years despite current balance-of-payments problems in the Ivory Coast and Senegal. However, the West African member states are subject to severe limitations, such as the inability to expand national credit unilaterally and the existence of ceilings on credit expansion. Current policies still point to an attenuated form of economic colonialism, with a 10 to 20 percent share of some states' GNP reverting to France in the form of industrial and private repatriation of capital.

Other societal factors such as interstate and intrastate cultural, linguistic and ethnic pluralism have stood in the way of pan-African economic progress. Africa is the most linguistically diverse continent in the world, with more than 2,000 distinct dialects spoken in the sub-Saharan area. Cultural fragmentation is also present in the tripartite structure of the collective psyche, where Islamic, European and African traditions lead an uneasy coexistence. Ethnic differences, if not rivalries, are also found within states. Nigeria, for instance, with an estimated 1980 population of 72,600,000 and a geographic area equivalent to the states of Texas and Colorado, held as many as eleven ethnic clusters, the largest (Hausa-Fulani type) being 21,050,000, or 29 percent of total population, and the smallest (Bororo or Nupe) being only slightly over 1 percent. (Some clusters, such as the middle belt of

Plateau Peoples, themselves comprise several distinct units.) Several ethnic units are less than 5 percent of the total population, yet have memberships of more than half a million persons. This ethnic fragmentation is paralleled on the linguistic level, with the major language (Hausa) understood by only an estimated 40 percent of the population, whereas the rest speak Yoruba (20 percent), Ibo and others of the Niger-Congo and Sudanic language families. For these reasons, English continues to be the official language but has the usual problems of a *lingua franca*, such as the inability to reach many non-urban, isolated groups.

Polyethnicity and multilingualism are compounded by further breakdowns at the economic level, such as an extraordinary increase in urban migration, oil wealth and to a doubling in size of many Nigerian cities in 1975–80, but migration is endemic in most other West African states (Morrison Paden *et al.*, 1983, ms., pp. 335–43). This phenomenon compounds the dualism which still characterizes this region; the rift between subsistence and modern economies is translated into territorial malintegration, i.e. a North–South regionalism *within* Nigeria, which strangely duplicates the North–South tensions at the global level. To these pressing needs in territorial and interethnic integration, one might add a third cultural task: mass-elite integration.

This is particularly visible in the fact that the indigenous private sector is still largely neglected in governmental policies. Ruling elites still tend to be trained more in European government schools than in US management programs, and the average, bright youth still aspires to be a high-ranking bureaucrat, not a businessman. This partly stems from cultural factors such as lack of trading tradition in some countries (Ivory Coast), the Islamic anti-usury custom, or simply the pervasiveness of corrupt business practices in countries such as Nigeria. All these 'bottom-up' components explain why 'top-down' policies, such as import substitution and indigenization have not reached their goals. Under the Nigerian Indigenization Decree, for instance, all enterprises must have full or partial Nigerian participation, classified in three groups: Schedule I identifies 39 types reserved exclusively for local management (bread-baking and retailing, for instance); another 39 types require 60 percent Nigerian involvement, and Schedule II stipulates 40 percent participation (Onah,.1979, p. xi).

Market conditions are still the major obstacle to a private sector take-off in this region: atomistic competition, limited communication and transport infrastructure, declining agricultural yields, prevalence of non-monetized production, shortage of skilled labor and managerial manpower and high birth and death-rates, all consistute a significant internal problem – compounded by external factors such as negative terms of trade, political risk, exports largely limited to oil and commodities, and a rising international debt.

Recent indices of economic trends, however, indicate a considerable market potential in this area. *Per capita* GDP for Nigeria and Ivory Coast rose, for instance, from US $153 to $329, and from $698 to $863 respectively in the 1965–77 period, which excluded both from the economic definition of a less developed country (LDC). Energy consumption more than doubled in both countries in the same period (in kgs of coal: 153 to 356 in the Ivory Coast, and 53 to 107 in Nigeria), and food consumption rose steadily. Oil production also led to a near-doubling of the percentage of the labor force in industrial employment in Nigeria during those twelve years (Morrison, Paden *et al.*, 1983).

If development is defined as 'a process through which a society moves from a given socio-economic condition to another more desirable [one] as a consequence of education in the appropriate attitudes and skills' (Onah, 1979, p. 7), the significant lag of the third sector can be directly attributed to a lack of grass-roots incentives. Local governments' 'top-down' policies have been largely ineffective: statutory protections, such as import substitution, do not work in the absence of indigenous managerial and technological know-how. Venture capital is often not accessible because of local conservative practices (loans reserved to safe, large-scale businesses). Direct government intervention, such as massive expropriations in the 1960s and 1970s, has proven disastrous in the face of risk-averse local credit policies. The establishment of parastatal firms in manufacturing, transportation and marketing, while solving short-term problems (such as AGRIPAC (Agricultural Products Distribution Branch of Programme d'Action Commerciale) and SICOFREL (Société Ivoirienne pour la Commercialisation des Fruits et Légumes) for domestic and export commodity trading in Ivory Coast) resulted in cannibalization of private enterprise by the public sector. Finally, indigenization has had relatively little success in Francophone Africa – because of a biased public view which sees business as exploitation and identifies capitalism with racism and colonial rule.

This bias has a particularly strong impact on the business-perceived function as the most openly commercial, i.e. marketing. A study recently commissioned by the Nigerian Council of Management Education and Training showed that it was 'the most neglected managerial function' in the country (Onah, 1979, p. xiii). Local planners tend to be more interested in the production of physical goods than in intangible marketing services, and inefficient marketing systems themselves may create a 'catch-22' situation, in as much as they afford employment for the otherwise unemployed. However, productivity will not increase if the proper incentives are not transmitted to producers, or if producers are not adequately informed of consumer demands for their products through the marketing system (Kaynak, 1982, pp. 25, 27). Drucker has claimed that marketing is the most effective agent of development in that it forms local entrepreneurs to optimize latent economic sources (Drucker, 1958).

Failing to see that marketing should still play a crucial role in such a situation, not as a stimulator, but as a *regulator* of demand has led to what could be called a pattern of *dysconsumption* in the sub-Saharan area. Economists have noted 'the noticeably distorted sense of value of many buyers, who buy for reasons other than utility' (Onah, 1979, p. 5). One might contrast the 'elite marketing' which often prevails with a 'basic-needs' concept of marketing, more synergistic with the goals of national development. In this perspective, increased local production would be paralleled by what Thorelli and Sentell (1982) call *consumer emancipation*. Current conditions often present aberrations such as the purchase of a luxury item, for status-seeking reasons, by consumers who might not even own all the basic goods necessary — or the neglect of affordable local brands for an overpriced, more prestigious imported one. Functional consumption would instead make the objective and subjective utilities of goods coincide. It would ideally be reached through a *bimodal* effort where commercial and social marketing would coexist and reinforce each other — particularly in regard to basic-needs goods. For instance, food products, pharmaceuticals or cosmetics would be marketed within the context of a nutrition and health-awareness campaign; textiles, housing and vehicles would be promoted within a policy of adaptation to socio-cultural heritage and local climatic and infrastructural conditions.

There is, of course, the danger of underlying authoritarianism, or economic paternalism, in this type of policy: how does one establish an ordinal ranking of utility for a given array of goods? According to whose norms will it be set? Consumers in LDCs have often been seduced, through uncontrolled promotion, into using Western-type products that they could usefully do without. But does not the *right to choose* include the right to make the same mistakes as those made by Western consumers in earlier times? For LDC consumers, self-realization may exist within a very precarious and narrow zone bounded on one side by free-market consumer manipulation, and on the other, by totalitarian interference with consumer choice.

The ideal objective of a *eurythmic* consumption, evolving smoothly along functional lines, might have to be accompanied by a redefinition of development itself. Social change has long been categorized in terms of a clear-cut polarity, a binary set of entities, whereby history is described as the movement from one state to another. Development, in particular, is seen as the passage from subsistence by mass production and consumption. This may amount to exchanging one set of constraints for another, subsistence living being replaced by *commodity dependence*, a new form of bondage leading Western consumers to live in a goods-intensive society whose needs are increasingly designed, prescribed and controlled by professionals and managers of large-scale businesses.

While it may be reactionary to sentimentalize 'vernacular' (i.e. traditional) society and extoll its virtues without stressing its hierarchical restrictions and economic limitations, one may consider an alternative, a less sharply dualistic concept of development which would broaden consumer and producer choices while allowing them to retain a degree of individualization and participation in traditional structures. In this system marketing could operate as a societal agent of the identity-formation. A more developed and accurate market research function, for instance, would promote self-perception as an index of development and change; the widespread tendency to be selective and additive in acculturation would be paralleled by *syncretic* marketing practices which incorporate some Western-type products without using them as perfect substitutes for local goods. Afrocentric marketing (in contrast to the Eurocentric marketing which still prevails) would also restore collective-mindedness into the system, where consumer self-realization would not be separated from group realization.

## Marketing Institutions in Africa: the Distribution System

There is now ample evidence, through cross-sectional and historical studies, of a specific channel development cycle driven by the growth of trade: purely traditional economies have short channels of distribution, developing economies have longer ones, and highly developed economies show a tendency to reduce the number of intermediaries (Moyer, 1965, p. 36). The dual economy typical of sub-Saharan Africa leads to the dysfunctional coexistence of radically opposite distribution patterns unintegrated and poorly linked to the production system.

The 'modern sector' is dominated by a few large distributors mostly engaged in the importation of consumer durable and non-durable goods. In Nigeria the most significant are the old colonial trading companies such as John Holt Ltd, Kaycee, Leventis Stores and Leventis Motors Ltd. Most are still foreign-controlled (on the average 60 percent ownership of the share capital in 1979 lies in foreign hands (Onah, 1979, p. 11). Some are vertically integrated, while others are horizontally integrated — reaching across several African states — which allows for considerable economies of scale. The savings, however, are most often not passed on to the consumer.

Most smaller indigenous firms cannot compete because of the prevalence of sole-agency arrangements either for imports of foreign products or for wholesale distribution of local manufactured goods.

Nigerian car-assembly plants, for instance, use car distributors like SCOA as their principal agents. Indigenous distributors lacking suitable manpower spread themselves too thin in an effort to over-diversify, and, when not excluded by sole agency rights, but only in very limited quantities with little bargaining power.

Even large-scale firms like Lever Brothers Ltd or local breweries have shown a lack of control of their channels through multiple pricing in a given locality. This distributive inefficiency does not exclude profiteering in retailing and non-retailing businesses; comparative yields in 1976 for Leventis Motors vs. Ford and CFAO vs. L'Oréal were, respectively, 35.7 against 4.8, and 18.2 against 1.4. Misintermediation and sole-agency arrangements therefore result for the consumer in overpriced goods and services (Onah, 1979, pp. 13-14).

Agricultural distribution is even more chaotic, not only for small-scale production, but also for cash crops. Marketing boards have in the past been unable to promote significant economic benefits, because of producer price-pegging, a defensive maneuver policy due to the fact that the Boards often operate in a monopsony-only situation. The Nigerian Cocoa Marketing Board, for instance, as the sole buyer of local cocoa for export, could play a major part in streamlining the distributive system, but interposes instead the usual crowd of intermediaries between producer and consumer. Rather than buy direct, it licenses trading companies as its agents. They, in turn, operate through middlemen who serve as buyers of farmers' produce. These may employ sub-buyers who hire 'runners' charged with collecting produce from outlying areas (Moyer, 1965, p. 37).

A socio-cultural obstacle to a streamlining of channels is the identification, in many African states, of different distributive functions with specific ethnicities. Reports on the trading methods of the Afrikpo of Nigeria, for instance, have isolated a group of Ibo, known as Aro, as specialized in a middleman's role, possibly because of their history as early slave traders and distributors to the Ibo markets for European iron, liquor and gunpowder, and native cloth and iron wares (Belshaw, 1965, p. 71). Similarly, an ethnically-defined channel arrangement exists in the collection of kola nuts in Nigeria. They are produced by Yoruba farmers and delivered by their wives to the nearest roadside market where the title of ownership is transferred to the Hausa middlemen. The Hausa traders, operating alone, or as buying agents, then move again from these bulk collecting points to the town or village for further resale before the product finally reaches the consumer (Moyer, 1965, pp. 36–7). Commodities, such as cassava flour, fowls or palm oil, have been reported to change hands as many as five times during the course of one day in several Yorubaland markets, with negligible profits at each transaction (Bohannan, 1962, p. 111).

The very proliferation of what one might call *micro-retailing*, with large-scale movement of traders to and from markets with local foodstuffs and cottage industrial products, appears from a Western perspective as a wasteful mismanagement of human resources. In the Akinyele ring of less than 300 square miles (777 square kilometers), on seven out of eight days, up to 5,000 Yoruba women converge on the market from a number of feeder villages or hamlets. Here again, vernacular traditions are a powerful force that discount simplification of the channel system. Market women are an institution of West African trade; they often trade on their own account and derive from market activities a degree of social recognition and economic independence which is not available elsewhere in their largely Islamic and male-dominated society. An arbitrary, centrally imposed reduction of their numbers would reveal their cosmetic function (as a screen for the endemic underemployment of labor in these regions), and entail a massive relocation of human resources which seems unfeasible at present. The women also perform two major functions (breaking bulk and, as itinerant traders, reaching rural dwellers) which will become obsolete only after significant improvement in national infrastructures and organized linkages between the subsistence and the modern sectors.

The Ivory Coast offers perhaps the best attempt of rational integration of these two systems. In 1972 the government created AGRIPAC, with 40 percent direct state ownership and 60 per cent semi-private ownership (by SONAFI, the Société Nationale de Financement); its distributive offshoot, DISTRIPAC, was set up in 1974 with a similar capital structure. Also, the PAC food chain, which comprises more than 240 stores in Abidjan and every town with a population above 3,000, operates on a franchise basis with local merchants. This arrangement offers significant advantages: 100 percent local employment, broader assortment of products and more standardized pricing. However, vertical forward integration is not to be seen as an absolute panacea because of the societal constraints and the sheer numbers of micro-retailers. A 1976 Ministry of Planning census for example counted 59,036 retailers in 36 cities of more than 10,000 each (Bollinger, 1977). A progressive distribution system would therefore have to strive for integration of the two sectors, with local producers reaching both the large-scale food chains and the wholesalers that sustain the small traders.

## Strategies for Indigenous Marketing

### Product and Price Policies

High product mortality, extreme brand loyalty and overvaluation of 'prestige' foreign goods are all endemic constraints in the West African region. Countries such as the Ivory Coast, Cameroon and Nigeria have a rapidly expanding middle-class base which represents a significant market potential. Within that class, however, the top layer of the upscale segment constitutes a Western-educated elite of 'early adopters' responsible for the introduction of European or US products and styles.

The ensuing 'elite marketing' concept, however, is not a good agent of economic development in that it tends to promote foreign prestige brands at the expense of local ones, and it is well adapted to the needs of the upper class, but creates dysfunctions at lower economic levels — such as loyalty to a foreign brand when a local substitute is available at lower prices. One study in three Yoruba markets showed, for instance, a total of 127 sellers displaying European cloth while only 3 were selling Yoruba material. Also 62 retailers were found to be selling local soap, tobacco, pots and baskets, vs 133 selling European beads, pipes, cigarettes and table ware (Bohannan, 1962, p. 117). A 1980 study showed high current and future demand for foreign appliances, household goods, clothing, cosmetics, automobiles, health and home care products, and processed foods (Kaynak, 1982, p. 188).

The key to success in local-product design for these categories would be to adapt them to suit the tastes, needs and economic characteristics of a particular national market, rather than follow a 'me-too' policy that would only result in a poor imitation of foreign goods. Labeling, for instance, should be simplified and more graphic than verbal to reflect varying levels of local literacy. Differences in family structure and power availability dictate a resizing policy: larger processed food containers to suit extended families, and smaller appliances to match the available energy. Maintenance and repair difficulties should be reflected in a higher reliability, durability and a change in tolerance for the local product. Because of the prestige appeal of foreign brands, local-product-and-company image could be formed on the basis of Western-oriented brand names and logos. When introducing new products attention should be paid to their economic benefits as well as *psycho-cultural compatibility*. The limited income of the average LDC consumer, for instance, favors a branded generic concept, with a reduced product line adapted to basic needs and savings realized on packaging. This concept has already been implemented by some pharmaceutical multinationals which market a separate LDC product line. However, these branded generics are sold to health institutions. Direct marketing to the consumer should take into account local sensitivities to attractive, brightly colored packaging. In the Ivory Coast, for instance, AGRIPAC built its own produce-packaging plant after market research showed that Ivorian buyers preferred imports because they were better calibrated and presented (Bollinger, 1977). Finally, local producers should focus on the *use-behavior*, i.e. the functions that the product performs (which may fluctuate widely across ethnic groups and social classes), and the way it fits into the total consumption system. The LDC marketing of a bicycle, for instance, should take into account both its primary and secondary purposes: transportation, and possibly status symbol in a poorer community.

Market research should establish a local psychographic base for product design — color symbolism, for instance, shifts from one ethnic group to another. There are also national and regional preferences: research has shown a marked preference for sharply contrasted colors, and for blue, white, yellow, red and brown for textiles sold in the Ivory Coast, with a North-South variation (brighter vs darker shades). Subtle gradations, such as a mauve/purple distinction, were not perceived by local consumers, possibly as reflection of their physical environment (Bollinger, 1977, p. 195).

Most importantly, an optimal marketing policy should always supply a product *and a process* as inseparable entities. It is the failure to implement this principle which led to catastrophic episodes like increased child mortality linked to mass sales of infant formula. The cause of the problem was not in the product itself, but in the fact that its marketing had not included proper consumer education regarding its use.

Like product planning, pricing policy should also include a degree of differentiation. For most West African consumers low income levels logically lead to a very high price elasticity of demand. This price consciousness, however, has been questioned on two counts: the upscale segment appears willing to accept a market-skimming policy — high quality, high-priced clothing, for instance, was found to be in great demand in Abidjan (Bollinger, 1977, p. 95). Because of non-standardized measures and mutliple pricing in micro-retailing, on the other hand, low-income consumers may be more sensitive to a 'gift' strategy (extra unit thrown in to close the bargain) or to non-price incentives such as providing special services, than to price reductions alone. In as much as pricing is demand-oriented, local producers may therefore enjoy more latitude than is commonly thought.

Major constraints originate less in the consumer than in national policies such as government price controls, which may result in hoarding, operationally defined as speculative storage against public policy. When prices are fixed at or below cost levels, similar businesses survive by black-marketeering, i.e. refusing to sell at controled prices. The price accepted by the consumer often ends up not only higher than the control price, but also higher than equilibrium price. Sole distributorship also creates a monopolistic situation where an exclusive dealer of a commodity with inelastic demand can increase profits by restricting output or hoarding (Onah, 1979, p. 37). Seasonal fluctuations may also lead a marketer to accumulate an oversupply of goods such as produce, before expected demand peaks, in order to profit from a rise in prices (Kaynak, 1982, p. 226). Commodity exchanges and national distribution systems such as AGRIPAC offer a partial solution to this problem.

## Promotional Policy

Contrary to what is commonly thought, the more developed West African countries have a relatively high level of advertising expenditure. In 1974 US $7,759,000 was spent on advertising in Nigeria; in comparison $8,009,000 was spent in Denmark, and $5,669,000 in Argentina (Onah, 1977, p. 103). Potential is even greater today in as much as the West African market is not even near the saturation levels of Europe and the US.

In accordance with a basic-needs concept, message emphasis should be as much, if not more, on information as on persuasion. Here again, social and commercial marketing should go hand in hand. Ethnic group-ings should be taken into account for linguistic considerations: al-though more than 200 dialects are spoken in Nigeria, commercials in basic English (but spoken by a Nigerian) can be effective in the three Eastern states and in Lagos. Yoruba is generally acceptable in Lagos, West and parts of Kwara state, whereas Hausa is the main medium of appeal in the North and Ibo in the East (*Nigeria Market Profile*, 1975, section 2). Advertising copy material should also be sensitive, not only to national, but also to regional beliefs and customs.

Media mix should also combine traditional and modern methods of information transmission. In the traditional sector where personal com-munication is important, particularly for new-product introduction, emphasis should be on intra-community communication and egocentric communication (Kaynak, 1982, p. 216). In the Ivory Coast, for instance, word of mouth was used in 1970–2 to launch the PAC food chain stores. Meetings were set up in each town where a store was to be opened, gathering opinion leaders (civil servants, administrators, elected officials, village chiefs) who heard the advertising message in French, then in the vernacular, and who were then asked to transmit it to all their acquaintances. Stores enjoyed a much more favorable reception than could have been obtained through impersonal media (Bollinger, 1977, p. 194).

Whereas the medium of choice for complex messages remains the press (the major Ivorian daily reaches 44 percent of urban adults), market research into the profile of the average reader suggests some limitations. For example, while one man out of two is reached by the newspaper, only one out of four women reads it. Radio has a much broader reach across gender, class and locality distinctions, and may be seen as a major agent of integration of rural areas into the modern sector, since it reaches 90 percent of urban dwellers, as well as 66 percent of the rural population (Bollinger, 1977). In 1972, the first messages in the vernacular were broadcast in the Ivory Coast — para-doxically, they did not promote local goods — they were stating the benefits of Nestlé's product for the consumers.

Other audio media of interest in West Africa are 'Sono-bus' or city buses equipped with sound systems broadcasting a 3-second commer-cial every 3 minutes in peak hours. Cinemas (103 in Nigeria and 51 in Ivory Coast in 1975–6) also include a commercial broadcast period, and can be further supplemented by mobile units reaching rural areas (33 circuits with an average capacity of 500 were serving about 20 Nigerian towns in 1975) (*Nigeria Market Profile*, 1975, section 6).

Finally, message execution is still largely suboptimal in that it does not follow a differentiation policy. Ninety percent of the turnover for Ivorian cinema advertising was still realized, in 1976, from standard commercials for major foreign brands like Coca Cola and Pepsi-Cola, Dunhill cigarettes, Colgate, Rexona, etc. Local manufacturers were either buying standard films (such as one for the watchmaking industry) which were dubbed to include their own brand identification, or in some cases, working through local agencies (S.I.C. and Y. Colmars) to produce their own commercials. Companies such as Bracodi, Blohorn, Brossette, Vedeyrt, Renault and Michelin were opting for the local commercials as well — thus showing a greater degree of cultural empathy than their US counterparts.

In conclusion, sub-Saharan Africa constitutes a considerable growth area for indigenous marketing, but also manifests an urgent need for national policies that will facilitate the adaption of marketing systems to a framework of economic development.

Present artificial market-control methods should be gradually abandoned in favor of a decentralized development of the third sector, which would lead to a better integration of the subsistence and monetized economic systems. Finally, widespread dysfunctions in the present consumption patterns may be minimized and eventually eliminated through better use of marketing research, leading to increased flexibility and efficiency in price, product, and promotional planning and implementation.

## References

Belshaw, Cyril *Traditional Exchange and Modern Markets*, Prentice-Hall, Englewood-Cliffs, 1965
Bohannan, Paul and Dalton, George *Markets in Africa*, Northwestern University Press, Evanston, 1962
Bollinger, Daniel *Le Marketing en Afrique*, vol. I *La Côte d'Ivoire*, Ceda, Abidjan, 1977
Drucker, Peter F. 'Marketing and Economic Development', *Journal of Marketing*, January 1958, 252–9
Kaynak, Erdener *Marketing in the Third World*, Praeger, New York, 1982
Moyer, Reed *Marketing in Economic Development*, Michigan State University Press, East Lansing, 1965
*Nigeria Market Profile* Rediffusion International Limited, London, 1975
Onah, Julius *Marketing in Nigeria*, Cassell, London, 1979

# Further Reading

*A Basic Needs Strategy for Africa* International Labour Office, Geneva, 1977

Abu-Lughod, Janet and Hay, Richard (eds) *Third World Urbanisation*, Maroufa Press, Chicago, 1977

*Accelerated Development in Sub-Saharan Africa* The World Bank, Washington, DC, 1981

Anderson, David J. *Commerce for West Africa*, Macmillan, London, 1977

—— *Economics of West Africa*, Macmillan, London, 1977

Anschel, K.R. *Agricultural Cooperatives and Markets in Developing Countries*, Praeger, New York, 1969

Bates, Robert *Ethnicity in Contemporary Africa*, Syracuse University Press, Syracuse, 1973

Bauer, P.T. *Economic Analysis and Policy in Underdeveloped Countries*, Duke University Press, Durham, NC, 1957

Bennett, P. (ed.) *Marketing and Economic Development*, American Marketing Association, Chicago, 1965

Berry, Sara *Capitalism and Underdevelopment in Africa*, Boston University Press, Boston, 1981

Binet, Jacques *Psychologie économique africaine*, Payot, Paris, 1970

Blake, David and Walters, Robert *The Politics of Global Economic Relations*, Prentice-Hall, Englewood Cliffs, 1976

Boddewyn, Jean *Comparative Management and Marketing*, Scott, Foresman, Glenview, 1977

—— and Marton, K. *Comparison Advertising: A World-Wide Study*, Hasting House, New York, 1978

Bryant, Coralie and White, Louise *Managing Development in the Third World*, Westview Press, Boulder, Colo., 1982

Cranch, A. Graeme 'Modern Marketing Techniques Applied to Developing Countries', in Boris Becker (ed.), *Dynamic Marketing in a Changing World*, Conference Proceedings, American Marketing Association, 1972, 34, pp. 183-6

Damachi, Ukandi and Diejomaoh, Victor *Human Resources and African Development*, Praeger, New York, 1978

Dholakia, N. and R. 'Marketing in the Emerging World Order', *Journal of Macro Marketing, 2*, 1, Spring 1982, 47-56

Doob, Leonard *Communication in Africa*, Greenwood Press, Westport, CT., 1979

Douglas, Susan and Wind, Yoram 'Environmental Factors and Marketing Practices', *European Journal of Marketing, 7*, 3, 1973-4, 155-65

Firat, Fuad 'Consumption Patterns and Macromarketing: A Radical Perspective', *European Journal of Marketing, 11*, 4, 291-7

Freedman, D.D. 'The Role of the Consumption of Modern Durables in Economic Development', *Economic Development and Cultural Change*, October 1970, 25-48

Gerstenfeld, A. and Wortzel, L. 'Strategies for Innovation in Developing Countries', *Sloan Management Review, 19*, 1, 1977, 57-68

Goldman, Arieh 'Outreach of Consumers and the Modernization of Urban Food Retailing in Developing Countries', *Journal of Marketing, 38*, October 1974, 8-16

Gugler, Joseph *Urbanisation and Social Change in West Africa*, Cambridge University Press, New York, 1978

Hail, Alfred 'Nigeria – a Big Market With a Bigger Future – But What Are You Doing About It?' *Trade and Industry*, May 1975, 296-300

Harper, M. 'Advertising in a Developing Economy: Opportunity and Responsibility', *European Journal of Marketing, 9*, 3, 1975, 215-33

Harvey, M.G. and Lusch, R.F. *Marketing Channels: Domestic and International Perspectives*, University of Oklahoma Press, Norman, 1982

Hinterhuber, H.H. 'A Framework for Marketing Strategies in the Developing Countries', *Journal of International Marketing and Marketing Research, 3*, 1, February 1978, 15–25

Hodder, B.W. and Ukwu, I.U. *Markets in West Africa*, Ibadan, 1969

Holas *Industrie et cultures en Côte d'Ivoire*, Centre des Sciences Humaines, Abidjan, 1965

Ikoku, E. *African Development with a Human Face*, Africa Books, London, 1976

Inocencio, E.S. *Advertising as an Agent of Social Change in the Underdeveloped Country*, American Academy of Advertising, Ann Arbor, Mich., 1967'

Izraeli, D. and Meissner, F. *Marketing Systems for Developing Countries*, Halsted Press, New York, 1976

James, J. and Lister, S. 'Galbraith Revisited: Advertising in Non-Affluent Societies', *World Development, 8*, 1, January 1980, 87–96

Kamanda wa Kamanda *Le défi africain*, ABC, Paris, 1976

Kotler, Philip *Marketing Management: Analysis, Planning and Control*, Prentice-Hall, Englewood Cliffs, 1980

Ladd, William C. *Francophone Africa. A Report on Business Opportunities in Eight Countries*, Overseas Private Investment Corporation, Washington, 1975

Lappé, Frances M. and Collins, J. *Food First: Beyond the Myth of Scarcity*, Ballantine, New York, 1977

Leff, N.H. and Farley, J.U. 'Advertising Expenditures in the Developing World', *Journal of International Business Studies*, Fall 1980, 64–79

Linde, V. *Marketing in Developing Countries*, University of Gothenburg Press, 1980

*Marketing Management and Strategy for the Developing World*, United Nations, New York, 1975

Meillassoux, Claude *Maiden, Meals and Money: Capitalism and the Domestic Community*, Cambridge University Press, New York, 1981

—— (ed.) *The Development of Indigenous Trade and Markets in West Africa*, Oxford University Press, Oxford, 1971

Morrison, Donald, Paden, John, *et al. Black Africa: A Comparative Handbook*, Free Press, New York, 1980 (new edn 1983)

Moyer, R. and Hollander, Stanley C. *Markets and Marketing in Developing Economies*, Irwin, Homewood, 1968

Nasir-ud-deen, K. *Marketing in Developing Countries*, National Book Foundation, Karachi, 1976

Nicosia, F. and Mayer, R. 'Toward a Sociology of Consumption', *Journal of Consumer Research, 3*, September 1976, 65–75

Nnoli, Okwundiba *Ethnic Politics in Nigeria*, Fourth Dimension Publishers, Enugu, 1978

Onah, Julius and Ejiofor, P.N.O. *Nigerian Cases in Business Management*, Cassell, London, 1978

Opayemi, M.S. and Hair, J. 'The Market Potential for Pharmaceutical Products in Nigeria', *Medical Marketing and Media*, July 1980, 23–7

Paden, John (ed.) *Values, Identities, and National Integration: Empirical Research in Africa*, Northwestern University Press, Evanston, 1980

Pyatt, G. 'Economic Strategies for Growth with Equity', *Economic Development and Cultural Change, 25*, April 1977, 581–7

Robinson, Pearl and Skinner, Elliott *Transformation and Resiliency in Africa*, Howard University Press, Washington, DC, 1983

Sommers, Montrose and Kernan, Jerome *Comparative Marketing Systems*, Appleton-Century-Crofts, New York, 1968

Thorelli, Hans and Sentell, Gerald *Consumer Emancipation and Economic Development: The Case of Thailand*, JAI Press, Greenwich, CT., 1982

US Department of Commerce 'Market Profile – Nigeria', *Overseas Business Reports*, February 1975, OBR 75–09, p. 30

Van Adam 'Futurs modèles de consommation dans les pays en voie de développement', *Revue française de Marketing*, juillet-auôt 1975, cahier *57*

Wilber, Charles (ed.) *The Political Economy of Development and Underdevelopment*, Random House, New York, 1969

# 8 MODELS-OF-MAN APPROACH TO FAMILY PLANNING[1]

## Ruby Roy Dholakia

## Introduction

The population problem in most developing countries have been caused by a faster decline in mortality-rates than in birth-rates, leading to higher-than-historical growth-rates. Not all see the higher growth-rates as a problem; but many countries view them as a boon because of their implications for market size, labor strength and national defense (Epstein, 1971; Heitleriger, 1976). However, more and more societies are adopting specific policies and strategies for limiting population growth (Stamper, 1973; Whitney, 1976).

### The Family-planning Approach

One approach to population control is that of family planning, which emphasizes conscious planning of families by individual parents. Most developing countries stress not only planned families but also small families, and actively encourage birth control. This emphasis on small families has emerged from repeated findings from knowledge-attitude-practice (KAP) studies indicating ideal sizes that are smaller than actual family sizes. It has been reinforced by the need to demonstrate economic progress measured in terms of *per capita* GNP for various purposes.

The family-planning approach has been implemented through programs of information, motivation and delivery of birth-control procedures. These programs attempt to create birth-control behavior through the individual acceptance of the following kinds of beliefs:

- families can be planned
- smaller families are better than larger families
- sex composition of children is not important
- spacing children over time is desirable
- specific procedures are available to prevent conception
- a specific procedure must be adopted to prevent conception

*Managerial Assistance*

In order to improve the design and effectiveness of family-planning programs, managerial assistance has been sought (Farley and Leavitt, 1971; Simon, 1968). Various techniques and concepts have been applied including segmenting markets on the basis of attitudes (Farley, Sexton, Smith and Takarski, 1974), age and parity of women (Roberto, 1972), and personal values (Bhandari, 1978).

Application of management technology has meant acceptance of goals and beliefs that families must be small, and that small families are inevitable if planning is accepted by individuals. Frequently, a specific number of children is explicitly recommended. For example, India not only advocates family sizes of two children, but portrays them always as consisting of one boy and one girl. Specific programs are then designed to inform, motivate and create acceptance of that norm and birth-control behavior.

## Models of Man

When strategies are designed to influence and control human behavior, implicit or explicit assumptions are made about the human being who is the target of change. These assumptions or models of man reflect program designer's belief about *why* individuals should conform, or *how* they can be made to conform. For example, the view of man as *Homo consumens* can be used to explain the consumption-enhancing activities of traditional marketing programs.

While relevant research is sparse, it is possible to identify five models of man that can be used to develop family-planning programs. (It is an empirical question whether all of them actually underlie any program.) These models have been assembled from a consideration of individual, social and cultural influences on family-planning behavior. Labelled the *macro, social, rational, risk-aversive* and *psychoanalytic* model of man, each of these views differs on its reasons for holding a particular position on family planning. While there can be considerable overlap in the traditional socio-economic characteristics of these models, their interaction creates a set of motivations that determine family-planning behavior. A summary of the models is presented in Table 8.1, and a brief description of each model is given below.

*Macro Man* is a model of man who is aware of and motivated by the aggregate effects of individual decisions. One's access to distribution of rewards is seen linked directly to larger issues such as size of GNP

Table 8.1: Models of Man in Family Planning

| Characteristic | Macro man | Social man | Models of Man<br>Rational man | Risk-aversive man | Psychoanalytic man |
|---|---|---|---|---|---|
| 1. Motivation | National need | Conformity to social norm | Family welfare | Minimum risk | Sexual satisfaction |
| 2. Socio-economic | | | | | |
| a. Location | Metropolitan centers | Rural | Urban-rural | Rural | Urban-rural |
| b. Education | High | Low | High-low | Low | Low |
| c. Income | High | Moderate | Moderate-low | Low | Moderate |
| d. Family structure | Nuclear | Extended | Both | Nuclear | Both |
| Sex role | Equal | Unequal | Limited equality | Unequal | Unequal |
| 3. Attitudes toward: | | | | | |
| a. Small family | Very positive | Negative[1] | Affluent-positive<br>Poor-negative | Negative[2] | Neutral |
| b. Sex composition of children | Favorable to both male and female | Favorable to male[1] | Favorable to male | Favorable to male | Neutral |
| c. Contraception | Very positive | Negative[1] | Affluent-positive<br>Poor-negative | Negative | Positive-weak |
| 4. Behavioral compliance | | | | | |
| a. Planning of families | High | Low | High-moderate | Low | Low |
| b. Completed family size | Small | Large | Affluent-small | Large | Large |
| c. Gap between desired vs actual | Nil-negligible | Small | Small | Moderate-large | Moderate-large |
| d. Timing of contraceptive decision | Early in life cycle | Late | Affluent-early<br>Poor-late | Late | Late |
| e. Choice of methods | | | | | |
| (i) Male vs female | Both | Male | Urban-both<br>Rural-male | Male | Both |
| (ii) Terminal vs non-terminal | Both sequentially | Terminal | Urban-both sequentially<br>Rural-terminal | Non-terminal | Non-terminal |

Notes: 1. It has been assumed that the social norm in most developing countries is for large families, preferably with a higher proportion of sons. These characteristics would differ for alternative assumptions about social norms.
2. It has been assumed that the historically high infant mortality-rates will affect the attitudes toward family planning, and will lead to a much larger completed family size than desired.

or rate of unemployment. There is symmetry in the belief that the individual and nation's interests are directly related.

In terms of specific attitudes and behavior, macro man in most developing countries is likely to favor small families, believe in active control of fertility behavior and value male and female children equally. Highly educated, environmentally aware and ideologically committed, macro man will be found in large urban areas and in employment positions involving power and control over others. Media exposure is high for both personal and mass media.

*Social Man* is motivated by desire to conform to social norms. Social units such as the extended family and village community impinge directly on the individual and mediate rewards and punishments. Decision-making is strongly influenced by authority positions such as family and village elders.

Social man is likely to favor large families — specially a large number of sons (Mamdani, 1972). Marriage is likely to take place early and fertility will be high. This model of man is most likely to be found in rural areas and living in extended families. With limited formal education, exposure to communication is likely to be channeled through personal media.

*Rational Man* is a model that emphasizes man's deliberate and conscious efforts to maximize one's own welfare. For some rational men, large families lead to increased welfare while others will require small families. This model of man hinges on deliberate choices made due to considerations at the basic family-unit level. The tendency of poor or agricultural people to have large families can be justified by the net increase in total family income (Neher, 1971).

One of the major influences on one's concept of welfare will be specific material conditions, and the means perceived to improve or maintain those conditions. Rational man can be found in urban and rural, rich and poor households, with extensive or limited formal education. This model of man will have preferences for specific family size and composition, and will be able to justify the preferences in terms of family needs and welfare.

*Risk-aversive Man* is able to see connections between aggregate effects and individual behavior, but the relationships are seen to be uncertain at the personal level. For example, infant mortality-rates may be known to be declining, yet there will be uncertainty about the health and survival of one's own children. Therefore, family-planning behavior will be motivated by efforts to reduce these risks and uncertainties.

Risk-aversive man may desire small families, but actual family size will be larger to provide the 'margin of safety' acceptable to the individual. This margin will be necessary to cover risks of not having heirs to carry on the family name (continuity), and of not having earning members to support old age (social security). Risk-aversive man can be found in rural and urban areas, and a major determinant will be personal experience of mortality-rates and health services.

*Psychoanalytic Man* is a model emphasizing deep personal psychological expectations and experiences. When expectations and experiences are congruent, the effect is positive and reinforcing. When there are discrepancies, behavior is negatively affected.

In terms of family planning, sexual relationships influence attitudes and behavior (Rainwater, 1960, 1965). When experiences of sexual relationships are satisfying, the psychoanalytic man will adopt methods that will achieve family-planning goals. On the other hand, if relationships are unsatisfying, then measures are likely to be implemented ineffectively.

In terms of socio-economic characteristics, the psychoanalytic man is likely to exist in urban and rural areas, in rich and poor, in educated and non-educated households. Attitude towards family-limiting behavior is likely to be favorable. However, when contraceptive methods are selected, there may be a tendency to select riskier methods or to practice with unconscious ineffectiveness (Rainwater, 1965).

## Model Validity

There is both indirect and direct evidence to support the preceding categorizations. In the present context of energy shortages, societal benefits (i.e. macro logic) are considered influential factors in creating energy-conservation behavior only among the upper social classes (Brooker, 1976; Murphy, Laczniak and Robinson, 1979). Individual characteristics of individuals who remain voluntarily child-free also tend to support this view (Jamison, Franzine and Kaplan, 1979).

Rainwater (1960, 1965) has found sexual relationships to be an important determinant of family-planning behavior, especially in terms of effectiveness with which birth control is practiced. The concept of alienation has been also used to predict and explain fertility behavior (Morris and Sison, 1974; Neal and Groat, 1977). Reviewing a study on Indian villages, Mamdani (1972) observed that compliance to social norms led to family-planning behavior that was not always in conformity with an individual's personal beliefs. Anker (1977) studied caste and village as two group-level variables, and found them to be highly associated with three measures of fertility — ideal size, completed family size and family-planning acceptance. Fishbein (1972) has used his extended model to incorporate social norms and motivation to comply as additional variables in understanding family planning behavior. Social-class norms have been found to determine family sizes, even in socially mobile families where both the class of origin and destination have their influences (Berent, 1951; Blau and Duncan, 1967).

The rational need for sons due to economic considerations (May and Heer, 1968), or the use of children as income earners (Neher, 1971), have led to large family sizes. While this view decreases with development when social security and pension plans reduce the dependence on children, this economic motive is still a strong determinant of family-planning behavior — being more important in rural than urban areas (Snider, 1980). Education and education aspirations have been found to create differences in the economic costs and benefits of children which affected family-limitation behavior in Taiwan (Mueller, 1972).

The influence of mortality-rates on family planning has been examined at aggregate levels (Shin, 1977), but it can be conceptualized as an element of risk in individual decision-making. By the mortality-rates of 1960, Indian couples would have needed 6.3 children to be relatively certain of having one son survive to support the parents (May and Heer, 1968). The concept of 'safety margin' has been viewed by some as irrational due to the costs involved in having children. However, this view of children as costs, not values, can be said to typify the middle and upper classes, who believe in extended and expensive socialization of children.

## Implications

By speculating that there is likely to be more than one model of man to describe and explain family-planning behavior, it leads to a problem of selecting one or some models of man for program management. A cursory glance at developing countries indicates that managers and administrators are more likely to use the macro model of man to design and evaluate family-planning programs. There is no empirical evidence, in India, for example, to support the two-child family-size norm or the one-son, one-daughter norm. Yet India has one of the largest birth-control programs in the world aimed at creating behavior based on this macro model of man.

The alternative models of man open up strategic choices, and very radical implications can emerge. The need for sons due to economic considerations can only be changed if income opportunities for females or for old age are substantially improved. The type of strategies adopted to achieve this will be very different from giving short-term incentives for sterilization (Rogers, 1972). Even decisions like labor-saving incentives for the agricultural man cannot be free from certain radical changes in social structures and relationships.

## Conclusion

Broadening the marketing concept is taking marketing technology to different and difficult contexts. The zeal to solve social problems can overlook many fundamental features and relationships of the problems, and lead to short-sighted program design. In the area of family planning it has often led to the adoption of a model of man that does not represent the social realities of the majority in the developing countries. It is possible to say that this limitation is creating a condition where:

• program failure is being attributed to the people's ignorance and intractability rather than to program irrationality and
• justifications are being developed for a 'compulsory' approach to family limitation.

## Note

1. This paper was presented earlier at the American Marketing Association Fall Conference, Chicago, 1980. Reprinted with permission.

## References

Anker, R. 'Effect of Group Level Variables on Fertility in a Rural Indian Sample', *Journal of Development Studies, 14*, 1977, 63-76
Berent, J. 'Fertility and Social Mobility', *Population Studies, 5*, 1951, 244-60
Bhandari, L. *Communication for Social Marketing: A Study in Family Planning*, Macmillan, New Delhi, India, 1978
Blau, P.M. and Duncan, O.D. *The American Occupation Structure*, New York, 1967
Brooker, G. 'The Self-Actualising Socially Conscious Consumer', *Journal of Consumer Research, 3*, September 1976, 107-12
Epstein, V.X. 'The Politics of Population in Latin America', in D. Chaplin (ed.),

*Population Policies and Growth in Latin America*, Lexington Books, Lexington, Mass., pp. 133–76

Farley, J.U. and Leavitt, H.J. 'Marketing and Population Problems', *Journal of Marketing, 35*, July 1971, 28–33

Farley, J.U., Sexton, D.R., Jr., Smith, R.H. and Tokarski, S.S. 'A Working Behavioral Segmentation System for a Family Planning Marketing Program', in *1974 Combined Proceedings of the American Marketing Association*, American Marketing Association, Chicago, 1974, 31–4

Fishbein, M. 'Towards An Understanding of Family Planning Behaviors', *Journal of Applied Social Psychology, 2*, 3, 1972, 214–27

Heitleriger, A. 'Pro-natalist Population Policies in Czechoslovakia', *Population Studies, 22*, March 1976, 123–36

Jamison, P.H., Franzini, L.R. and Kaplan, R.M. 'Some Assumed Characteristics of Voluntarily Childfree Women and Men', *Psychology of Women Quarterly, 4*, 2, 1979

Mamdani, M. *The Myth of Population Control: Family, Caste and Class in an Indian Village*, Monthly Review Press, New York, 1972

May, D.A. and Heer, D.M. 'Son Survivorship and Family Size in India: A Computer Simulation', *Population Studies, 22*, July 1968, 199–210

Morris, N.M. and Sison, B.N. 'Correlates of Female Powerlessness: Parity Methods of Birth Control and Pregnancy', *Journal of Marriage and Family, 37*, February 1974, 708–12

Mueller, E. 'Economic Motives for Family Limitation: A Study Conducted in Taiwan', *Population Studies, 26*, 3, November 1972, 393–403

Murphy, P.E., Laczniak, G.R. and Robinson, R.K. 'An Attitudinal and Behavioral Index of Energy Conservation', in K.E. Henion II and T.C. Kinnear (eds), *The Conserver Society*, American Marketing Association, Chicago, 1979, pp. 82–91

Neal, A.G. and Groat, H.T. 'Alienation and Fertility in the Marital Dyad', *Social Forces, 56*, Summer 1977, 77–85

Neher, P. 'Peasants, Procreation and Pension', *American Economic Review, 61*, June 1971, 380–9

Rainwater, L. *And the Poor Get Children*, Quadrangle Books, Chicago, 1960

—— *Family Design: Marital Sexuality, Family Size and Contraception*, Aldine, Chicago, 1965

Roberto, E.L. 'Social Marketing Strategies for Diffusing the Adoption of Family Planning', *Social Science Quarterly, 53*, June 1972, 33–51

Rogers, E.M. *Field Experiments on Family Planning Incentives*, Michigan State University, East Lansing, Mich., 1972

Shin, Evi Hang 'Socioeconomic Development, Infant Mortality, and Fertility: A Cross-sectional Longitudinal Analysis of 63 Selected Countries', *Journal of Development Studies, 13*, 4, July 1977, 398–412

Simon, J.L. 'Some "Marketing Correct" Recommendations for Family Planning Campaigns', *Demography, 5*, 1, 1968, 504–7

Snider, A.J. 'Parenting Motives Change to Love', *Manhatten Mercury*, 24 March 1980, 7

Stamper, B.M. 'Population Policy in Developing Planning: A Study of Seventy Less Developed Countries', *Reports on Population/Family Planning, 13*, May 1973

Whitney, V.H. 'Population Planning in Asia in the 1970s', *Population Studies, 30*, July 1976, 337–52

# 9 THE PUBLIC SECTOR AND THE MARKETING OF BIRTH CONTROL IN LDCs[1]

G.S. Kindra, Ruby Roy Dholakia and Prem Pangotra

## Introduction

For centuries, societies were confronted with the problem of ensuring a sufficiently sized population. Today things have changed. Better medical and sanitation facilities and other health improvements have reduced mortality-rates faster than birth-rates have fallen, creating what is known as the 'population problem'.

Views on the population increase differ: some see it as a boon because of its implications for market size, labor strength and national defense (Epstein, 1971; Heitleriger, 1976). But the increasingly common view is that population growth be limited (Ridker, 1976) because the demographic transition theory is not relevant for developing countries (Teitelbaum, 1975). In one survey 80 percent of the developing countries surveyed had an official policy on population, but only 53 percent of these countries supported a population-reduction program for demographic reasons (Nortman and Hofstatter, 1980).

Technically, planning for population control means deliberate influence over all attributes of a population, including its age/sex structure, geographical distribution, racial composition, genetic quality, total size and growth. Since no government attempts such full control, current population policies are concerned only with the growth and size of populations. The three determinants of these attributes are the birth-rate, the death-rate, and migration. Since in the context of the present-day world the scope of migration to check population growth at the intra-national level is extremely limited, high population growth in a number of less developed countries (LDCs) has been explained with increasing or non-decreasing birth-rate and sharp declines in mortality-rate. Decrease in infant mortality, high life expectancy, better health, and consequently higher productivity, logically point toward the raising of small families.

## Alternatives for Population Control

A review of the literature yields the following six courses of action available to any country in respect of its population problem:

(1) *To do nothing* specific that directly affects population growth except to provide better health and sanitation facilities. Developmental resources are allocated to the building of infrastructure, industries, agriculture and employment opportunities. It is assumed that fertility behavior will change in response to changes in living conditions of the population.

(2) *To employ a mass-communication strategy* to inform and educate the public about the benefits of planned families. This involves an educative and persuasive strategy in order to provide cognitive and affective inputs so that fertility behavior is directly affected. Both mass media and more personal sources of communication are mobilized for these purposes;

(3) *To provide services* directly. For example, contraceptives are made available through clinics and other channels. The programs are responsible not only for disseminating information about population control, but also for direct servicing of the population's needs. This is a more action-oriented strategy, and the logistics of the problem are quite dominant.

(4) *To manipulate the balance of incentives and disincentives* to achieve desired rates of growth. Extrinsic rewards and punishments are manipulated in order to promote the desired fertility behavior. Incentives such as family allowances (for larger families), and tax schemes (for larger or smaller families) can be designed to reward or punish specific forms of fertility behavior.

(5) *To shift the weight of social institutions and opportunities* in the desired direction. The barriers to desired family sizes — roles of women, availability of social security — are seen to be structural in nature and requiring change. Rather than depending on improvement in socio-economic conditions to produce these changes and changes in fertility behavior, action is taken directly to alter them. This is a more revolutionary approach as it involves fundamental changes in the social structure and values in order to produce development and fertility control.

(6) *To coerce behavior* through various forms of direct and compulsory sanctions. Licences for having children, compulsory sterilization after a specified number of children and temporary sterilizing

agents placed in water systems are some ways to implement a coercive strategy. The essential assumption here is that voluntary measures are inadequate or ineffective, and population goals can only be achieved through some compulsory sanctions.

In the following sections the authors will first examine the population programs of LDCs and the role of the public sector in them. A framework for planning population control in LDCs will then be developed. Both these topics will be examined by drawing upon the family-planning program in India.

## Population Programs in India

Not only do many LDCs officially support population programs, but also the public sector is primarily responsible for the planning, organizing and implementing of them. This involvement is quite a historic event; the demographic transition in the developed countries has occurred without direct intervention by the public or private sectors.

How are these programs performing? A review of period 1965–75 showed a 'substantial fertility decline in Asia, quite a bit in the Americas, some in North Africa and almost none in black Africa' (Mauldin and Berelson, 1978, p. 89). Mauldin *et al.* find a strong relationship between fertility decline and program effort, and go on to recommend a family-planning program of at least moderate strength if a country wishes to reduce its birth-rate substantially. These implications are examined in greater detail for India.

### The Case of India

With 2.4 percent of the world's land area, India has about 15 percent of the world's population. From 1901 to 1951, that is in 50 years, there was an increase in population of 123 million. Since 1951 the rate of growth has assumed a quicker pace. Within the 20 years since then, population has increased by 187 million. The rate of growth, which was 1.1 percent per annum in the 1960s, reached 2.5 percent per annum in the late 1970s. Currently, there are about 21 million births and 8 million deaths a year, adding 13–14 million to the existing population every year. In the year 2000 the population will have reached 1,600 million (see Figure 9.1).

One of the first nations in the world to support a family-planning program, the Government of India has rapidly changed its role from one of

Figure 9.1: Projections of India's Population

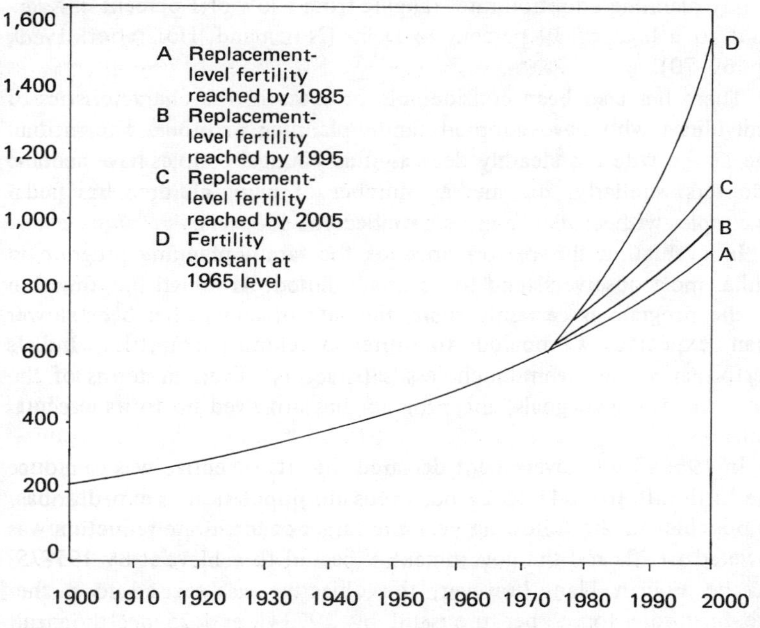
1,600
1,400
1,200
1,000
800
600
400
200
0
A Replacement-level fertility reached by 1985
B Replacement-level fertility reached by 1995
C Replacement-level fertility reached by 2005
D Fertility constant at 1965 level
D
C
B
A
1900 1910 1920 1930 1940 1950 1960 1970 1980 1990 2000

Source: *Population Bulletin*, November 1970.

providing information and communication to that of action and research orientation. In 1978 the family-planning budget constituted 0.52 percent of the total government budget and over 11 percent of the country's health budget (Nortman and Hofstatter, 1980, p. 35). This was the largest-ever budget for family planning (though not in *per capita* terms) – 78 percent of which was allocated for delivery of contraceptive services (Nortman and Hofstatter, 1980, p. 40).

*Program Analysis*

In terms of performance, the birth-rate in India had been reduced to 34–35 per thousand population by 1978 (Nortman and Hofstatter, 1980, p. 10); i.e. a decline of 16 percent between 1965 and 1975 (Maudlin and Berelson, 1978, p. 110). By March 1979, 22.6 percent of married couples (with the wife aged 15–44) were protected by some form of contraception, primarily sterilization (Nortmand and Hofstatter, 1980, p. 69). Performance varies considerably within the country, being much higher in urban areas. Performance also varies by states, with family-planning adoption-rates ranging from a low of 1 percent in Nagaland to a high of 39 percent in Delhi (Nortmand, Hofstatter, 1980, pp. 69–70).

There has also been considerable progress in the characteristics of individuals who have adopted family-planning methods. The median age of the wife has steadily decreased as younger couples have become adopters; similarly, the median number of living children has fallen as couples with smaller families have become adopters.

In evaluating the performance of the family-planning program in India, most observers tend to be disappointed. Although the direction of the program is certainly right, the rate of change has been slower than expected. Compared to other developing countries, India's performance has been much less satisfactory. Even in terms of the government's own goals, the program has not lived up to its expectations.

In 1966–7 the government declared that its objective was to reduce the birth-rate from 41 to 25 per thousand population as expeditiously as possible. In the following year the target of birth-rate reduction was lowered to 22, and the government expected to achieve it by 1978–9. In the Fourth Plan, however, the objective was revised to reduce the birth-rate to 32 per thousand by 1973–4 and 25 per thousand population by 1980–1. The Fifth Plan noted that the birth-rate had gone down by only 4 points, i.e. from 39 to 35 per thousand in the previous Fourth Plan period. The report noted that 'in the light of this trend, it does not appear feasible to bring the birth rate down to 25 per thousand population by the end of 1980–1.' (*Fifth Five Year Plan*, 1976.) It was subsequently planned to reduce the birth-rate to 30 per thousand at the end of the Fifth Plan and to 25 per thousand at the end of the Sixth Plan, that is, by 1983–4. Further revisions may be expected.

While the information and communication on family planning seems to have reached 80 percent of the population, only 22 percent have complied behaviorally. What are some of the problems?

## Obstacles to Lower Birth-rates

The first obstacle to higher rates of change in fertility behavior is the characteristics of the population and environment. The age composition of the population is such that even a family size of two children will lead to a significant increase in population size. Further, two children are by no means the most desired family size (Mamdani,

1972). With high infant mortality-rates, birth-control behavior (especially sterilization) becomes particularly risky. India has an infant mortality-rate five times that of Singapore and Taiwan — countries with more remarkable fertility declines. By the mortality-rates of 1960, Indian couples would have needed 6.3 children to be relatively certain of having one son survive to support the parents (May and Heer, 1968).

The second obstacle is the mix of contraceptive services delivered by the public-sector system. Because of logistic and administrative complexities, male sterilization is emphasized, although other services are made available. As a method, sterilization is relevant only to those couples that have already achieved their desired family sizes. The program, therefore, appears to ignore the needs of the majority of the population. Cross-country comparisons show that higher fertility declines are associated with programs based on multiple methods (Potter, 1971). Even among those programs emphasizing one method, sterilization appears to be less effective to eligible couples as a contraceptive method (see Table 9.1).

Thus, given the age distribution of the population, infant mortality-rates and prevalent norms of family sizes, terminal methods such as sterilization are not likely to be effective. Yet many knowledgeable experts continue to recommend it, and the Indian program continues to emphasize it.

And thirdly, the entire expenditure of the family-planning program is met by the central government, while the responsibility for implementation of the program rests with the states. As the *Fourth Five-Year Plan* (1970) puts it: 'Family Planning will remain a centrally sponsored program for the next ten years and the entire expenditure will be met by the Central Government' (p. 393). Such a system has been observed to lead to lack of commitment on the part of the states. In order to get maximum involvement of state governments, the programs must have their financial commitment as well. Further, the state governments have to retain a high priority for the programs at the inter-ministerial level by involving all related ministries actively. This becomes far more viable when the programs are conceptualized on the basis of a more comprehensive policy of population control. With significant financial commitment, the state governments are certain to increase their involvement. It would also help to grant to the state governments more administrative and financial flexibility to modify the national programs, or plan on their own in the context of the demographic, economic and social situation in their own states.

Table 9.1: Family-planning Methods Mix and Effectiveness

| Mix of methods[a] | Number of countries[b] | Effectiveness % MWRA using contraception[c] | 1965–75 crude birth-rate decline[d] |
|---|---|---|---|
| A. Single[e] | 5 | 19.2 | 9.0 |
| 1. Oral | 4 | 19.74 | 10.4 |
| 2. Sterilization | 1 | 17.0 | 16.0 |
| B. Multiple[f] | 10 | 30.2 | 17.9 |
| 1. Oral, IUD | 4 | 23.75 | 11.75 |
| 2. Oral, sterilization | 4 | 37.5 | 21.5 |
| 3. IUD, sterilization | 1 | 17.0 | 24.0 |
| 4. Oral, IUD, sterilization | 1 | 40.0 | 22.0 |

Notes: a. Methods included: intra-uterine devices (IUD), pills and injectibles, sterilization and abortion. Methods classified as 'others' not included.
b. Countries selected for which information available from both sources. Nepal, Philippines, Singapore and Taiwan excluded, even though information available because 'other methods' account for more than 25% of adoption.
c. Current contraceptive use among married women of reproductive age (MRWA) taken from Nortman and Hofstatter, 1980, Table 21.
d. Decline in crude birth-rate taken from Mauldin and Berelson, 1978, p. 96.
e. Dominantly single method assumed when *one* method accounted for more than 50% of adoption, and second method accounted for less than 20%.
f. Multiple methods assumed when two or more methods accounted for more than 60% of adoption, and second method accounted for at least 20% of total adopters.
Source: Nortman and Hofstatter, 1980, Tables 16 and 21; and Mauldin and Berelson, 1978, p. 96.

## Strengthening Program Effort

The ability to affect birth-control behavior through strong programs tends to attract support from many quarters. There is evidence from cross-country comparisons that indicates higher declines in birth-rates to be associated with stronger programs (Mauldin and Berelson, 1978). However, for India and many other developing countries, a stronger family-planning program is not an automatic choice. At least two very distinct and alternative paths are available in this context. The fundamental differences in the two approaches are illustrated in Table 9.2.

The first alternative for LDCs is to improve their socio-economic conditions as prerequisites for a strong program. Analysis of cross-country comparisons reveals that program strength and program effectiveness is very much dependent on social setting, and one of the requisites for an *effective* campaign is a rapidly changing socio-economic environment. This is an *indirect* approach to changing family-planning

Table 9.2: Social Setting, Program Effort and Political Ideology

| Communist countries | Social setting | Program effort | 1965–75 crude birth-rate decline % |
|---|---|---|---|
| | | | M[a]:    23 |
| | | | R[b]: 5–40 |
| China | Upper-middle | Strong | 24 |
| N. Vietnam | Lower-middle | Strong | 23 |
| Cuba | High | Moderate | 40 |
| N. Korea | High | None | 5 |
| Non-communist countries | | | M: 19.25 |
| | | | R: 0–32 |
| India | Lower-middle | Moderate | 16 |
| S. Vietnam | Lower-middle | None | 0 |
| Costa Rica | High | Strong | 29 |
| S. Korea | High | Strong | 32 |

Notes: a. M = mean %.
b. R = range of % values.
Source: Mauldin and Berelson, 1978, p. 110.

behavior. Possibly, only with this approach can India and other LDCs expect to have a stronger program and a sustaining decline in birth-rate as in countries like Singapore, Hong Kong, Taiwan, South Korea (Mauldin and Berelson, 1978).

The second alternative is to fundamentally change the social values and institutions that support large family-size norms. India would have the example of countries like China and North Vietnam to follow; these were the only two countries which had a *strong* family-planning program even though their socio-economic setting was not considered to be complimentary (Mauldin and Berelson, 1978). These two countries had much higher declines in birth-rates between 1965 and 1975 than India and other developing nations.

It is quite readily apparent that the first alternative is a time-dependent process where the focus is on the socio-economic conditions; the second alternative is too radical and represents a very different political ideology. However, in the absence of these alternative routes, a stronger family-planning program can attempt to achieve its objectives only at great societal costs. This was evidenced in India during the years 1975-7 — the two years in India's political history when normal democratic processes were put aside under the rule of 'National Emergency'. Family planning became an arena of intense effort, and even the word 'compulsory' was used to characterize the strategic stance. It is not surprising that in 1976 program acceptance increased 80 percent, and the total number of acceptors of government-supported services reached 12.8 million (Nortman and Hofstatter, 1980). In keeping with the strategy, acceptors of sterilization increased 200 percent in one year. Although the period of political crisis is over, there remains in the family-planning program pressures to generate results in an environment where changes in fertility behaviour must come from the masses who are poor, uneducated and rural, and with their own, different, concept of family welfare. In the following section a marketing-oriented approach to birth control — a third alternative — is discussed in some detail.

## A Framework for Marketing Birth Control

The approach discussed below has been derived from the Sketch Plan concept (Hoffman and Jakobson, 1979) developed at the University of Wisconsin Regional Planning and Area Development Project. While this concept is not a generalized formal theory or model for planning, it does set up a heuristic guide for planning under conditions of uncertainty and complexity.

The Sketch Plan framework of a planning system for population control in the context of the preceding discussion is presented in Figure 9.2. This model has been developed at a level broad enough to be meaningful to the situations prevailing in most LDCs.

The model describes the process of planning based on the societal goal of controlling population growth and its translation into control practices at individual family-level. The core concept of the model is that if we want people to adopt the small-family norm and practice birth control, the marketing program designed to accomplish this must create, sustain and perpetuate conditions so that families at the unit-level, *want* to limit their size, are *able* to limit their size, and have the potential *capability* of limiting their size.

Marketing ought to consider these factors in specific contexts, and incorporate suitable strategies in the programs of promoting population control.

Families *want* to practice birth control when a motive or incentive is present. This factor becomes extremely crucial to the success of programs when enforcement through non-marketing means (i.e. compulsion) is ruled out. Kotler defines incentives as 'Something of

Figure 9.2: Marketing Framework of the Task of Family Planning

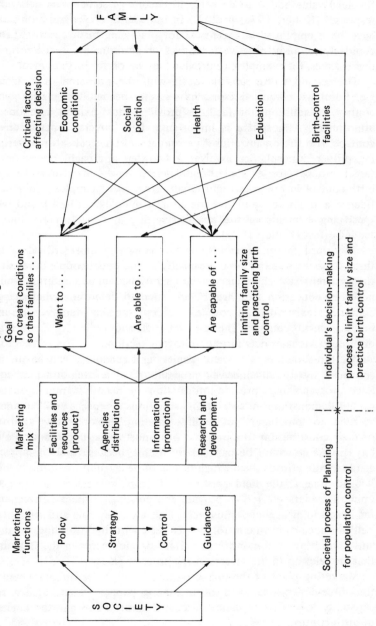

financial value added to an offer to encourage some overt behaviour response' (Kotler, 1975, p. 202). In India cash, cookware, radios etc. have been employed as incentives for practicing birth control. LDCs could also employ negative incentives or punishment, in the form of higher taxes, for examples, to provide motivation for birth control.

The second factor, *ability*, deals with the provision of facilities, e.g. hospitals, clinics, doctors, nurses, etc. needed to practice birth control. In addition, the facilities provided must exhibit a conducive atmosphere. Atmosphere is important when 'buyers' come in direct contact with the organizations' personnel and physical setting. Designing proper atmospherics involves a two-step approach; one defining target groups (for example, middle-class, newly married seekers of birth-control information) and target effect (for example, inspire confidence and comfort and give the clinic a middle-class look); and two, specifying elements of the physical setting that are to carry the intended effect (Kotler, 1975).

The third factor, *capability*, is probably the most critical of the three. It seeks to examine the capacity of the target couple in terms of their current state in society as judged by economic condition, social position, education and health; and then to determine whether preconditions exist for that couple to accept the small-family norm and practice birth control. The motivational and capability factors are discussed in greater detail in the following section.

All three factors, i.e. want, ability, and capability can be further enhanced by a well-conceived program of advertising and publicity. Such programs must provide information on incentives; moreover they should demonstrate in 'slice-of-life' situations the 'peace and happiness' accrued to 'purchasers' of family planning, demonstrating approval of their contribution to a program of utmost social importance. Publicity programs would be particularly useful, because their non-propaganda nature affords them a high degree of believability.

And finally, the field personnel (doctors, canvassers, nurses, paid opinion leaders etc.) that provide the personal contact between the family-planning agencies, must recognize their key role and attempt to 'sell' the idea of birth control, service the clients by informing, assisting and consulting, and monitor important developments in the field area that are relevant to the success of the program (Kotler, 1975).

Marketing plans of the public sector should, therefore, be aimed at the three-dimensional goal of increasing people's want, ability and capability towards acceptance of a small-family norm and the practice of birth control.

## A Prescription for Birth Control in LDCs

Considering the magnitude of the population problem in India, Pakistan, Bangladesh, and a large number of other LDCs, it is important to ask with respect to any policy for population control: Can it develop into a self-generating process in the society, or must it forever remain a concern of the bureaucracy to impose on the society? The success of programs, in the long run, should be viewed from such a perspective. In terms of a scenario of an ideally successful program, in the long run, it would be characterized by some such visible effects in society as:

• direct and visible benefits to people practicing birth control and raising small families
• economic growth characterized by decreasing unemployment, rising *per capita* income, decreasing shortages of essential commodities and higher levels of general education
• people possessing the economic security and education to exercise preference for small families for their own welfare and for the welfare of society
• increased involvement of people in development programs
• birth-rate close to zero growth
• induction of other people into birth-control programs through a ripple effect

Ultimately, the policy for economic and social development has to sustain the family-planning measures and turn the movement to induce a self-generating process in society. It should be emphasized that while the immediate concern for slowing the growth of population may demand high priority for family-planning programs, in the long run the policy must acquire a much broader base in economic and social reality.

From the perspective of the family, the motivation to accept the small-family norm depends on four tangible and identifiable factors: economic condition, social position, education and health. The decision to practice birth control depends further on the availability of facilities and several other factors which cannot be generalised, e.g. a strong preference for male children in some societies, a norm regarding age of marriage, etc.

To alter a social system so as to regulate births in accord with the demands of the collective welfare of society would require adequate provision for social welfare services, social legislation and social reforms.

The program should not be merely eclectic, popularizing contraceptive methods to ensure the success of family planning, but should also aim at the effectiveness of the national educational policy, employment policy, industrial policy, and in general the country's economic policy. Further, this approach should be built into the programs gradually but strategically, to present the overall perspective to the people and thereby ensure their involvement.

### Motivating Birth Control

As stated earlier, families want to practice birth control when a motive or an incentive is present. In the design of incentives the following steps are recommended:

(1) Specify objectives for which incentives are being used.

(2) Specify recipient. In the case of family planning in India, the recipient should be the consumer, the doctor or the canvassers that bring in men for vasectomy.

(3) Will the incentive be in the form of reward, punishment or both?

(4) Determine form of incentives, i.e. specify whether the incentive will be in the form of food, cash, health care, free education, lottery ticket, etc.

(5) Specify time of payment. This will vary according to the 'product' being sold. For example, in the case of sterilization, immediate payment is appropriate, whereas yearly incentive will be appropriate when the couple has been sold the idea of using birth-control pills.

(6) Determine optimum amount of incentives.

It is important to recognize that even in a traditional and complex society like Indian society, people at all levels are fully aware of their biological role in reproduction, and do not view the birth of children as an accidental or indiscriminate phenomenon. The choice of the number of children to be had is a deliberate one made by the people. Some sort of motivation based upon their knowledge of contextual reality is in-built in the process. In developing countries with critical population problems, planning for population control ought to go beyond stressing the right of parents to have the number of children they desire, to their responsibility not to exceed the number of children society desires. The crux of the problem is to introduce some kind of societal control over the desire to have children. However, people will adopt a birth-control measure and pursue it on their own if it fits in with their concept of rationality. It is certainly not enough to pose the issue in terms of the acceptance of birth-control devices. In the words of Kingsley Davis.

If it were admitted that the creation and care of new human beings is socially motivated, like other forms of behavior, by being a part of the system of awards and punishments that is built into human relationships, and thus is bound up with the individual's economic and personal interests, it would be apparent that the social structure and economy must be changed before a deliberate reduction in the birth-rate can be achieved. (1967)

Motivating birth-control should attempt, therefore, to overcome the obstacles to smaller families. These are: (a) high infant mortality in rural areas; (b) strong preference for male children; and (c) desire for more children as potential earning hands and as a form of social security for the family.

The approach to the first issue should be one of concerted efforts on the part of the government to extend health services to the rural areas by whatever measures necessary, such as substantial monetary incentives to medical professionals to work in the villages. A simultaneous effort should be made to carry out campaigns to popularize traditional and modern practices of preventive medicine. The basic problem in having a female child is the implication that the family marriage incurs a heavy financial burden, while a male child brings in a dowry, which, in relative terms, is usually a source of substantial wealth. There are other associated factors which are religious, economic and social. All these point to a solution − the social emancipation of women by affording them the means of education, employment, income and abolition of the dowry system. The third obstacle should be overcome by making the labor of the child and the mother more costly in comparison to simple labor-saving devices and tools. It is often imaged that the small and marginal farmer does not need mechanical devices because of the plentiful labor supply at his command through his own children and women. But unless this supply, now so accessible to him, is made to prove comparatively more costly than an array of readily acquired agricultural tools and implements, birth-control programs in rural areas are unlikely to make any significant impact. The problem of old-age security for parents has to be dealt with by a strong commitment on the part of the government as well. The developing countries must come up with a well thought-out program for sickness insurance, unemployment insurance, and old-age pension. Possibilities should also be explored in the Indian context of the approaches based on allowing economic advantages to accrue to the single as opposed to the married person, and to the small as opposed to the large family. This is one of the major strengths of the population control program in China.

## Selecting the Capability Factor

The capability factor discussed earlier seeks to examine the target couple in terms of economic conditions, social position, education and health; and then to determine whether preconditions exist for that couple to accept the small-family norm and practice birth control. Further, as the case of India suggests, a situation of wide variations of population growth-rates exists at state and district levels, and for different social strata. This suggests that significant reductions of the national birth-rate cannot be achieved unless preconditions for the attainment of their respective goals are first created at the family and higher levels, such as social groups, communities, districts, states, regions, etc. What this means for the Sketch Plan is that it makes no sense to direct intense program efforts at high expense to families, areas or groups who either/or:

(a) do not have a problem of high birth-rate;
(b) will practice birth control even without the program;
(c) will be insignificantly affected by an intense mass program;
(d) do not have the preconditions needed to justify the rationale of birth control.

Thus, recognizing that selective processes and selective constraints characterizing the situation, planning should adopt a differential approach. The strategy should be to concentrate the program efforts into strategic areas, to achieve the maximum potential of the programs. One approach, for example, is to develop a typology of all districts in terms of levels of development, and then select the top two or three districts in each state for intensive programs of birth control. For the country as a whole, the Sketch Plan should explore the process of preparing state plans and regional plans which can be interwoven into the national plan for population control rather than the other way around.

The capability and consideration emphasizes the role of promotion-and-research development in the planning for population control. In the Sketch Plan we can envisage the role of promotion as the key role in planning, administration and organization, and research. The role of research should be to develop new technologies, new management techniques, techniques of precondition analysis, media campaigns and data analysis.

## Summary and Conclusion

The broadened concept of marketing is taking the practice of marketing into many non-traditional areas such as family planning and population control. It is the task of marketing management to identify public needs and to design and provide services that satisfy those needs (Farley and Levitt, 1971). The challenge lies in designing effective strategies to meet the needs of the population programs.

There are also many opportunities for marketing management to improve the performance of current programs (Simon, 1968; Wilder and Tyagi, 1968). At the very micro-level, there are tremendous opportunities for improving the orientation of program personnel to the needs and characteristics of the market (Demerath, 1967). Various tools and techniques — the technology of management — can be applied so that the goals are more adequately defined and programs are designed to be consistent with such goals.

These conflicts have been brought out in this chapter by focusing on India, where the public sector has been involved in the largest and oldest family-planning program in the world. Program performance in that country has been modest, even disappointing. To improve this performance, a marketing-management orientation should be adopted. One approach to the management of birth-control marketing was discussed under the so called Sketch Plan framework. This approach was based on the recognition that acceptance of a small-family norm is interwoven with the freedom to make that choice. This is an important point because even though segments of the LDC population are desirable of accepting the small-family concept, they are often deprived of the means-and-objectives motivation for accomplishing the same. This framework suggests that marketing plans should be aimed at the three-dimensional goal of increasing the population's desire, ability, and capability toward acceptance of the small-family norm and the practice of birth control. The framework also suggests that in consideration of the wide geographical variations in population growth, *per capita* income, and the level of development in general, programs should be designed in a segmented manner to suit the socio-economic nature of each group.

## Note

1. Parts of this chapter were presented earlier at the Academy of Marketing Science Conference, held at Miami Beach, Summer 1983.

Selected parts of the chapter were also presented at the American Marketing Association's Annual Macromarketing Conference, Emory University, Atlanta, 1981.

## References

Davis, Kingsley 'Population Policy: Will Current Programs Succeed?', *Science, 158*, 3802, 10 November 1967, 730–9

Demerath, N.J. 'Organization and Management Needs of a National Family Planning Program: The Case of India', *Journal of Social Issues, 23*, 4, 1967, 179–94

Epstein, V.X. 'The Politics of Population in Latin America', in D. Chaplin (ed.), *Population Policies and Growth in Latin America*, Lexington Books, Lexington, Mass., 1971, pp. 133–76

Farley, J.U. and Leavitt, H.J. 'Marketing and Population Problems', *Journal of Marketing, 35*, July 1971, 28–33

——, Sexton, D.E., Jr., Smith, R.H. and Tokarski, S.S. 'A Working Behavioral Segmentation System for a Family Planning Marketing Program', *Proceedings*, American Marketing Association, 1974, 31–4

*Fifth Five-Year Plan*, Planning Commission, New Delhi, 1970

*Fourth Five-Year Plan*, Planning Commission, New Delhi, 1970

Heitleriger, A. 'Pro-natalist Population Policies in Czechoslovakia', *Population Studies, 22*, March 1976, 123–36

Hoffman, M. and Jakobson, L. 'Sketch Plan, A Conceptual Framework', Discussion Paper, University of Wisconsin, Regional Planning and Area Development Project, May 1979

Mamdani, M. *The Myth of Population Control: Family, Caste and Class in an Indian Village*, Monthly Review Press, New York, 1972

Mauldin, W.P. and Berelson, B. 'Conditions of Fertility Decline in Developing Countries, 1965–1975', *Studies in Family Planning, 9*, May 1978, 89–147

May, D.A. and Heer, D.M. 'Son Survivorship and Family Size in India: A Computer Simulation', *Population Studies, 22*, July 1968, 199–210

Nortman, D.L. and Hofstatter, E. *Population and Family Planning Programs: A Fact Book*, 10th edn, Population Council, New York, 1980

Potter, R. 'Inadequacy of one One-Method Family Planning Program', *Studies in Family Planning, 2*, 1, January 1971, 1–6

Simon, J.L. 'Some Marketing Correct Recommendations for Family Planning Campaigns', *Demography, 5*, 1968, 504–7

Teitelbaum, M. 'Relevance of Demographic Transition Theory for Developing Countries', *Science, 188*, 2 May 1975, 420–5

Wilder, F. and Tyagi, D.K. 'India's New Departures in Mass Motivation for Fertility Control', *Demography, 5*, 1968, 773–9

## Further Reading

Bhandari, L. *Communication for Social Marketing: A Study in Family Planning*, Macmillan, New York, 1978

Blaikie, P.M. *Family Planning in India: Diffusion and Policy*, Holmes and Meier, New York, 1975

Bose, Ashis 'Some Emerging Issues in Family Planning Administration', in Jagannadham, V. (ed.), *Family Planning in India, Policy and Administration*, 1973

Cassen, R.H. 'Development and Population', *Economic and Political Weekly*, Special Number, August 1973

*First Five-Year Plan*, Planning Commission, New Delhi, 1953

Gulhati, R. 'India's Population Policy: Critical Issues for the Future', *Public Policy, 26*, 3, Summer 1978, 415–54

IBRD *Population, Policies and Economic Development*, Johns Hopkins University, Baltimore, Ma., 1974

Kotler, P. *Marketing Management: Analysis, Planning and Control*, 1st edn, Prentice-Hall, Englewood-Cliffs, NJ, 1967

—— *Marketing for Non-Project Organizations*, Prentice-Hall Inc., NJ, 1975

Kristensson, Folke *Manniskor, foretag och regioner*. (People, Establishments and Regions), Translated by Hans Lingsom, Almquist and Wiksell, Stockholm, 1967

—— and Levy, S.J. 'Broadening the Concept of Marketing', *Journal of Marketing, 33*, January 1969, 10–15

—— and Zaltman, G. 'Social Marketing: An Approach to Planned Social Change', *Journal of Marketing, 35*, 3, 1971, 3–12

Lapham, R.J. and Mauldin, W.P. 'National Family Planning Programs; Review and Evaluation', *Studies in Family Planning, 3*, 3, March 1972, 29–52

Martin, N.A. 'The Outlandish Idea: How a Marketing Man Can Save India', *Marketing/Communications, 296*, 1968, 56–60

Mukherjee, R. *Family and Planning in India*, Orient Longman, 1976

Ridker, R. (ed.) *Population and Development: The Search for Selective Interventions*, Johns Hopkins University Press, Baltimore, Ma, 1976

Roberto, E.L. 'Social Marketing Strategies for Diffusing the Adoption of Family Planning', *Social Science Quarterly*, June 1972, 33–51

Rogers, E.M. *Field Experiments of Family Planning Incentives*, Michigan State University, East Lansing, Mich., 1972

*Second Five-Year Plan*, Planning Commission, New Delhi, 1957

Singh, Karan 'Strategy and Segmentation of the Birth Control Market: This Side of Family Planning', Working Paper, Department of Communications, University of Illinois, Urbana, Ill., 1972

—— 'National Population Policy', *Yojana*, New Delhi, 1 July 1976

*The Statesman*, 2 December 1979

*Third Five-Year Plan*, Planning Commission, New Delhi, 1961

# 10 THE MARKETING-EDUCATION TASK IN THIRD WORLD COUNTRIES[1]

## Christopher A. Ross and Ronald McTavish

### Introduction

Among marketers there is a tendency to assume that essentially North American or Western European marketing ideas can be readily transplanted into the Third World environment. This chapter discusses the peculiar features of developing countries, stresses the need for modifications to marketing-course content, and makes recommendations to the educator.

### Some Characteristics of Developing Countries

While the characteristics of developing countries are generally seen to be 'different' from those of the developed countries, knowledge of the true nature of Third World countries is relatively sparse. Nevertheless, there is a tendency — even if logically attractive — to assume that the Third World is developing, in the sense that it is moving towards the contemporary situation in the developed world. According to this view, the marketing educator requires only a simplified watered-down version of contemporary approaches to the subject matter, in order to make a contribution to the developing world.

In fact, present-day conditions in the Third World are often substantially different from those of the advanced countries prior to their industrialization. In other words, the 'similar path' model is probably a serious misrepresentation of reality, based as it is on the questionable assumption that developing countries are evolving and will continue to evolve in the same manner as developed ones (McGree, 1971).

The marketing educator needs to be aware of some further characteristics of Third World countries. One set of characteristics relates to the poverty of these countries: low *per capita* incomes, high illiteracy rates, a predominance of agriculture and other primary production, and a dependence on commodity exports. Another characteristic is that industrialization is often a supreme national goal: it dominates economic policies and will probably continue to do so for a considerable time to come. Government regulations and controls are also quite pervasive.

But despite such considerations, the Third World consists of a highly heterogeneous group of countries. In size of population, these countries range from India with more than 700 million inhabitants, to Barbados with less than 1 million. Some are much further advanced than others: Brazil, a newly industrializing country, possesses a major industrial center in its São Paulo region, and Argentina has ten times the *per capita* GNP of 'least developed countries', (for example, Haiti and Rwanda). The oil-exporting countries, with their vast wealth, constitute a distinct subset. A wide range of political ideologies, representing all segments of the political spectrum, can also be observed.

It seems clear, therefore, that the relative homogeneity of value systems and practices amongst developed Western societies is not likely to be replicated in developing ones, where the balance between traditional culture, the implicit disciplinary values of industrialization, and concepts of the role of the state, are immensely diverse. If there is something which might be described approximately as a system of European (and North American) values and constructs of performance and organization, the same could not be said, for example, of Africa (Montgomery, 1982).

This heterogeneity is paralleled by a similar diversity within individual countries. Santos (1979), writing from a standpoint of regional economics, suggests that a developing country needs to be thought of not as a single homogeneous entity, but as consisting of what he calls two subsystems, the 'upper' or 'modern circuit', and the 'lower circuit'. These circuits are obvious, at a superficial level, to any visitor to a developing country where frequently modern department stores thrive side by side with well-developed street vending and village markets.

Santos argues that in the process of national development and in accommodating the demands of dynamic modernization, the economic system evolves into two circuits. The upper circuit — the one most recognizable to the developed-country marketer — is characterized by capital-intensive production, large-scale distribution and the use of advertising. In short, this circuit is more oriented towards the advanced capitalist world. The lower circuit, on the other hand, is traditional and primitive; its features include small-scale manufacturing and crafts, small-scale trade, and many varied services.

While the educator may feel more at home in the upper-circuit environment, an important problem is that little is known in concrete terms about the lower circuit of the urban or domestic economy (Saylor, 1967). Although it may seem bizarre to suggest that the educator needs to know more about the role of hawkers and peddlers in some countries, in fact without this understanding the marketing professor is handicapped. After a brief discussion of the nature of marketing, the rest of this paper discusses the need for modifications to traditional marketing frameworks and applications such that the impact of these characteristics can be taken into account.

### Approaches to Marketing in Developed Countries

There exists a considerable literature on the nature and scope of marketing (see, for example, Kotler and Levy, 1969; Luck, 1969; Bartels, 1974). A complete discussion would therefore be a lengthy process. However, two things may be said briefly for the present purpose. One is that because marketing is a discipline originated and developed in the advanced countries, the managerial approach to marketing, which emphasizes the marketing manager seeking to optimize the marketing-mix elements in a large manufacturing organization, is still universally taught. Certainly, many practitioners prefer to view marketing in this light. Secondly, this approach is typically supported by the teaching of sophisticated concepts and techniques, for example, attitudinal market segmentation and preference mapping. One can see immediately, therefore, that this approach is liable to run into trouble in developing countries unless appropriate modifications are made to suit particularly the 'lower circuit'.

However, as is now widely acknowledged, it is too simple to restrict marketing solely to the managerial aspect since the scope of marketing is exceptionally broad. Hunt (1976) proposes that marketing has three major dimensions: micro/macro; profit sector/non-profit sector; and positive/normative. A consensus is gradually emerging that this three-dichotomy model with eight cells is the most comprehensive representation of the domain of marketing to date.

From the viewpoint of the Third World marketing educator, it will be useful to know how and to what extent each element of the model applies. Are macro-marketing concerns broadly similar to those encountered in the developed world, or are there important differences? What are the special problems of non-profit-sector marketing, or of the individual entrepreneur? These and similar issues are discussed below using Hunt's framework as a guide.

## The Scope of Marketing in Developing Countries

### *Macro-marketing*

In developing countries macro-marketing issues are frequently raised by indigenous academics or by students, and this questioning reflects a real concern for the economic well-being of the countries. Problems range from the role of marketing as an engine of economic development to questions about the necessity for the discipline at all. The marketing educator needs to have an informed point of view on these issues — issues which are broad, varied and often controversial.

The vexed question of the relationship between marketing and economic development is frequently raised, and at least two camps in the debate can be discerned. There are those, for example, who see marketing as a progenitor of growth (Drucker, 1958; Weisenberger and Humphries, 1976). According to this view, marketing mobilizes latent economic energy and it develops entrepreneurs and managers. The other side of the debate sees the level of marketing technology as a function of economic development (Bartels, 1981). There is no easy resolution to this issue, and until more concepts and theories are developed and more empirical research undertaken, the debate will continue. But the issue is central to any discussion of marketing in developing countries and thus requires some degree of conceptualization on the part of the marketing academic. This issue has been dealt within greater detail elsewhere in the book.

The idea that consumer sovereignty weakens as industrialization progresses is another important issue for debate. Nigerian experience suggests, for example, that as peoples and governments move further and further into their industrialization programs, buyers are seen to have fewer and fewer opportunities to ask questions about standards of terminology, packaging and advertizing, product quality and other matters (Onyebuagu, 1978). Onyebuagu thus strongly advocates a consumer-affairs division of government which would seek consumer protection not only through product warranties, but also by conveying the message that educated, informed consumers are necessary. Little is known about how many Third World governments have actually established consumer-affairs departments, but is the need for and the relevance of consumer protection and indeed a consumerist movement (Akereka, 1980) evidence of weakening consumer sovereignty? The marketing educator must have informed responses.

Connected to the belief in weakening consumer power, is the view that in a developing country production of goods is the primary concern, not marketing. Because goods and services are in short supply in many developing countries, it is deceptively simple to argue that since the available supply is consumed, satisfaction is being maximized and thus marketing is not necessary. But what is really being proved is that something is better than nothing: company A's brand may be sold out only because insufficient quantities of B — the preferred one — cannot be found. In other words, a great deal of consumer dissatisfaction may be masked in the scarcity/seller-market economies which typify the Third World. This is not a refutation, however, of the view that in terms of scarcity a de-marketing approach may be required (Kotler and Levy, 1971).

In their efforts to control their own destinies and to stimulate the development of their societies, developing countries have tended to institute a system of central economic planning with all its concomitant controls and with the implication that decisions by the state are supreme. Some countries, for example, Tanzania and Guinea, have deliberately set out to build a society along socialist lines (Berg, 1968). Another example is Grenada in the Caribbean. Countries such as Trinidad and the Philippines, without any attempt at labeling or promulgating a definite ideological position, have simply instituted economic controls in the belief that development, justice and equity would be better served. Within this planning environment, objections are often raised by those who question the fit between marketing concepts and frameworks on the one hand and strong state involvement in the economy — state capitalism or socialism — on the other. Educators must thus give careful thought to the compatibility of profit-seeking entrepreneurship with this kind of environment.

Those who venture into the macro (non-profit) field need not look too far for challenging problems. The educator needs a thorough grasp of the problems and opportunities involved in improving the efficiency of distribution systems for health care, education and social services. Many developing countries, such as India and Thailand, have adopted family-planning programs. Adult education and the eradication of illiteracy is another daunting task. Jamaica tried improving the level of savings of its citizens through a marketing approach. The efficiency of 'aid'-distribution systems presents similar problems. The importance of these programs demands that the educator include relevant concepts and frameworks within the ambit of the course.

## Micro-marketing

Discussion of marketing-management issues at the level of the individual firm leads us into the heartland of conventional marketing — the management of the '4 Ps'. Despite the growth of interest in other areas, this is still a major pedagogical domain, and one in which the practitioner's interest has always been strong.

Marketing management traditionally uses a framework which places the manager in a position of control over the four key areas of product, price, promotion and distribution. In many less developed countries, however, these variables are very much uncontrolable. Many consumer products, for example, refrigerators, stoves, and basic food products such as chicken, milk and corned beef, are subject to price control. Although the broad issue of such control is properly a 'macro' one, its impact at the micro-level is obvious in terms of the restrictions placed on the marketing manager. Moreover, the marketing manager faces other important and daunting issues in the price field: low levels of *per capita* income lead to considerations of equity and justice in pricing, not simply charging what the traffic will bear.

Other mix elements are also influenced by government control. Distribution is a case in point. In Jamaica and Guyana, for example, the distribution of agricultural cereals and commodities is controlled by the State Trading Corporations. In Jamaica too, food products considered luxuries were restricted to the geographical areas frequented by tourists. Such problems, while obviously not totally absent in the industralized world, are of key importance in the developing one, and therefore need careful evaluation by the educator.

The scarcity/sellers' market mentioned earlier also impacts on marketing decision-making within the firm. Third World marketing managers may, for example, find it difficult to measure the success or failure of their brand on its own merits. This difficulty in obtaining crucial market information is worsened where the manager does not know the potential size of the market because of the shortage situation. (This is in addition to the overriding problem of obtaining accurate market information because of the lack of official data and the serious obstacles to conducting field research.) It follows, therefore, that product-development activities are hampered. Again, because production is always at maximum level, there are dangers of deterioration in product quality, and in the ability to meet consumer demands for variety. In the case of promotion there may be a loss of creativity by advertizing executives because of lack of challenge and pressure. Furthermore, because of the predominance of an allocation rather than a marketing philosophy, salesmanship and merchandizing ability may suffer. In short, companies operating in sellers' markets for prolonged periods face real problems of decline in marketing competence —

problems which educators cannot ignore.

So far nothing has been said about the type of company that predominates in the Third World. Small enterprises — less than fifty employees — are the norm in the manufacturing sector. While small-scale business is also important in the developed world, its pervasiveness and intensity make it a unique feature of developing societies. The educator must therefore make the problem of small-business marketing a key concern.

The special features of particular markets in developing countries must also occupy the educator's interest. Agricultural marketing is a good example. Because these countries rely on the production and export of primary products, the educator needs to be familiar with the problems of their marketing, both by small peasant farmers and by cooperatives. This in turn calls for a willingness to become familiar with peculiarly developing-country products, for example cassava and yam flour. To the extent that the sale of such products is organized officially by the state, there is also a need to know about how government boards and agencies go about their marketing. It is also worth mentioning here that state agencies, using tender boards, may be the focal point for the purchase of all sorts of capital equipment to support major infrastructural projects, new roads, dams, forest clearing. The way in which these purchases are effected leads one into the field of organizational buying behavior, on which very little published research is available as far as practice in these countries is concerned.

The peculiarities of other markets should also be mentioned. In the case of industrial marketing, the full paraphernalia of industrial-marketing concepts and methods has limited applications. The developing economies traditionally import their capital equipment, though much depends on the degree of industrialization reached by the individual country. Factors hampering the development of capital-goods industries include the historical dependence on primary production, the typically unspecialized nature of the labor force, and the need to provide after-sales service and maintenance facilities. Frequently, the method of distribution is by a sole agent seeking monopoly profits in return for committing the necessary capital (Ugoh, 1979). Thus, the educator interested in this market may find his activities confined to distribution problems.

In addition to the problems of industrial marketing, questions are also raised about the factors influencing the export success of manufactured products. These questions come about because in spite of their continued reliance on primary exports, many Third World countries, such as Pakistan, Columbia and Malaysia, are developing policies designed to stimulate their manufactured exports. Students and business people are consequently very much interested in factors and strategies which influence export success. Does success lie in product development, particular kinds of products, or in the kind of technology utilized? Do export incentives work, and are they worth the cost? Are factors internal to the firm and its managers more important for success than factors in the domestic and foreign markets? Can only large firms export successfully? These and similar issues are frequently raised during class discussions.

The intent of the discussion up to this point is not to deny the importance of marketing in the developing world, but rather to emphasize the need to rethink, reshape, and adapt the approach to the subject. It is a plea for relevance, not an attempt to destroy or attack the discipline.

## Teaching the Third World Student

We now turn from the question of *what* to teach, to a consideration of *to whom* and *how*. This section thus discusses what is special about the educator's 'audience' in the developing world — the students — and highlights problems of teaching methods.

One important characteristic of students is their rurality. The bulk of students in the universities are the sons and daughters of middle-class families coming from predominantly rural societies. The majority of developing countries have only fledgling stock markets, mail order is often non-existent; and in some countries there is limited circulation of newspapers and no television. Many students are unfamiliar with the modern factory and office, with large department stores, and with modern banking practices, including use of credit cards and even the basic process of writing a check. The extent of their knowledge, in many instances, is limited to simple transactions in retail outlets. In consequence, students tend to be unfamiliar with the world of commerce (Onah, 1981). In contrast, students of the industrial society usually have a working knowledge of business transactions and market-ing institutions. They have 'industrial minds'.

The marketing educator in the Third World thus has to instruct students who possess a 'non-industrial' mind. In addition, there is a prevalent attitude that most people have little impact on the economy anyway, so why bother to attempt change. This is reflected in the Latin

American saying of 'Que sera, sera!' (Whatever will be, will be), or the almost identical concept in Muslim countries — 'Inshallah' (God willing). These factors taken together produce the result that, typically, students do not recognize the need for urgency in business, they do not recognize the critical role of planning, and the importance of time and deadlines in the development of marketing strategy. Faced with a formal exposure to decision-making and planning, many fail to see the merits of detailed steps, anticipation of possible problems, and contingency planning. Such attitudes can actually operate as barriers to industrialization in an economy (Terpstra, 1978).

In addition, the kind of formal pre-university education followed by the typical business student does little to prepare him or her for the process of decision-making. Educational systems in many developing countries are patterned after the pre-World War II model. The emphasis, in these systems, is on the process of analysis, understanding, and the development of the whole man — an emphasis with real merit. However, little if any attention is paid to decision-making. Thus, Nunes (1977) remarks that this system produces analysts but no decision-makers, thinkers but no doers, those who understand the meaning but not the meaningfulness.

A final point is the attitude of students towards the professor himself. Deriving to an extent from the hierarchical authority structure of the village system, there is a tendency for the professor to be regarded as a remote, authoritarian figure. It is true that conventional social structures are under pressure to change as countries move towards greater economic development, social mobility, and national self-consciousness. But the professor can expect to be held in awe by some students, a consideration which has implications for their reaction to teaching methods.

What are the consequences of these factors for the conduct of the marketing class? Special problems are posed, in particular, for instructors using the case method. Because of the students' lack of familiarity with commerce, the teacher first has to interpret the material — a process which includes the explanation of basic business terminology — before the class can begin the analysis process. This observation holds even with the use of indigenous cases. Typically, such cases deal with companies and situations which are very similar to those which exist in North America. Cases at the University of the West Indies, for example, deal with the problems of upgrading the image of a local perfume brand, or the problem of structuring the sales force by territory, product or customer. For consumer behavior, a case may illustrate the process and forces which influence the consumer when buying a car or house. Thus, it is not unfair to say that for many 'local' cases the casewriter portrays the situation from an industrial-country perspective. In a developing country the industrial segment (the upper circuit) of society is precisely the segment with which the student is least familiar. Moreover, having presented the case to the class, the educator may find that students analyze the case quite well, but conceptualize the decision-making process poorly.

In part, because of student attitude towards the professor, teaching methods and evaluation systems based heavily on group discussion and class participation may have to be introduced gradually. Caution in doing so is also desirable even for more advanced classes if they have not hitherto enjoyed exposure to a variety of teaching methods. Lack of space and other physical limitations may discourage work in small groups. Finally, budget restrictions may prevent the emergence of learning-resource units, common in North America, to provide various back-up services such as films or the administration of teaching evaluation programs. The professor will thus often find himself very much dependent on his own resources; and certainly very careful thought about the most appropriate methods will be obligatory.

Overrriding these problems is the difficulty of obtaining adequate and relevant text and case material. Compared with the huge range of texts available in North America, the supply of material relevant to the Third World is virtually non-existent. Dependence upon texts reflecting the experience of the developed world suffers from various drawbacks. There is a danger of adopting a 'large-firm' stance and using ill-suited cases. But, perhaps more important, the educator may, consciously or unconsciously convey the dominant values and ideologies of the industrialized world. Whether these are compatible with what is desirable in the Third World is open to debate, and is often debated. Marketing (and particularly advertising because of its conspicuousness) is open to the judgement that it promotes 'false' values. The professor may have to answer such questions as: Is marketing socially useful? What is the role of marketing in a socialist society? These questions often emanate from fellow academics such as economists and sociologists with whom the educator has to work. A greater availability of texts dwelling on the contribution of marketing to the developing country would obviously be of great help. But in the absence of these, the professor needs to develop his own viewpoints and to defend the discipline with reasonable arguments.

The foregoing is not intended to be entirely discouraging to the teacher. On the positive side, students are often friendly, cooperative, outgoing and eager to learn and to experiment — ideal material for the use of a range of methods. The writers have found in these countries a refreshing absence of what might be called ethno-centricism. Although possessing as much national pride as anyone else, the students do not automatically see themselves or their countries as the pivotal point in world affairs — an attitude which can at times be encountered, and to an extent pardoned — among students in the leading industrialized countries. There is thus a strong receptivity to new ideas, and a lively interest in the happenings in other countries. The teacher of international marketing or of comparative marketing institutions can usually count on a receptive audience.

**Possible Future Trends**

Bearing in mind the diversity of countries making up the Third World, one is likely to see in the future considerable differences in the emphasis placed on marketing education from one to another. This in turn will depend upon a variety of factors such as the rate of industrial growth, finances available for educational development at the higher level, and government policies. Also, where the country can support multiple universities, as in Nigeria, there will be differences between them in terms of curriculum content and type and variety of course offered. Generalization is thus difficult, but if a majority of countries are dedicated to economic development, and even if we view marketing as a consequence of growth, the scope for marketing and marketing education should grow.

Reinforcing the idea of inter-country diversity is the point that growth in marketing education is a function of the speed of acceptance of the marketing concept itself, which in turn is a function of the efficiency of communications networks available within the country. To the extent that these are of mixed development and sophistication, the spread of marketing ideals is likely to be patchy. But in some countries the speed of acceptance of modern business concepts will be accelerated by the efforts of international agencies such as the United Nations, whose development program, in for example Kenya, involves helping to build the industrial infrastructure of the country, and providing a variety of specialized managerial advice and training. If these efforts continue in future and if they help to build indigenous cadres of skilled entrepreneurs and managers, marketing and marketing education can only flourish.

There are grounds for believing, too, that once it has taken root the demand for marketing education will increase quite rapidly. The establishment of national economic planning in some countries, with stated goals to be achieved within prescribed time-limits, indicates an intention, if not to force the pace of economic development, then at least to accomplish it with reasonable speed. Marketing education will not only accompany such planned economic growth, rather more education will be demanded *in anticipation* of the growth, as a preparation for it. National manpower planning, allied with indigenization programs now in place in some countries, seek to meet current development requirements as well as to build pools of locally trained manpower for the future. Marketing education forms a crucial part of this process, and will therefore grow correspondingly.

Continued growth, however, will depend on the contribution to development and the perceived usefulness of the discipline. For marketing education to provide these benefits, a great deal of adaptation must be made on the basis of environmental and student characteristics and on the needs of these countries. Such adaptation is still in its infancy, and should be a matter of great concern both to those who currently teach marketing in the Third World, and also to those who may one day find themselves teaching in the environment, an increasingly likely possibility given the interest of Third World governments in employing academics from developed economies (Kirpalani, 1975).

**Recommendations to the Professor**

Clearly, the teaching of marketing in a developing country requires a different orientation and focus from what one would expect in a developed society. Some of the consequences of the Third World environments for the educator have already been touched upon. It might be useful, however, to offer a summary of main recommendations. These recommendations are categorized into attitudinal and behavioral considerations.

Teaching in the Third World demands a willingness to adopt the 'right' attitude. An essential requirement is the ability to come to terms with a new culture and to be responsive to its peculiarities. This process is not easy. Developing 'cultural sensitivity' is — and indeed should be — the result of a reasonably long immersion in the culture. A corollary of this is to avoid an ethno-centric view of things. An educator bred on a diet of industrialized-country marketing must be willing to examine the discipline and its applications from different vantage points. In particular, the educator must try for an understanding of why certain practices and institutions exist before evaluating their usefulness for marketing. The educator must recognize that the basic orientation required is that marketing is fundamentally the management of demand and of exchange, the maximization of consumer satisfaction or the minimization of consumer dissatisfaction, against a background of sellers' market and strong state involvement, with the purpose of achieving whatever objectives the organization sets for itself.

From a behavioral standpoint, several recommendations are suggested:

(1) *Study the environment in which you find yourself* Field visits to government offices, and manufacturing concerns, as well as discussions with marketing personnel in distribution outlets, and elsewhere, are useful if they can be arranged. Adopt the view that very little can be taught 'from the book'.

(2) *Research into the really basic issues* Recognize that social concerns must be considered in all decision-making; macro issues are just as important as micro issues; that inputs of small-business marketing, agricultural marketing and export marketing are of key importance; that the foundations of the marketing discipline will be thoroughly questioned from the standpoint of social usefulness and relevance in state-run scarcity economies; and that many basic issues are very different from those in the Western world: for example, the role of pricing in a socialist economy, and the functioning of agricultural distribution in a situation of chronic shortages.

(3) *Build local teaching materials* Be willing to develop your own case material by direct contact with companies working in the areas, or by study of reports in newspapers and trade 'journals' if available. Seek out case material developed by marketers in other universities in the same or similar country.

(4) *Talk to local businessmen* Try to obtain a view of how the indigenous marketer views marketing. If marketing is a social process embracing all activities in the exchange of goods and services between producers and consumers, then it is certainly no new phenomenon even in a developing country. The seasoned practitioner has no difficulty in accepting the validity of the discipline, and he can impart much of his industry's and country's special problems.

(5) *Find out how the local marketing system works* The arrangement

and periodicity of local markets may be characteristic of a single country and hence quite unique. In some markets the inherent tendency is for trade, even in the open markets, to follow the line or bond of family relationships: the buyer seeks out a relative's stall or store for purchase; the seller gives a fairer deal to his relatives. These and other features will be of second nature to the student, therefore the educator must also possess this knowledge. There is an increasing awareness that marketing improvements will flow from adapting traditional marketing systems, not trying to transplant mass-marketing technology from the developed world (Meissner, 1981). This, too, underscores the importance to the educator of being familiar with the existing arrangements and their functioning.

(6) *Be familiar with the literature on economic development* The educator lacking knowledge of conditions in some developing countries will be shocked by what he finds, for example the huge disparities between the rich and the poor, and the appalling conditions in some cities. These reflect the process of growth and change. The educator will be less than effective if he is unfamiliar with this change process, with the distortions and dislocations which can accompany it, and with the role that marketing can play in this process.

(7) *Be familiar with the country's economic plans* Where the country practices central economic planning, and makes its objectives known, it is obviously useful to study the industries, regions and products earmarked for development. This knowledge is important for its own sake, and lends a greater relevance to teaching. This can also be an excellent source of background data to augment case writing.

## Conclusion

This chapter makes a case for product adaptation, in the content of marketing education. The case rests on the peculiar features of the environment in Third World countries and of the student and academic population. Of all the professions which might be required to research and gain an understanding of a given environment so as to produce a 'product' (education) to match that environment's requirements, none is better equipped to do so than marketing with its long tradition and preoccupation with identifying and satisfying consumer needs.

But to define the task is not the same thing as saying that it will be easy to accomplish. The opposite is true. A great deal of product adaptation, market knowledge, and customer sensitivity is required, particularly since the yardstick of profitability is not the only measure of performance used to gauge the marketing performance of companies. Societal goals are also paramount.

## Note

1. A slightly different version of this chapter has been published in the *Journal of Marketing Education,* Vol. 6, no. 3 (Spring 1984), pp. 20-27. This version appears with the publisher's consent.

## References

Akerele, Bayo 'The Relevance of Consumerism for a Developing Economy', *Nigerian Journal of Marketing*, vol. 2, December 1980, 44–51

Bartels, Robert 'The Identity Crisis in Marketing', *Journal of Marketing*, vol. 38, October 1974, 76

—— *Global Development and Marketing*, Grid Publishing Inc., Columbus, Ohio, 1981

Berg, Elliot J. 'Socialist Ideology and Marketing Policy in Africa', in R. Moyer and S.C. Holloway (eds), *Markets and Marketing in Developing Economies*, American Marketing Association, Chicago, 1968, pp. 24–47

Drucker, Peter F. 'Marketing and Economic Development', *Journal of Marketing*, vol. 22, January 1958, 252–9

Hunt, Shelby D. 'The Nature and Scope of Marketing', *Journal of Marketing*, vol. 40, July 1976, 17–28

Kirpalani, V.H. 'Opportunity/Problems in the International Transfer of Marketing Skills/Technology to the Third World', in Edward M. Mazze (ed.), *Combined Proceedings*, American Marketing Association, Chicago, 1975, pp. 285–8

Kotler, Philip and Levy, Sydney J. 'Demarketing, Yes, Demarketing', *Harvard Business Review*, vol. 49, November–December 1971, 74–80

—— and —— 'Broadening the Concept of Marketing', *Journal of Marketing*, vol. 33, January 1969, 10–15

Luck, David 'Broadening the Concept of Marketing – Too Far', *Journal of Marketing*, vol. 33, July 1969, 54

McGee, T.G. *The Urbanization Process in the Third World*, Bell and Son, London, 1971

Meissner, Frank 'Capital Intensive Supermarket Technology Can't Serve Needs of Poor in Third World or U.S.', *Marketing News*, 27 November 1981, 13

Montgomery, Malcolm M. 'The Societal and Economic Role of the Multinational Enterprise, Particularly with Reference to the Issues of the Transfer of Technology and Managerial Skill in the Context of Global Development', presented at the Annual Meeting of European Foundation for Management Development, Dublin, 6–9 June 1982

Nunes, Frederick E. 'Education Analysis and Indecision', in *Handbook*, Department of Management Studies, University of the West Indies, Kingston, Jamaica, 1977, pp. 19–20

Onah, J.O. 'Teaching Marketing Management to a Developing Economy – the Nigerian Experience', unpublished manuscript, Department of Marketing, University of Nigeria, 1981

Onyebuagu, C.S. 'Promoting Consumer Interests: The Case for Less Developed Countries', *Nigerian Journal of Marketing*, vol. 1, February 1978, 20–1

Santos, Milton *The Shared Space: The Two Circuits of Urban Economy in Underdeveloped Countries*, Methuen, London, 1979

Saylor, Ralph C. *The Economic System of Sierra Leone*, Duke University, Durham, DC, 1967

Terpstra, Vern *The Cultural Environment of International Business*, South-Western Publishing Co., Cincinatti, Ohio, 1978

Ugoh, S.U. 'The Economic Consequences of Sole Agency Distribution in a Developing Economy', *Nigerian Journal of Marketing*, vol. 1, February 1978, 11–13

Weisenberger, T.M. and Humprhies, Keith D. 'Marketing's Role in Economic Development', in H.W. Nash and D.P. Robin (eds), *Proceedings of the 1976 Conference*, Southern Marketing Association, 1976, pp. 17–19

# 11 MARKET IMPERFECTIONS AND ORGANIZATIONAL STRUCTURE: THE LDC PERSPECTIVE[1]

Jan J. Jorgensen, Taieb Hafsi and Moses N. Kiggundu

## Introduction

In an earlier work reviewing 94 articles on management and administrative practice in less developed countries (LDCs), the authors found that managers in LDCs are able to use North American theories and techniques when effects can be narrowly circumscribed to the organization's technical core (Kiggundu, Jorgensen and Hafsi, 1983). When the organization interacts with its environment, however, the results are unpredictable. Here we use these same articles to examine the structure of organizations in LDCs and what causes the structure to change over time.

## Structure as a Response to Imperfect Markets in LDCs

Input-output analysis of the LDC economy typically shows a great many empty cells, indicating a lack of inter-industry linkages within the domestic economy. The environmental support system is lean; resources are not available in the needed form, or are available only sporadically. Consequently, organizations must be highly self-contained. They must internalize many services which organizations in industrial countries routinely obtain through the market. Uncertainty of resource supply leads to hoarding behavior by organizations. Input inventories are larger than needed in some areas, inadequate in others. Inputs are purchased when available rather than when needed, or when optimally priced. Inappropriate inputs may even be purchased in hopes of using them as bargaining chips with other organizations. Market imperfections force the organization to use payment in kind, providing employees with goods and services that are not easily obtained in the market.

These buffering activities swell the overhead costs of organizations, making them less efficient than their counterparts in industrial countries.

172

Subsidiaries of multinational corporations (MNCs) are exceptions to the rule. These subsidiaries depend on the parent and affiliates for key inputs. It is, therefore, hardly surprising that nationalized subsidiaries perform badly. Nationalization cuts off the external support system, and opens the subsidiary to wide-ranging societal demands.

Because of scarcity, organizations that successfully gather resources become targets for resource raiding and extra-economic demands. Public-sector organizations and multinational firms routinely raid each other's managerial and technical cadres. Proprietors of family firms risk liquidity crises by converting cash balances into unneeded inventory to resist claims by relatives and kinsmen (Walden, 1980).

Foremost among the extra-economic demands is the requirement that organizations maximize employment. For example, in 1964 and 1970 the Government of Kenya negotiated tripartite agreements between itself, the private sector and trade unions, in which private firms agreed to take on 10 percent additional employees (ILO, 1972, pp. 91 and 95). In India private-sector firms are expected to maximize employment as well as profits (Glen and James, 1980). Although the factor endowment of developing countries favors labor-intensive production methods, tariff structures and exchange-rates frequently subsidize imports of capital goods (Guisinger, 1981). As a result, labor-saving machinery is combined with overstaffing. Furthermore, firms face community demands for extraordinary social services which are difficult to resist (Presthus, 1961; Crosby, 1976; Henley, 1977).

Finally, market competition is weak; organizations often enjoy monopoly power, behind which inefficiency flourishes. Rimlinger (1976) documents how established organizations can use political power to eliminate a successful new competitor.

## Implications for Structure

Organizations and markets are normally considered alternative forms of coordination. In LDCs one finds imperfect markets and thin organizational networks. Developing countries are not fully organizational societies. The density of inter-organizational networks is low. The number of organizations is small relative to total population. The distribution of organizations is highly skewed to many small organizations, very few medium organizations and some very large foreign and state-owned organizations.

State organizations tend to be overly large and private organizations overly lean in their administrative components. Sinha (1979) found size to be unrelated to changes in the scale of activities of state organizations. In periods of expansion, they grow faster than their activities; when demand for their activities contracts, they shrink very little, if at all. Subsidiaries of MNCs have relatively lean administrative components because key administrative tasks are performed by the parent. Recruitment of managers is hampered by distrust of outsiders and the general shortage of such skills in society. A multiple-firm family enterprise will deploy the same relative in several firms to conserve managerial talent and to facilitate control and coordination (Flores, 1972).

Functional specialization tends to be blurred within LDC organizations, and the functions of departments often overlap. For example, personnel departments of private firms carry out public-relations functions (Henley, 1977). Functional overlaps are also common in state-owned firms (Presthus, 1961).

## Structural Types

We focus on five major types of firms in developing countries: the entrepreneurial firm, the industrial cluster, the multinational subsidiary, the state-owned enterprise, and the state bureaucracy.

### Entrepreneurial Family-owned Firm

The entrepreneur is owner and manager. He reduces environmental uncertainty through personal horizontal and vertical integration, heading the local branch of organizations that affect the firm's success. For example, the entrepreneur may be simultaneously president of the firm, chairman of the local branch of the political party, head of the parents' association, officer in the local credit union or trade association, and officer in the local chamber of commerce or Rotary Club, and head of the local branch of the ethnic, religious, or caste welfare association (Hamer, 1981, p. 207).

Because of weak capital markets, the entrepreneur diversifies risk by engaging in several businesses at once. The firm becomes a cluster of disparate enterprises linked by the entrepreneur and other family members (Flores, 1972). Because limited opportunity to liquidate assets raises the barriers to exit, unsuccessful ventures are shelved rather than liquidated. They can be reactivated if market conditions change. Such risk minimization impairs efficiency, and may overextend the managerial capacity of the entrepreneur.

## The Industrial Cluster

There are few medium-size private firms in developing countries. Partnerships tend to be unstable, and medium-size firms that develop from family enterprises are structured into clusters. In South Korea, India, Pakistan and East Africa these clusters of firms resemble the *zaibatsu* industrial groupings of Meiji Japan. As Tsurumi (1982) points out:

> Functionally, the emergence of pre-war *zaibatsu* combines reflected the evolution of internalized markets for such scarce resources as capital, technology, trained labor, and managerial skills. Without waiting for uncertain developments in the external . . . markets for the resources, the prewar *zaibatsu* structure enabled its affiliate firms to share scarce resources and rapidly to diffuse technological and managerial innovations among themselves. (p. 88)

Eventually, the industrial grouping's affiliates evolve a functional division of labor: some affiliates specialize in manufacturing, others in marketing or finance. Some industrial clusters remain closely controled by the founding family; in others control shifts to professional managers.

## The MNC Subsidiary

The multinational-firm subsidiary is characterized by its truncated structure. Most planning, financial and logistical functions are performed by the parent. The subsidiary is dependent on the parent for key inputs and for external marketing channels (Shapiro, 1981). The subsidiary manages local inputs, notably personnel functions necessary for the operating core.

## The State Bureaucracy

The key characteristics of the state bureaucracy are as follows: deep personal insecurity among bureaucrats, sanctions to prevent lateral communication among subordinates, greater loyalty to family and clan than to the organization, ritualistic adherence to formal rules, and lack of initiative (Milne, 1970). Formal 'paper' qualifications are reversed; loyalty to hierarchical status is valued more than effectiveness; and patron-client relationships create steep micro-hierarchies within the state bureaucracy (Moris, 1977, p. 79). Transfers are the only sanctions invoked against top officials who fail to do their jobs; problem people are simply shuffled around within the system (Moris, 1977, p. 79). The concentration of wealth, status, education and power in society makes large government organizations the foci of power for the upper class (Deva, 1979). By doling out bureaucratic jobs to supporters, the upper class maintains patron-client relations. Corruption becomes a means of reconciling privilege with equality before the law (Deva, 1979).

Although the state bureaucracy is the most powerful organization in society, its ability to mobilize the efforts of citizens is limited. Potentially explosive urban masses are placated by food subsidies, which weigh heavily on farmers and foreign-exchange reserves. When the demands of the state become too burdensome, farmers retreat into the subsistence economy or seek better markets through smuggling.

*State-owned Enterprises*

State-owned enterprises (SOEs) are important elements in the economy of LDCs, even in countries that favor private enterprise. Some SOEs date to the colonial period, for example, marketing boards set up to stabilize revenues for the government and farmers. Some were founded to provide services (rail, electricity) which would help attract foreign investment. Others were founded as a substitute for foreign investment. When local entrepreneurs could not start an industry the choice lay between foreign ownership and state ownership, and governments before and after independence often opted for the latter course. After independence, some foreign firms in key sectors were nationalized to give the state leverage in economic policy.

That SOEs are failure-prone is not surprising. SOEs are often established in high-risk or low-return sectors spurned by private investors (Mendoza, 1977). Profitability is only one of the conflicting goals set for SOEs. Moreover, the goals change as government priorities shift. Governments find it difficult to resist the temptation to intervene in the management of SOEs to obtain a short-term political advantage. The strategic management autonomy of the SOE is at best fragile. Uncertainty undermines its medium and long-range planning capacity, and creates a mood of cynicism among managers. There are also examples of waste among SOEs. Marketing boards face a variation of Parkinson's Law: the bureaucracy expands to consume the surplus available. What should have been a mechanism to smooth fluctuations in government and farmer revenue becomes instead a self-perpetuating drain on revenue.

**What is Needed in Organizational Structure?**

A recurrent theme in the development literature is the appropriate organizational structure for developing countries; centralized versus decentralized, and organic versus mechanistic.

*Centralization vs Decentralization*

Decentralization appears to enhance the effectiveness of both administrative bureaucracies and commercial firms. Comparing 25 countries, Montgomery (1972) found land reform was most effective when administered through local authorities rather than central agencies. In India, Negandhi and Reimann (1972) found relatively decentralized firms to be more effective in both competitive and non-competitive market conditions.

There is constant tension between popular demands for decentralization of bureaucratic power and the central government's desire to retain effective control (Muwanga-Barlow, 1978). On the one hand, decentralized structures involving local participation appear most effective for community development programs (Montgomery, 1972; Korten, 1980), and on the other, the government argues, centralization is needed for efficient and equitable allocation of scarce resources. It fears decentralization will intensify regional conflicts and create power bases for local opponents of the central government (Smith, 1972; Mills, 1979; Sinha, 1979). Centralization creates its own justification by attracting the most able to the central government, leaving local government to the less capable or less experienced (Mills, 1979). To maintain stability in outlying provinces, the central government must rely on local traditional authorities who enjoy legitimacy (Smith, 1972).

The tension between central allocation of scarce resources and local demands for participation will lessen only gradually with improvements in the capacity of the economy to generate goods and services.

*Organic vs Mechanistic Structures*

Nearly two decades ago Victor Thompson (1964) noted that public-administration models imported from the West emphasize stability and control. He argued that countries facing rapid change need organic structures embodying flexible roles, adaptation and creativity. Rondinelli (1976, 1982) argues that structures imposed on LDCs by international aid agencies are excessively rigid and overly concerned with top-down control. In a similar vein, Korten (1980) presents the case for flexible community-development structures steered by popular participation.

Milne (1970) injected a new dimension into Thompson's schema by drawing a distinction between formal and informal organization structures. The Burns and Stalker organic model (1961) cannot be implemented in developing countries because the necessary preconditions are absent: interpersonal trust, loyalty to the organization, egalitarian norms, and a degree of organizational slack in physical resources. The formal organization in developing countries is a dysfunctional caricature of the bureaucratic model. It is excessively rigid and hierarchical. Milne notes that the success of mechanistic bureaucracies in industrial countries depends on the simultaneous existence of an informal organic organization whose members internalize the bureaucracy's formal mission. The informal organization is goal-functional because of interpersonal trust, loyalty to the organization, and faith in the reward system. By contrast, the informal organization in LDC bureaucracies is goal-dysfunctional. Members do not trust each other, and have little faith in the organization's ability to provide rewards and security (Milne, 1970).

Effectiveness therefore requires a degree of decentralization and an informal structure based on interpersonal trust and faith in the reward system. How do we get there from here?

## Change Catalysts

Catalysts changing the structure of LDC organizations may have positive, negative, or mixed effects. We begin by outlining the more general catalysts that affect all organizations, and conclude by discussing structural change within specific types of organizations.

### Growth and Specialization

As an organization grows, it must develop new coordinating mechanisms. General growth is accompanied by increased functional specialization and the development of specialized administrative skills to coordinate the new division of labor. This in itself lessens the concentration of authority in the organization (Kooperman and Rosenberg, 1977). Furthermore, the technology embodied in a new activity shapes the structure of that unit of the organization: the task determines the (optimal) structure (Gable and Springer, 1979).

The introduction of new machinery forces a restructuring of work arrangements. Fleron (1977, p. 472) observes that technology is itself a cultural artifact that embodies the dominant values of the culture in which it was developed. Production machinery is designed with a certain division of labor in mind, even a certain form of labor control. The ideology of technological neutrality can, however, legitimize the rearrangement of work, ostensibly to maximize the usefulness of the technology.

Increased technical specialization forces the restructuring of organizations, even stagnant bureaucracies. There are two pitfalls in the technocratic route to overcome bureaucratic stagnation. First, the new units may be delegated insufficient authority to do the technical task. In this case, the specialized units will also stagnate. Secondly, it is possible to have too much success, to create a ruling class of technocrats. Some authors (Loveman, 1976; Tapia-Videla, 1976) see this happening in Latin America. They argue that technology has become a repressive tool for reshaping society and suppressing popular participation.

## Widening Externalities

It may seem tautological to argue that increased material prosperity is a catalyst for change in developing countries. The lack of material goods is, after all, the definition of underdevelopment. Yet material shortages are cause as well as effect. Earlier we noted that lack of inputs in the marketplace forced organizations to create internal buffers. Similarly, consumer-goods shortages take people away from work to stand in line. Shortages take people's minds from their work. Food shortages and other scarcities make workers less efficient.

Only if consumer goods are available can economic incentives work (Presthus, 1961) and make the reward system appear legitimate. For both workers and peasants, increased effort depends not so much on increasing the value of payoffs, but on improving the probability of expected payoffs (Popkin, 1979). The availability of parts and other inputs lessens the organization's needs to stockpile, and reduces repair time for breakdowns. Reduction of resource scarcity would remove the most compelling argument for bureaucratic centralization. When the private sector is weak the state becomes mired in the intrigue of allocating jobs, resources, goods and services. Only by increasing the capacity of the private sector to provide goods and services can allocation decisions be shifted from the political/bureaucratic sphere to the marketplace.

## Growth of the Working Class

The creation of a working class with no alternative livelihood increases the power of both the state and employers. Workers without access to land cannot evade state demands by retreating into the subsistence sector. Growing unemployment gives managers greater power to structure work in ways which go against cultural norms (Niehoff, 1959).

The transition from migrant labor to a working class also causes grave problems: severe pauperization, exploitation and political ferment. Too fast or too slow a transition may lead to revolution or reaction. Yet, on the whole, those countries which have made the transition have experienced rapid economic growth. Those countries that have experienced the most economic misery are caught in a halfway house in which laborers still have some ties to the soil.

Research on leadership style shows mixed results. Some find leadership in LDCs to be employee-oriented and participative compared to depersonalized and task-oriented leadership in industrial countries (Helmich and Papageorge, 1976). Others find that within the same country locally owned firms are more task-oriented and autocratic than foreign-owned firms (Deyo, 1978). Still other studies find technical requirements to be more important than external-authority patterns in determining the authority pattern of an organization (Kakar, 1971; Farris, 1972).

We suggest that leadership style varies with the degree of proletarianization. The style is paternalistic when most workers are migrant workers, and when the market is unable to supply necessities of life at a price workers can afford. Leadership style becomes more task-oriented once workers have been blocked from returning to the soil. Only with increased prosperity can leadership once again become more employee-oriented.

## Product Life-cycles and Economic Cycles

Leadership style is also related to the product life-cycle and economic cycle. Task-oriented leadership (Theory X) is needed in firms producing mature, standard products for the world market. Employee-oriented leadership (Theory Y) is possible in firms that are protected from international competition, either because of tariff protection or because of natural protection in the early stages of the product life-cycle. Similarly, task-oriented leadership becomes necessary and more legitimate during economic downturns, and employee-oriented leadership becomes necessary to retain employees during economic booms.

## Organization-specific Change Catalysts

### *The Entrepreneurial Family Firm*

Succession problems are the central catalysts for change in any family firm that has managed to survive several decades. According to Davis (1968), succession crises can take three forms. If there is a strong founder and weak offspring or no willing successor, then the firm will collapse or be sold to outsiders. If there is a conservative founder in conflict with a more progressive successor, then the firm will probably adapt and survive. If there is a split between the siblings — e.g. highly educated ones in administration, less educated ones in technical posts — then one faction will buy out the other, enabling the firm to survive (Davis, 1968).

Technical and financial requirements will also alter family control. Growth may involve increased organizational specialization in which units acquire some autonomy based on specialized function, but strategic decisions remain in family hands. Lenders and new investors may successfully demand changes in decision structures. Going public (rare) involves changes in authority patterns, and exposes the firm to the risk of takeover as family holdings become dispersed.

### *The Industrial Cluster*

Family-controlled industrial clusters can undergo the same succession crises as smaller firms. The clusters are more likely to engage in exports and foreign direct investments. Although private firms are usually reluctant to venture beyond the sheltered domestic market, growing firms eventually exhaust the local market's potential and have to turn to international operations. For some, the outward impetus springs from a desire to escape local bureaucratic restraints. Whatever the motive, internationalization of the private firm exposes it to international competition that forces it to become more efficient. In standard products and services (such as engineering), firms from developing countries often discover that their lower managerial and technical salaries give them a competitive advantage against larger multinationals.

### *State-owned Enterprises*

For state-owned enterprises, the key catalysts for change are growth, technology, financial autonomy and internationalization. In a study of 31 Egyptian SOEs, Badran and Hinings (1981) found that increased size was positively correlated with increased technological complexity and less concentration of authority. Increased technological complexity led to decentralization of authority. Conversely, higher dependence was associated with lower technological complexity, smaller size, and less structured activity.

State-owned enterprises become less dependent on government by winning the rights to charge prices adequate to cover operating costs, or even to finance expansion (Mishra, 1980). Success in self-financing, however, undermines the case for state-ownership. Commercialization leads to increased demands for privatization (Sexty, 1980).

Growing deficits and non-economic pricing can also provide the impetus for change. The deficit may exceed the government's financial capacity to provide a subsidy. Consequently, the government may be forced to restructure, commercialize or sell the enterprise.

Because of growth or the nature of their business (for example, airlines), more and more SOEs expand their operations beyond national boundaries. Competition abroad enables the firm to legitimize demands on members which would be unacceptable within the closed national environment.

A crucial variable in the effectiveness of SOEs is the instability of its board of directors (supervisory board) and top management. Too often these change every year or two, leaving little opportunity for consolidating change. Insecurity of tenure prompts managers to create a docile retinue of subordinates, which only pushes insecurity downward. The effort is futile because, in the end, managers are removed from above and not because of rebellion from below.

## The State Bureaucracy

The state bureaucracy changes slowly because of its sheer size and complexity. It is shielded from many external forces; inertia prevails.

For example, education provides an uncertain catalyst for bureaucratic change. When available only to the few, education acts as a bulwark of privilege. When available to many, it serves as an instrument of mobility. None the less, rapid mobility based on education sharpens conflicts between generations within the bureaucracy. Threatened by the technical expertise of young officials, older officials cling to prerogatives based on seniority. The introduction of new ideas and techniques is thereby delayed.

Another potential catalyst consists of external financial intermediaries, notably the International Monetary Fund and the World Bank, whose loans are conditional upon acceptance of administrative and economic reforms. These agencies have scored some success in individual government departments and public utilities. Sometimes, however, these agencies become unwitting tools in interdepartmental battles within the state bureaucracy. Once labeled as the ally of a particular ministry, such as finance, their 'objectivity' is compromized.

A strong external threat can infuse a stagnant state bureaucracy with a new sense of mission — exposing the hollowness of its legitimacy. Yet, even stripped of legitimacy after invasion or economic ruin, many a state delays reform, tottering from crisis to crisis.

Although populist legitimacy requires some attention to the needs of the common man, the state bureaucracy best serves the interests of its own members and of power-holders in the wider society: landlords, the urban middle class, the military. Change in societal power relationships is thus the main exogenous catalyst altering its structures and functions, but even violent revolution brings no guarantee of bureaucratic change. Successive peasant rebellions in China led to renewal and consolidation of bureaucratic power (Wolf, 1969, pp. 113-16). A military coup does little to change the bureacuracy. With few exceptions, juntas are very dependent on the civilian bureaucracy. In countries with civilian government the bureaucracy is often completely subservient to the ruling political party. The emergence of a strong middle class can affect the bureaucracy. For example, in India the growing middle class forced the bureaucracy to become autonomous from the Congress Party (Subramaniam, 1977).

## Conclusion: Linking Knowledge to Action

### Implications for Western Firms

Developing countries are becoming increasingly important for the Western economies. For example, the share of Canadian exports going to developing countries rose from 7.4 to 10.7 percent between 1970 and 1980, whereas the share going to Europe declined from 18.7 to 13.9 percent. If these trends continue, then within five years the developing countries are going to be more important than Europe for Western export trade. Furthermore, increased trade increases the probability of Western direct investment in developing countries.

What, then, are the practical implications of the market-imperfections perspective for Western firms that invest in developing countries? The parent firm must be prepared to internalize the market for many goods and services required by the subsidiary. This requirement raises the strategic issue of where to locate the ancillary support units. As Shapiro (1981) notes, locating all the needed support services within the subsidiary makes it a good corporate citizen, but makes nationalization a more viable option for the host government. Locating all the support units outside the host country makes the subsidiary a less tempting target for nationalization, but creates the image that the firm has little empathy for the host country's development. The appropriate location strategy lies somewhere between these two extremes. The location of support services will depend on the following factors: (a) the level of trust between the investor and host government; (b) the bargaining power of the two parties; and (c) cost factors. The cost factors may be larger than expected. For example, the larger the number of skilled expatriates assigned to a subsidiary, the more dependent the subsidiary is on the parent for these skills. Yet studies show that it costs 2.5 to 3 times the home rate to base an employee in a developing country. This differential arises from the fact that the firm must provide the expatriate employee with home-standard goods and services — not easily obtainable in the LDC market.

## Implications for Managers of LDC-based Firms

How can organizations be made more effective in LDCs? Our analysis has practical implications for managers in developing countries. We observe that organizational structure in LDCs is a response to market imperfections. Therefore, managers cannot slavishly copy organizational models from industrial countries, where markets for capital, labor and resources are well developed. Instead, they must structure organizations to internalize the market for inputs that are not easily obtained externally.

Furthermore, the recurring theme of legitimization in catalysts for restructuring patterns of work suggests that managers must be sensitive to opportunities that allow improvements in efficiency and effectiveness to be implemented with less resistance. The introduction of new machinery legitimizes changes in work arrangements and supervisory patterns. Growth is accompanied by increased specialization that allows some delegation of authority. Unemployment weakens cultural barriers to new patterns of work. Increased availability of consumer goods in the market helps develop the reward system. Internationalization justifies new demands on both managers and workers.

## Note

1. Support for this chapter comes from Canadian Social Sciences and Humanities Research Grant No. 410-82-0495.

## References

Badran, Mohamed and Hinings, Bob 'Strategies of Administrative Control and Contextual Constraints in a Less-developed Country: The Case of Egyptian Public Enterprise', *Organization Studies, 2*, no. 1, 3–21

Burns, T. and Stalker, G.M. *The Management of Innovation*, Tavistock, London, 1961

Crosby, John 'Personnel Management in a Developing Country', *Personnel Management, 8*, September 1976, 19–23

Davis, Stanley M. 'Entrepreneurial Succession', *Administrative Science Quarterly, 13*, no. 3, 1968, 402–16

Deva, Satya 'Western Conceptualization of Administrative Development: A Critique and an Alternative', *International Review of Administrative Sciences, 45*, no. 1, 1979, 59–63

Deyo, Frederic C. 'Local Foremen in Multinational Enterprise: A Comparative Case Study of Supervisory Role-tensions in Western and Chinese Factories of Singapore', *Journal of Management Studies, 15*, October 1978, 308–17

Farris, George F. and Butterfield, Anthony 'Control Theory in Brazilian Organizations', *Administrative Science Quarterly, 17*, no. 4, 1972, 574–85

Fleron, Frederic J., Jr 'Afterword', *Technology and Communist Culture*, Praeger, New York, 1977

Flores, Filemon 'The Applicability of American Management Practices to Developing Countries: A Case Study of the Philippines', *Management International Review, 12*, no. 1, 1972, 83–9

Gable, Richard W. and Springer, Fred J. 'Administrative Implications of Development Policy', *Economic Development and Cultural Change, 27*, July 1979, 687–703

Glen, Thaddeus M. and James, Charles F., Jr. 'Difficulties in Implementing Management Science Techniques in a Third World Setting', *Interfaces, 10*, February 1980, 39–44

Guisinger, Stephen E. 'The Measurement of Investment Incentives: The Rental Cost of Capital Approach', paper presented to the Academy of International Business Meeting, Montreal, October 1981

Hamer, John H. 'Self-Interest and Corruption in Bukusu Cooperatives', *Human Organization, 40*, no. 3, 1981, 202–10

Helmich, Donald L. and Papageorge, Andrew 'Cross-Cultural Aspects of Executive Leadership Styles', *Akron Business and Economic Review, 7*, no. 4, 1976, 28–33

Henley, John S. 'The Personnel Professionals of Kenya', *Personnel Management, 9*, February 1977, 10–14

ILO *Employment, Incomes and Equality: A Strategy for Increasing Productive Employment in Kenya*, International Labour Office, Geneva, 1972

Kakar, S. 'Authority Patterns and Subordinate Behavior in Indian Organizations', *Administrative Science Quarterly, 16*, 1971, 298–307

Kiggundu, Moses N., Jorgensen, Jan and Hafsi, Taieb 'Administrative Theory and Practice in Developing Countries: A Synthesis', *Administrative Science Quarterly, 28*, March 1983, 66–84

Kooperman, Leonard and Rosenberg, Stephen 'The British Administrative Legacy in Kenya and Ghana', *International Review of Administrative Sciences, 43*, no. 3, 1977, 267–72

Korten, David 'Community Organization and Rural Development: A Learning Process Approach', *Public Administration Review, 40*, September–October 1980, 480–512

Loveman, Brian 'The Comparative Administration Group, Development Administration, and Anti-development', *Public Administration Review, 36*, November–December 1976, 616–21

Mendoza, Gabina A. 'The Transferability of Western Management Concepts and Programs, and Asian Perspective', in L.D. Stifel, J.S. Coleman and J.E. Black (eds), *Education and Training for Public Sector Management in Developing Countries*, Rockefeller Foundation, New York, 1977, pp. 61–71

Mills, G.E. 'Local Government in a Small Developing State: Jamaica', *Journal of Administration Overseas, 18*, July 1979, 180–92

Milne, R.S. 'Mechanistic and Organic Models of Public Administration in Developing Countries', *Administrative Science Quarterly, 15*, March 1970, 57–67

Mishra, R.K. 'Pricing in Public Enterprises', *Indian Journal of Public Adminstration*, October–December 1980, 987–1008

Montgomery, John D. 'Allocation of Authority in Land Reform Programs', *Administrative Science Quarterly, 17*, no. 1, 1972, 62–75

Moris, Jon R. 'The Transferability of Western Management Concepts and Programs, an East African Perspective', in L.D. Stifel, J.S. Coleman and J.E. Black (eds), *Education and Training for Public Sector Management in Developing Countries*, Rockefeller Foundation, New York, 1977, pp. 73–83

Muwanga-Barlow, C.H. 'The Development of Administrative Sciences in English Speaking Africa', *International Review of Administrative Sciences, 44*, no. 1–2, 1978, 93–105

Negandhi, Anant R. and Reimann, Bernard C. 'A Contingency Theory of Organization Re-examined in the Context of a Developing Country', *Academy of Management Journal, 15*, no. 2, 1972, 137–46

Niehoff, Arthur 'Caste and Industrial Organization in Northern India', *Administrative Science Quarterly, 3*, March 1959, 494–508

Popkin, Samuel L. *The Rational Peasant: The Political Economy of Rural Society in Vietnam*, University of California, Berkeley, 1979

Presthus, Robert V. 'Weberian vs. Welfare Bureaucracy in Traditional Society', *Administrative Science Quarterly, 6*, June 1961, 1–24

Rimlinger, Gaston V. 'Administrative Training and Modernization in Zaire', *Journal of Development Studies, 12*, July 1976, 364–82

Rondinelli, Dennis A. 'International Assistance Policy and Development Project Administration: The Impact of Imperious Rationality', *International Organization, 30*, no. 4, 1976, 573–605

——— 'The Dilemma of Development Administration: Complexity and Uncertainty in Control-Oriented Bureaucracies', *World Politics, 35*, no. 1, October 1982, 43–72

Sexty, Robert 'Autonomy Strategies of Government Owned Business in Canada', *Strategic Management Journal, 1*, October–December 1980, 371–84

Shapiro, Alan C. 'Managing Political Risk: A Policy Approach', *Columbia Journal of World Business, 16*, no. 3, Fall 1981, 63–9

Sinha, A.K. 'Organization Building in a Developing Country: A Study of the Central Department of Food in India', *International Review of Administrative Sciences, 45*, no. 2, 1979, 176–82

Smith, B.C. 'Field Administration and Political Change: The Case of Northern Nigeria', *Administrative Science Quarterly, 17*, no. 1, 1972, 99–109

Subramaniam, V. 'Politicized Administration in Africa and Elsewhere: A Socio-Historical Analysis', *International Review of Administrative Sciences, 43*, no. 4, 1977, 297–308

Tapia-Videla, Jorge I. 'Understanding Organizations and Environments: A Comparative Perspective', *Public Administration Review, 36*, November–December 1976, 631–6

Thompson, Victor A. 'Administrative Objectives for Development Administration', *Administrative Science Quarterly, 9*, June 1964, 91–109

Tsurumi, Yoshi 'Japan's Challenge to the U.S.: Industrial Policies and Corporate Strategies', *Columbia Journal of World Business, 17*, no. 2, Summer 1982, 87–95

Walden, Thorn 'Entrepreneurial Illiquidity Preference and the African Extended Family', in Tom Pinfold and Glen Norcliffe (eds), *Development Planning in Kenya*, York University Geographical Monographs no. 9, Toronto, 1980, pp. 119–39

Wolf, Eric R. *Peasant Wars of the Twentieth Century*, Harper and Row, New York, 1969

# 12 A GENERALIZED MODEL OF COMPARATIVE MARKETING: FORMAL DEVELOPMENT, METHODOLOGICAL IMPLICATIONS AND EXAMPLES

Hamid Etemad

## Introduction

In a comprehensive review of the literature of the past 25 years, Boddewyn concluded that, 'Comparative marketing is still relatively green' (1981, p. 61). El-Ansary and Liebrenz went beyond Boddewyn. They began with the premise that, 'Comparative marketing appears to be a term still misunderstood' (El-Ansary and Liebrenz, 1982, p. 59). Barksdale and Anderson argue that, 'There is a consensus that the published research does not add up to very much' (Barksdale and Anderson, 1982, p. 52). The main objective of this chapter is, therefore, to develop a framework to allow for a systematic and methodological analysis in comparative marketing that will respond to the above criticisms.

After a comprehensive review of the literature from a historical and methodological perspective, this chapter will develop a general model for comparative marketing. The features of the model will then be discussed, and the shortcomings of descriptive marketing, which covers most of the past literature in comparative marketing, will be pointed out. To further explore the implications of the model, two examples are presented and analyzed.

## A Short History: The Field of Comparative Marketing in Perspective

Comparative Marketing (CM) as a field of research and study emerged in the 1960s. Several publications appeared earlier, (e.g. McNair, Teele and Mulhean, 1941), but the bulk of pioneering work was presented in the 1960s.

In the earlier part of the 1960s most authors focused on the institutional activities in different markets. For example, Hall, Knapp and Winston (1961) reported similarities and differences in the structure of distribution in Canada, Great Britain and the United States. Jeffreys and Knee (1962) studies retailing in 18 Western European countries. Bartels edited a collection in which wholesaling was compared in 15 countries (1963).

Although these authors laid the initial foundations, the field lacked an accepted and consistent methodology or basis for comparison. To remedy this, Cox (1965) suggested 'flow approach' to comparative marketing, and this was later extended by Jaffe (1969, 1976). Cundiff focused on adoption of technology in 15 countries (1965), and reported that it was directly related to their stage of economic development. Studying channels of distribution in 8 countries, Wadinambiaratchi (1965) reached a similar conclusion: the channel structure was reflective of the stages of economic development. Shapiro's classic piece (1965) focused on the role of marketing (and comparative marketing in particular) in economic development. Boddewyn (1966, 1969) suggested another framework and methodology for comparative marketing. He proposed an actor, process, function, structure, and environment-oriented comparison.

The latter part of the 1960s continued to witness new research and ideas. The idea of a systematic framework for comparative marketing was suggested by Fisk (1967). Liander *et al.* (1967) began to develop and use a taxonomy in comparative marketing. Sommers and Krenan (1967) focused on comparative-buyer behavior, and found that the influence of cultural values was a significant determinant of product success in different nations. Bartels (1968) suggested a conceptually appealing formal framework for systematic comparison in comparative marketing.

The decade of the 1970s brought widespread qualitative growth to the field of comparative marketing. Researchers covered numerous aspects of the field and significant positive steps were taken. For example, Douglas (1971) examined the patterns of marketing structure in five countries.[1] Arndt's research elaborated on temporal and economic patterns (including lags) in comparing channels of distribution (Arndt, 1972).[2] Goodnow and Hansz (1972) tested Litvak's and Banting's hypothesis, and established an empirical relationship between overseas market conditions and entry strategies.[3]

On the consumer-behavior dimension, Sheth and Sethi developed 'A Theory of Cross-Cultural Buyer Behaviour' (1977).[4] Douglas and Dobois (1967) re-emphasized the cultural sensitivity of cross-cultural consumer behavior in general (Sommer and Krenan, 1967) and its implications for advertising and communication in particular. Urban extended the cross-cultural dimension of her 'Life Style Pattern' analysis (1965) to 'Profile Women in International Markets' (Douglas and Urban, 1977) and also developed a 'Cross National Comparison of Consumer Media Use Pattern' (Urban, 1977). Finally, Shimaguchi and Lazer (1979) provided an environmentally insightful[5] description of Japan's inefficient (by Western standards) channels of distribution in terms of channel organization and characteristics which have remained utterly puzzling to non-Japanese researchers for a long time.

The field of comparative marketing did not experience a rapid growth and development on the theoretical and conceptual front in the 1970s. The slow rate of progress is attributed to several factors. These factors cover a wide range, varying from the relatively difficult nature of the field (as compared to domestic marketing for example) to the limitation of research funding, which resulted in the restriction of the scope and depth of research efforts (Barksdale and Anderson, 1982, p. 52). None the less, several theoretical and conceptual pieces stand out. As early as 1970 Holt and Turner edited a collection of papers entitled *The Methodology of Comparative Research* (1970). This collection has remained underutilized. Brislin, Lornner and Thorndike (1973) detected the need for further theoretical and methodological development in comparative marketing research, and published their book *Cross-Cultural Research Methods*. This work is also underutilized.

Although there were earlier calls for general methodological care and prudence, Wind and Douglas pointed out in 1971 (also 1980) that comparative studies require a 'specific' research design to respond to (or control) the inherent differences and difficulties in the field. Demetrescu published a similar 'outline' for 'Comparative Marketing Systems' in 1976. Concerned with the lack or improper use of prudent methodology, Green and White (1976) examined the field and observed that, 'Many of the methodological issues involved in the conduct of cross-national research are being ignored' (p. 81). Among the ignored issues, Green and White emphasized the concept of 'equivalence' (p. 81). The concept covers a wide range, from functional to conceptual equivalence, as well as research-instrument comparability. Lack of equivalence, according to these authors, is the most damaging methodological flaw in cross-cultural research and, by implication, in comparative marketing (Green and White, 1976, pp. 81–2). In the same vein, the issues of construct validity and lack of rival hypothesis testing were questioned by Van Raaij (1978). Despite a real need, the field still remains rather weak as far as theoretical, methodological and conceptual development are concerned. Boddewyn's view is that, 'CM studies are frequently disappointing in terms of theorizing' (1981, p. 64). Lack of strong and solid 'theorizing', and methodological under-development have led to underconceptualization (relative to market-ing) in research and study of comparative marketing. These deficiencies appear to be the primary reasons for alleged 'emptiness' in the field of comparative marketing (Barnes, 1980).

*Summary of Alternative CM Frameworks*

Among the several distinct conceptual frameworks suggested to date, Bartels's is the oldest (1963, 1968). His pioneering work is environ-mentally oriented and conceptually elaborate. Despite its richness, it has remained underutilized and somewhat ignored. Boddewyn has argued in the past, and still maintains, that Bartels overemphasized the environmental dimension of CM, and that has been responsible, to a great extent, for its slow rate of adoption and use (Boddewyn, 1969, 1981).[6]

Boddewyn suggested that marketing scholars should focus on some aspect of marketing at the time rather than on the entire marketing system and its associated environment. Boddewyn's substitute frame-work is logically sound and internally consistent. It includes five major related components: actor, process, structure, function, and environ-ment (1966, 1969). Except for the Boddewyn–Hollander compendium (1972), Boddewyn's framework remains equally underutilized.

Fisk's general systems approach to comparative marketing (1967) suggests that marketing scholars should focus on goals, organizations and productivity of marketing systems, while allowing for the major constraints imposed by different political, economic and governmental institutions. In fact, if one accounts for all constraints, Fisk's sugges-tions become highly environmentally oriented and hence similar (if not identical) to Bartels's. The main improvement or advantage over Bartels, however, may lie in the well-developed methodology of the systems. This may allow scholars to use the system's methodology to better focus on a particular aspect (or part) of marketing as a sub-system, while paying full attention to the effects, influences and/or constraints imposed by other subsystems.

Cox's flow approach (1965) was extended later by Jaffe (1976). It consists of six components: input, process, output, goals, constraints and feedback. Within the context of this model Jaffe suggested that comparative marketing research should focus on marketing process and its associated flows — including ownership, physical possession, communication, financing and risk. According to Jaffe, these flows form an 'invariant point of reference', and are essential parts of all distribution channels and all marketing systems' (Jaffe, 1976).

Although the field of CM has witnessed a great deal of progress in terms of refinement and further elaboration of the original ideas since the early 1960s, it faces massive difficulties and challenges. According to Barnes, CM is still 'remarkably empty' (1980, p. 91). Despite the severe exaggeration in Barnes' characterization of the field of CM, it appears that the extreme diversities in the marketing environments, goals, institutions and practices in different countries (e.g. industrialized versus developing countries) have deterred methodological and substantive development. The relatively underdeveloped state of methodology seems to be responsible for massive measurement difficulties that plague CM studies (e.g. lack of 'functional' and 'conceptual' equivalence (Green and White, 1976, pp. 81-2). Therefore, this chapter intends to develop a formal methodology to deal with a range of issues that plagued the field. On the basis of the pioneering nature and relatively high dissemination of Bartels's work in the scholarly community, his conceptualizations will form the basis for further formal development in this paper. The introduction of a similar formal development to other alternate conceptual frameworks (e.g. Boddewyn, Cox, Fisk, etc.) results in a greater degree of exactitude and 'equivalence' than is present in current literature.[7] Without such a formal methodology and subsequent rigorous testing, the development of a complete theory of CM remains unlikely. In summary, in view of the field's vast diversity, some degree of formalization is helpful, if not necessary, and Bartels's pioneering work forms the basis for such formal development in this chapter.

## *Descriptive and Comparative Marketing in Perspective*

Despite the richness of Bartels's conceptualization, marketing scholars have not used it for the most part. As a result, Bartels's framework still remains untested and not fully developed. This is partially because of the difficulties involved in conceptualizing the environment of marketing and then accounting for the environmental effects on marketing processes. Another reason for the underdevelopment seems to be the absence of a clearly stated purpose for comparison(s), and of justification for introducing further complication (e.g. the environment, its relations with marketing processes, etc.). According to Bartels a substantial portion of CM literature was (and I maintain that it still is) 'descriptive' as opposed to 'comparative' (e.g. Boddewyn and Nath, 1970; Buxton, 1973; Carson, 1974; Carman and March, 1979;

Figure 12.1: Model for Comparative Analysis

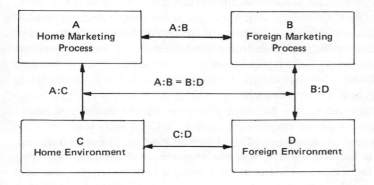

Source: Adapted from Bartels (1968).

Ehrenberg and Goodhart, 1968; Goldman, 1967; Harris, Still and Grask, 1978; Nagashima, 1977; Urban, 1977). Several authors have argued that any comparisons of marketing process (or parts thereof) in two countries provide 'valuable' information and should be recognized and categorized as such (e.g. Boddewyn, 1966, 1969, 1981).

Such categorization may satisfy the denotative meaning of 'comparative' and might also be informative. However, comparison of marketing processes in two locations with due respect to their context – that is the relationship between the marketing process (or parts thereof) and its associated marketing environment – can be much more informative and hence more 'valuable'. Simple comparison of seemingly similar (or different) marketing phenomena, regardless of their underlying contextual relationship, may fail to uncover their true functional context. It also implies a higher chance of violating 'functional' and 'conceptual equivalence' (Green and White, 1976, p. 82), and this may make for a fruitless (if not misleading) comparison.[8] Figure 12.1 can help to clarify the distinction between 'comparative' and 'descriptive'.

Where:

A represents the marketing process in the home country,
B represents the marketing process in the foreign country,
C represents the environment of the home country, and
D represents the environment of the foreign country (Bartels, 1968, p. 59)

A comparison of marketing processes (A:B), without a proper consideration for their respective environments is a 'descriptive' statement (Bartels, 1968, p. 59). Although, such a comparison may identify the similarities or the differences of the two marketing systems, it is of very little value for it fails to specify the reasons for these. The relative ease of descriptive analysis seems to be the primary reason for such casual and somewhat uncritical comparing or contrasting of marketing processes in different countries.

A description of a marketing process within the confines of, and in relation to, its environmental context (A:C or B:D) was called the 'statement of environmentalism' (Bartels, 1968, p. 59). Such a description is useful in many ways. For example, in designing a marketing plan (an ex ante analysis at firm level) a firm can hypothesize and test for the relationship between the components of its marketing plan and its relevant marketing environment (e.g. manipulate advertising to estimate sales-advertising-environment response functions). Or, in order to increase marketing efficiency and increase the chances of achieving marketing objectives, a firm may decide to test for the environmental sensitivity of different components (e.g. any of the four P's (product, place, price and promotion) individually or collectively) of its marketing plan. When it is believed that at least some of the components are environmentally sensitive (can be influenced by outside factors), identification of the 'state of environmentalism' (e.g. A:C or B:D) and the actual state of the environment assumes greater importance. Consumer products, and hence the marketing of these products (e.g. personal hygiene items), are generally believed to be more environmentally sensitive than industrial products (e.g. mainframe computers) and their associated marketing. Even a mild environmental sensitivity requires a firm to establish and perhaps improve upon the relationship between its marketing practices and its environment. A high degree of environmental sensitivity may require a firm to forecast the future state of environment before deciding on marketing policy (for example, see Terpstra, 1978, pp. 529–62). In general, assessing the marketing strategy-environment relationship allows a firm to analyze and revise this relationship continually in order to improve upon its future efficiency. Therefore, the state of environmentalism formally characterizes the relationship between marketing processes at different levels (e.g. at firm, industry or country level) and the environment.[9]

Bartels defines 'comparative' marketing as the comparison of two marketing processes in relation to their environments (i.e. A:C versus

B:D). This type of comparison, as stated earlier, is much more meaningful and, of course, more difficult than casual and uncritical comparison of descriptive information. Stated differently, 'Comparative study is not simply a description of either the marketing or environmental differences, but rather a comparison of relationships between marketing and its environment in two or more countries,' (Bartels, 1968, p. 59).

The following notation was used by Bartels to illustrate comparative marketing in two countries:

$$A:C = B:D \tag{1}$$

Jaffe (1980) adopted Bartels's model and symbolism and extended Bartels's static two-country model to allow for more than two-country comparisons in the following fashion:

$$A:B = A_1:B_1 = A_2:B_2 \ldots A_n:B_n \tag{2}$$

Where As and Bs denote marketing systems (Jaffe's terminology)[10] and their corresponding environments for different countries, respectively.

**Analysis of the Extended Model**

In light of expanding international marketing and rapidly changing environments, the extension is an overdue and welcome addition. In this work Jaffe generalized the two-country comparison model (expression (1)) to arrive at a multi-country comparison framework (expression (2)). Bartels's model is of a static, or at best, a comparative static variety. However, in his supporting argument, leading to expression (2), Jaffe unwittingly introduced an element of dynamism into his analysis. This newly introduced argument used slightly questionable logic and terminology.

Jaffe wrote: 'Some parts of the environment of a certain foreign country (D) may change into a new environment (D-1),' (1980, p. 85). 'When D-1 starts to influence its marketing system causing it to change in some way (B-1), the relationship between D-1 and B-1 will be constant again,' (1980, p. 85).

Jaffe's argument presents the reader with at least two new concepts that were not present in Bartels's original paper. First, a causal relationship between the environment and the marketing system is implied;

and secondly a notion of equilibrium or constancy in the relationship is introduced.

The notion of a causal relationship between the marketing process and its environment, (i.e. whether a change in the environment causes change in the marketing processes, or marketing innovation leads to environmental changes, especially in developing countries) is not a settled issue in international marketing literature. In some instances new marketing processes, usually introduced by international marketers, act as change agents and lead to profound environmental changes, i.e. economic growth and development (for example, see Baldwin, 1954; Bauer, 1954; Bonnen, Eigher and Schmid, 1964; Boulding and Singh, 1962; Dholakia and Firat, 1976; Drucker, 1958; Fisher, 1954; Haring, 1965; Holton, 1953; Mentzer and Samli, 1981; Miller, 1967; Riley, 1970; Sherbini, 1965; Slater, 1965, 1976, 1977).

In other instances the environment is treated as a series of constraints to marketing processes to which they must adapt (e.g. Douglas and Dubois, 1977; Douglas and Wind, 1977; Wind and Douglas, 1973). Hence, the direction of the influence is unclear and far from constant. In addition, in a dynamic and longitudinal analysis, causality is not usually a simple one-way relation.

## Defining the Environment

Bartels did not define environment explicitly. This may have hindered the further development of his model. In a game-theoretic approach to international marketing at the firm level, Holton (1970, pp. 8-10) identified players and their alternate strategies. These can be viewed as good proxies and an active environment. Following Ansoff and Ackoff[11] the notion of 'stakeholders' was proposed by Wind and Perlmutter (1977, p. 131). Stakeholders are, 'All those individuals, groups and organizations which contribute to the viability and legitimacy of the organization,' (1977, p. 131). Holton, Wind and Perlmutter came very close, but they did not define the environment explicitly, nor did they define marketing environment specifically.

All aspects and dimensions of a society's life are not equally influential on marketing processes. Certain elements or dimensions of the environment interact with and influence marketing processes much more powerfully than others.

## Definition

The relevant or influential environment is that part of the environment that influences or is influenced by marketing processes. Symbolically,

Figure 12.2: Influential Environment of Marketing

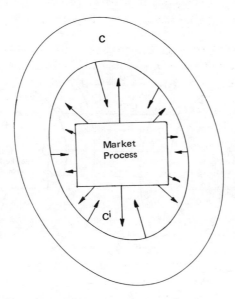

this will be denoted by $C^i$ and referred to as influential environment hereafter. Figure 12.2 illustrates this schematically. Of course $C^i$ is a subset of the overall environment C. Thus $C^i$ must be contained in C or $C^i \subset C$ at all times.

The influential environment of $C^i$ is a subset of the entire environment C ($Ci \subset C$) and hence must be distinguished from the entire environment. The criteria for the influential environment's boundary condition play an important role in discriminating between $C^i$ and C. C replaces $C^i$ by default.

The complement of $C^i$ (or the non-influential part of the environment, not contained in $C^i$) will be denoted by $C^n$ ($C^n \subset C$). The shape, composition, and evolution of $C^n$ will have very little or no effect on the marketing processes. Conversely, the shape, characteristics, behavior and evolution of $C^i$ is of great interest. In summary, the entire environment of a country is comprised of two parts: (1) influential and relevant, $C^i$, that must be identified and fully understood; and (2) the non-influential part, $C^n$, which remains inactive.

The distinction between influential environment ($C^i$) and the overall environment (C) is not a trivial one. The use of $C^i$, means a proper 'identification' or 'specification' (for example see Kmenta, 1971,

Figure 12.3: A Graphic Representation of Bartels's Modified
Framework[a]

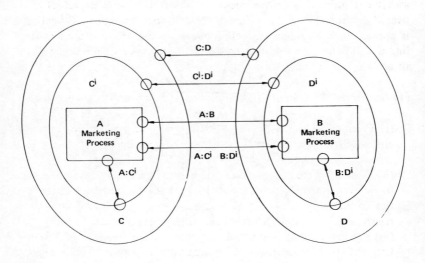

Note: a. Where A:B, $C^i$:$D^i$ and C:D are descriptive statements;
A:$C^i$ and B:$D^i$ are statements of environmentalism; and
A:$C^i$ vs B:$D^i$ is a comparative statement
Legend:   ———— Boundary line.
          —o— Boundary for the entity under consideration for comparing and
               contrasting.
          ←———→ Comparing and contrasting entities.

pp. 439–50; Kelejian and Oates, 1974, pp. 244–52; Pindyck and Rubinfeld, 1976, pp. 127–39). Proper identification is necessary for proper
measurement and evaluation of the relationship between the marketing
processes and the influential variables (or elements of) the environment. A proper identification/specification is also the first necessary
step in correct assessment of the relationship between A and $C^i$, (or B
and $D^j$). The use of C, as opposed to $C^i$, is bound to expose the
marketer to an unduly large set of environmental variables which
increase the chances of misspecification of the relationship, and of
accepting some spurious relations.

Accepting the above argument and the resulting decomposition
forces one to modify Bartels's framework and reformulate Jaffe's
extension. The following modification in Figure 12.3, based on the

above discussion, is a useful start. In contrast to Figure 12.1, where two separate boxes are housing the 'home environment' (C), only one box, representing home marketing process (A), is nested within its own associated influential environment $C^i$ which in turn is a part of the overall environment C (see Figure 12.2). Corresponding modification is applied to the foreign marketing processes and the environment. In line with Figure 12.1 and the discussion (Bartels's original framework), three categories of analysis are still possible.

(1) *Descriptive Statement:* Three types of analysis are feasible here:

  (i) Comparing and contrasting marketing processes in two differ-ent countries without reference to their corresponding marketing environment A:B (e.g. buyer behavior in US and France);
  (ii) Comparing and contrasting the relevant marketing environments in two countries $C^i:D^i$ (e.g. availability, rates and other characteris-tics of commercial ratio and television in two countries, laws and regulations pertaining to advertising in two countries, etc.);
  (iii) Comparing and contrasting the entire environment in two coun-tries C:D (e.g. comparison of populations, geography, legal systems, socio-political systems, economic structure, cultural background, etc.)

Items (i) and (ii) above can provide useful marketing and environ-mental information without reference to each other. Item (iii) may provide a great deal of general information, most of which may be irrelevant to marketing and/or not specific enough. The probability of overcrowding and information pollution is substantial.

(2) *State of Environmentalism:* The relationship between marketing processes and marketing environment or influence in a given country ($A:C^i$ or $B:D^i$) is defined as the state of environmentalism. This state-ment is invaluable for better control of marketing activities within a given environment. Furthermore, it is the cornerstone of comparative marketing. Without a full understanding of the relationship of market-ing activities (i.e. at firm-level) or marketing processes (i.e. at industry or country-level) and their associated influential environment(s), com-paring and contrasting is not very practical.

(3) *Comparative Statement:* A systematic comparison of at least two statements of environmentalism characterizes comparative marketing. Stated differently, this is the comparing and contrasting of comparable aspects of dimensions of marketing in different markets, with proper

reference to their associated marketing environments (or context). Symbolically, that is:

$$A:C^i \quad vs \quad B:D^i \qquad (3)$$

A comparative statement can be very powerful and can help to establish the following:

(i) It can distinguish universal marketing principles from others. A universal principle is one which transcends country boundaries and remains invariable across environments. The nature and hence the functioning of these principles are not culture bound and should be applicable universally. Once established, these principles should be applicable in all environments. Universal rules and principles have formed the cornerstones of scientific theories. Such universal marketing principles can accomplish much toward constructing 'marketing theory' (Boddewyn, 1981; Shapiro, 1965).

(ii) It can describe the contextual effects of the environment. In view of these, international marketers can decide on the degree of adaptation (of marketing activities) that is required to transfer them from one environment to another. Hence, the limitation of environmentally bounded strategies (i.e. activities, processes and systems) is recognized and treated accordingly.

(iii) It can provide a substantiated perspective on the transferability of marketing knowledge and practices from one country to another. A large number of marketing scholars have argued that more efficient marketing can substantially enhance the economic development of developing countries (for example see: Bauer, 1954; Boulding and Singh, 1962; Drucker, 1958; Holton, 1953; Sethi and Etemad, 1984; Etemad, 1982; Shapiro, 1965; Slater, (1976). But, the question of transferability of marketing knowledge in terms of its acceptability to and compatibility with the host environment still remains unresolved. (Dholakia and Dholakia, 1982; Firat and Dholakia, 1982)

## Toward a Generalized Model of Comparative Marketing

Comparative marketing holds great potential for enriching marketing theory and the understanding of marketing's capability and constraints. Shapiro (1965) saw these potentials, but warned against expecting a comprehensive theory because of the practical difficulties of comparing 'total' marketing systems. Time has proved that Shapiro's prediction was correct. The literature still lacks a universal theory of marketing and a set of universal marketing principles; and the theory of comparative marketing, as Boddewyn reports (1981), is still in its infancy.

If a universal or non-environmentally specific theory of marketing is to emerge in the future, the practical difficulties of the field should not deter researchers, as they can be gradually overcome. Small but cumulative and logical attempts can slowly pave the road. In that vein, any systematic development should be welcomed. Based on substantial research, Bartels's observation that marketing is composed of 'twofold character: technical and social' (1968, p. 57), was and still is a constructive step. As a technical process, Bartels wrote: 'Marketing consists of application of principles, rules or knowledge relating to the non-human elements of marketing' (1968, p. 57). As a social process, he explained that 'Marketing is a complex of interactions among individuals acting in role positions in various systems involved in the distribution of goods and services,' (1968, p. 57).

Segmentation of marketing to 'social' and 'technical' seems to be logical. This postulates that marketing is comprised of two subcategories: One contains only the rules, principles and knowledge that are independent of human elements and therefore are expected to remain invariant across boundaries and individuals; the other contains a complex set of 'interactions among individuals', and is, by definition, societal and culturally bound'.

Some may take issue with the above way of decomposing marketing on the grounds that the lines of demarcation cannot be clearly or easily delineated. Proponents, however, point out to a solid body of marketing knowledge in general, and marketing research techniques in particular that are adopted from other disciplines (e.g. statistics, biometrics, economics, econometrics, etc.), and are proven to be independent of their application environment and hence universally applicable. The results of applying such a set of principles, rules, and knowledge to marketing is not intrinsically environmentally specific, unless researchers unwittingly introduce human, social or cultural biases into their analyses. Even when such biases are introduced, the end results should remain much less environmentally bound than that set of knowledge that is primarily concerned with human elements, their mutual relationships, characteristics and consequent behavior. The latter belongs very clearly to the social side of marketing. The state of marketing represented by 'technical' and 'social' processes in any society, however, must be reflective of the society's state of technical and social development. This suggests that further decomposition of influential environment ($C^i$) may also permit a higher degree of refinement and equivalence in future analysis.

In view of the above, and especially in the absence of any other logical suggestion, Bartels's formulation seems to be a good start. 'Marketing processes' therefore, is decomposed into 'technical' (i.e. AT or BT) and 'social' (i.e. AS or BS) processes. In a parallel manner, the environment of marketing is divided into its technical and social components. The technical environment (i.e. $C^{it}$ or $D^{it}$) of marketing is logically a subset of a society's technical infrastructure; and hence the degree of its richness, advancement and evolution is directly related to that of the technical infrastructure in the country. The technical sophistication of marketing is expected to be related to the society's overall technical advancement, but the degree of correspondence may vary from one society to another.[12] By the same token, the social environment of marketing ($C^{is}$ or $D^{is}$) must also be a subset of the social structure of the society and hence its structure, characteristics and evolution must resemble that of the societal and perhaps cultural structure. With slight change in notation, the above two decompositions are incorporated into the symbolic characterization of the comparative statement in the following steps:

(i) marketing processes, A, is composed of (i.e. =) technical process, AT and (+) social processes, AS (or A = AT + AS)
(ii) similarly, B = BT + BS
(iii) the influential environment $C^i$ is composed of (=) technical, $C^{it}$, and (+) social $C^{is}$; where $AT \subset C^{it}$ and $AT \cap C^{is} = \phi$
(iv) similarly, $D^i = D^{it} + D^{is}$; where $BT \subset D^{it}$ and $BT \cap D^{is} = \phi$
(v) $(AT:C^{it} + AS:C^i) \text{ vs } (BT:D^{it} + BS:D^i)$           (4)

To avoid the strict mathematical meanings of (:) and (=), and to minimize confusion, the above expression is rewritten as:

$$(AT/C^{it} + AS/C^i) \approx (BT/D^{it} + BS/D^i) \tag{5}$$

where $AT/C^{it}$ should be interpreted as AT within the context of $C^{it}$ (or AT conditioned by $C^{it}$) and $\approx$ represents the act of comparison.

Expression (5) is a concise statement of comparative marketing. It simply states the 'what' and 'how' of the comparison. It also suggests that a division (i.e. technical and social) in marketing activities and their associated environment should be applied. A dichotomous and perhaps multiple segmentation can potentially help to improve the quality of the comparison in several ways:

(i) it allows CM research to be divided into much more refined categories than it currently is:
(ii) further categorization permits future differentiation and refinement in definitions, boundaries, scope, research methodology and hence much improved results;
(iii) it allows for a much more focused comparison in concepts, functions, processes and systems by permitting sharper distinction in the unit and level of analysis on one hand and better detection of contextual (e.g. environmental) effects on the other hand;
(iv) comparing, contrasting, and perhaps testing of well-defined concepts and tightly formulated hypotheses will be much easier, and their potential contribution to the eventual construction of a solid body of knowledge in marketing will be much higher than otherwise;
(v) finally, well-formulated and tested hypotheses with full consideration for their environmental context, can effectively discriminate between universally applicable rules and principles, and others which are environmentally bound or culturally specific. This permits marketers to make appropriate adjustments if their transfer from one environment to another becomes necessary.

A generalized statement requires a further change in notation, but the substance and form remain unchanged. That is:

$$(MT/E^{it} + MS/E^i)_1 | \approx (MT/E^{it} + MS/E^i)_2 \ldots \approx (MT/E^{it} + MS/E^i)_j$$
$$\approx \ldots \approx \ldots \approx (MT/E^{it} + MS/E^i)_n \qquad (6)$$

where: MT and MS are technical and social parts of marketing, respectively,

$E^i$ is the influential part of a country's entire environment (E) and hence $E^i \subset E$;
$E^{it}$ is the technical part of $E^i$ and hence $E^{it} \subset E^i$; subscript j (from 1 to n) refers to different countries included in the analysis.

Ideally, expression (6) should be further expanded to accommodate comparison of marketing activities, dimension, concepts, processes and systems across their corresponding environments. Although such a formal expansion is beyond the scope of this paper, a description of the steps involved is helpful to the better understanding of the above model and its implications. They are as follows:

(i) define the scope, level and unit of analysis, including the boundaries;
(ii) define the components of the activity, dimension, concept, process and/or marketing system desired. This step is analogous to defining and distinguishing marketing's technical and social aspect, when the level of analysis is relatively aggregate. For a given level of analysis, the marketing function can be divided into many components as: $(m_1, m_2, \ldots m_k, \ldots m_k; m_k \Sigma M)_j$;
(iii) similarly, identify the corresponding relevant dimensions of the environment, that is $(e_1, e_2, \ldots e_p, \ldots e_p; E^i)_j$;
(iv) establish the state of environmentalism in different countries (i.e. $j = 1 \ldots n$) by determining the relationship between the marketing activity, dimension or process and the relevant/influential environment. At a highly macro-level this relation may take a form similar to $M = F[E^i]$, $Mt = F_t[E^{it}]$, $MS = Fs[E^i]$, etc; where M, MT, MS, $E^{it}$, $E^i$ are macro variables. At the micro-level, however, M may be replaced by a subset or vector of M (e.g. $m_1, m_2, \ldots m_k, \ldots m_k; m_k \Sigma M$)); F is replaced by a series of relationships (e.g. structural relations); and $E^i$ is replaced by another subset or vector from the relevant/influential environment (e.g. $(e_1, e_2, \ldots e_p, \ldots e_p; e_p \Sigma E^i)$;
(v) any component can then be compared with its counterparts within the context of their respective environmental components (e.g. $(m_1 : e_1)_j \ldots (m_1 : e_1)_t)$.

## Implications of the Generalized Model for International Marketing – a Micro Analysis: From a Firm's Viewpoint

In the following pages the generalized model (expression (6)) will be applied to a firm's international entry strategy to show its applicability and usefulness. The model is equally applicable to other components of a firm's international marketing strategies. To keep the arguments as simple as possible, a narrow definition of international marketing will be used. International marketing is defined as a conduct of marketing across the boundaries of only two countries. However, results of the argument remain valid for multiple-country definition.

Looking at expression (6) an international marketing manager is faced with several choices that expose him to different sets of strategic alternatives. Assuming that the manager is fully familiar with the marketing processes $m_k$, ($m_k \Sigma M$), in the environment $e_p(e_p \Sigma E^i)$, and the relationship between $m_k$ and $e_p$ ($m_k = f[e_p]$) in his own country (home country), his first decision is to determine the range of the environmental flexibility of his firm's international marketing operation. A firm's environmental flexibility is dependent on its willingness and ability to introduce, implement and accommodate change (or variations) in marketing policies (due to environmental diversity). Two extreme cases are examined below.

1. *Low Flexibility and Low Degree of International Orientation.* A highly domestically oriented international marketing manager is expected to find very little environmental flexibility in his organization. This may translate to a great desire for operating in foreign environments which are as similar to that of the domestic operations as possible. This will lead the firm to find a host country with the environment that is most similar to that of its home country (e.g. western provinces of Canada to the United States). A minimum amount of reorientation or changing of marketing policies is required. International marketing in such a market will expose the firm to a large market with maximum environmental overlap. Under extreme similarity of the environments, there will be little need for any change in the firm's marketing strategy. Maximum enviromental similarity, including the technical and industrial structures, and the competitive conditions of the firm's industry in the two countries, permits the firm to extend its home marketing policies to the new market without any appreciable adaptation.

Assuming that the environmental similarity continues over the length of operations in the host country (e.g. exporting for five years), the crucial first step is to find a host-country environment which is the most similar to that of the home country at the point of entry. Application of any taxonomical procedure classifying a country's environments ($E^i$) can be very helpful here. However, it must be noted that the set of variables (V) entered into the classification scheme must be related to, and influential in, the marketing strategy of the firm. In other words, they must characterize ($E^i$) but not necessarily $E^n$ ($E^n = E-E^i$; $V = v_j$ $\Sigma E^i$ and $v_j \not\subset E^n$, for all j, (where V is the set of variables included in the classification analysis). In the short run identifying the environment that is most similar is the necessary condition for a minimum amount of change in marketing policies at the point of entry. However, it may not be sufficient in the long run. It is possible that the changes over time cause incremental diversion and lead to increasing differences in the two environments. Hence, the necessary and sufficient condition for the success of those firms with low flexibility wishing to extend home marketing strategy with minimal or no adaptation, to the host country, requires 'over-time' similarity or 'equivalence' of the marketing environments. The notion of time in general, and its over-time equivalence in particular, remains highly neglected in comparative marketing.

Assuming that over-time equivalence or similarity cannot be forecasted, extension of home marketing strategy is not a prudent policy, especially for firms with a low ability to adapt in time to change. As the environment changes over time, the gap between the old marketing strategy and the new environment may grow wider causing more environmental incompatibility. Incompatibility may, in the extreme, lead to severe losses, in spite of all precautions and prudence at the beginning of operations.

A low willingness and ability to adapt to new changes is generally attributable to a low sensitivity to the environment or to environmental changes. In stable or stagnant environments this may not cause very many problems. However, in highly volatile environments a low ability exposes the firm to increasing incompatibility over time. The firm will either fail to manage, or the environmental incompatibility will force change. Both cases expose the firm to higher probability of losses.

Accommodating change is a costly activity. Therefore, similarity between home and host environments may minimize short-run costs. However, similarity of the environments at the time of entry cannot guarantee similarity over time. Furthermore, this similarity cannot be substituted for the true relationship between the firm's marketing strategy and the host's environment.

A firm's decision to expand into international markets by entering into the most similar ones has certain advantages. Since marketing strategies need not change at the entry time, the immediate cost of adapting home-country marketing policies (i.e. initial set-up cost) will be minimal. In the case of small firms, especially those that lack resources, experience or expertise, the above strategy may be the only one available in the very short run; however, it is a risky strategy in the longer run. The potential cost savings must be balanced against potential losses. Furthermore, the trade-offs between short-run profits and longer-run potential losses must also be considered. Potential environmental changes must be forecasted as much as possible. Costs of incremental or total change in marketing policies (from home to host country) should be considered in the face of over-time environmental incompatibility and hence unrealized potential profits. For small and/or inflexible firms, the consequences of environmental compatibility may prove to be unbearable.

2. *Highly Flexible Firms and Varying Environment.* For firms enjoying a wide range of flexibilities (high ability to adapt to environmental changes), the degree of similarity or dissimilarity of home and host environment may not be of ultimate importance. Rather than using similarity as a selection criterion, they may use other criteria (such as market size, growth-rate, portfolio effect or profit potential) as long as the costs and benefits of the results justify the criterion. In comparison to the previous case, their willingness — and thus their ability to accommodate change — does not confine their search for potential markets only to similar markets (which is a subset of all markets). Rather, these firms rely on flexibility and include diversity, and hence, do a thorough job of international marketing.

When environments are assumed to hold no similarity (that is $C^i \cap D^i = 0$), the firm's marketing strategy in the two countries may not be similar or comparable, and the two operations should be viewed as fully isolated cases. Hence, marginal cost being equal to marginal revenue could be a criterion for maximizing profits in each location. That is:

$$(MC = MR) \quad \text{and} \quad (MC = MR)$$
$$\text{home} \qquad\qquad \text{foreign}$$

This criterion may take the firm to large and profitable but costly markets, with a total disregard for home-country strategies or practices. This case is similar to a holding company operating across boundaries.

Real cases will fall in between the above two extremes, where some adaptation of marketing strategies is required. In the former case a full extension of marketing strategies is a possibility. But for the latter case, a full adaptation of marketing strategies is required. Furthermore, in the former case, the firm may shy away from diversity, and hence remain a domestic marketer in its outlook. Under such circumstances, not only is the firm exposing itself to possible longitudinal incompatibilities (between its marketing strategies and the host-country environment) but also it deprives itself of knowledge about other dissimilar markets. When other marketers capitalize on their learnings from their diverse markets and incorporate them into their domestic marketing strategy, a firm with domestic outlook (the first case) will soon feel competitive pressures, even at home, that cannot be easily counteracted. This will be so because of at least two main factors: (1) The portfolio effect of diverse markets reduces average losses; and (2) a partial extension and partial adaptation of home marketing strategies to other markets will increase the global efficiency of marketing strategies. Both effects are powerful, and a firm with a low flexibility and/or constrained resources is not strategically equipped to counteract them properly.

## Summary and Conclusion

A properly formulated comparative marketing strategy is a necessary asset for identifying the cause of success or failure in different marketing environments. A concise statement of comparative marketing is necessary for doing so, and the lack of it can cause confusion. Although the literature has created the impression that comparative marketing can be a substitute for micro-international marketing decisions, this is clearly not the case. Hence, future research must look into the contextual effects of different environments on marketing strategies, processes and systems.

This paper presents a concise statement of comparative marketing which can be used as a model for carrying out 'comparative analysis'. It suggests careful decomposition of marketing and marketing environment into their components at different levels of analysis. It further suggests that a statement of environmentalism must be established (between the marketing and marketing environment components) before any 'comparative analysis' is carried out.

Comparative marketing can be very helpful on many fronts. At the theoretical level, for example, the extension of home marketing strategies to other environments carries the implication that either the strategy's underlying rules, concepts and principles are universally applicable, or the environments are highly similar.

The emerging field of comparative marketing has dealt with some of the above issues. For example, the issues of universality (or lack of) of marketing principles, the conditions under which marketing strategies can be extended and the degree of environmental similarity dominated the early years of the study of comparative marketing. Some of these issues still plague the field. The relatively underdeveloped state of theory and methodology is responsible for the lack of systematic solutions to problems in the field. The formal developments presented in this paper provide a logical foundation in that regard.

At the firm level, a contextual or environmentally adapted marketing strategy stands a greater chance of success than does a marketing program that has not fully absorbed these effects. This assumes an even greater role in international marketing. Specifically, the contextual effects of a foreign environment can contribute substantially to the success or failure of international or foreign marketers. In general, those who fail to do a 'comparative' analysis to detect similarities and/or differences are more prone to extend home marketing practices to the new markets. Such an extension may affect the future success of the firm unfavorably when differences outweigh the similarities. At the host market (or industry) level, however, the extended strategy (new to the host country) may require a new set of changes. These may not be compatible with the environment, and hence cause more harm than benefit.

Two cases were examined in terms of implications and applicability. Because of the diversity of international marketing environments, firms with a low degree of adaptability will face difficulties in their international marketing endeavors. Should they not alter their low adaptiveness, they would find that dissimilar markets (as compared to those at home) are unacceptable. Above all, the fast pace of evolving markets would expose them to the risk of environmental incompatibility – even when they decide to enter into a similar market. In due time, the difficulty of international marketing operations forces them to retreat to their home markets. This reinforces their original home (domestic) orientation. In the face of crumbling tariff and other protective barriers, however, they will find no refuge in their previously safe home markets. Their home market may have already been invaded by other international marketers.

Those firms, however, which are not constrained, are prepared for diversity and are ready to accommodate change by adapting their policies, will experience higher success-rates in international markets. This in turn may lead to further orientation toward multi-environments and high adaptability to variations. Such an orientation may take the firm to highly volatile, different, and rapidly changing but profitable environments. They will not lose their home market at the cost of expanding into international markets, and their varied experiences may improve their international and domestic marketing. Their customers will benefit as well.

## Notes

1. Douglas and Dubois (1977) dealt with some of the social and cultural dimensions of several European countries in their paper. Before doing so, however, they presented a framework for the analysis of marketing behavior in a cultural setting. They showed, for example, how advertizing for two products (i.e. Omega watches and the Renault 5 car) had to be adapted for the apparent cultural differences in different countries.

2. Wadinambiartchi studied the relationship between the channels of distribution and stages of economic development in eight countries: Japan, Brazil, Venezuela, Puerto Rico, Turkey, Egypt, India and Tropical Africa. He reported that the relationship 'appears to be well-founded'. In his study, however, he also reports that the marketing institutions and their activities seem to be highly reflective of their environments in terms of social, cultural and economic dimension of the societies. In that regard, this study is a contribution to 'comparative' marketing.

3. Goodnow and Hansz examined the relationship between entry strategy into overseas country markets and environmental gradients in different countries. They used Litvak's and Banting's (1968) 'temperature gradient' for those countries. Their study reveals that there is a perceived relationship between the environment and the strategy selected. Fifty-nine environmental characteristics for 100 countries were inputed into a hierarchial grouping procedure which divided them into 16 'hot' countries, 34 'moderate' countries and 50 'cold' countries. The strategy profile for hot countries gravitated toward high degree of involvement and commitment, high amount of allocated resources and longer time perspective. The strategy profile for 'cold' countries conveyed the opposite. Hence, for 'hot' countries which are much more similar to the US than other countries, US firms' perception was that they had more control over the operation (including marketing) and hence were willing to invest more than otherwise. The implicit suggestion of entry strategy, environmental correspondence, and its relationship with that of the home environment is an interesting result.

4. Seth's and Sethi's theory of cross-cultural consumer behavior still remains untested. They advocate a better understanding of consumer behavior on an international basis. Such a theory or understanding can provide the necessary foundations for systematic development in international and comparative marketing, and its absence can only contribute to confusion and incomparability.

5. Shimuguchi's and Lazer's is an excellent study for it sheds light on Japanese channels of distribution. These remain highly ineffective, inefficient and expensive by Western standards. In some cases they act as a 'barrier' instead of contribution to the smooth movement of goods and services, and in that regard they are puzzling. The authors' environmentally oriented analysis of channel behavior provides a clear perspective that would not have been possible without environmental content.

6. Boddeweyn argues that any comparison, so long as it reveals new information, is valuable. He cites several examples (see Boddewyn, 1981, p. 62). The argument presented here is not in favor of or against journalistic reporting of any given phenomenon in two or more markets. It is a necessary guideline for description to avoid inappropriate reporting and the conveying of misleading impressions or incomplete information (without context).

7. The above review of the literature is a selected portion of published research in comparative marketing studies. For a more comprehensive review of the literature, see Boddewyn (1982), and Barksdale and Anderson (1982).

8. Green and White addressed four specific but interrelated issues in cross-cultural research. They are: (i) functional equivalence of the phenomena under

study; (ii) the cross-cultural equivalence of concepts; (iii) research-instrument equivalence; and (iv) equivalence in connotation as well as denotation of the research instrument after translation into different languages. See Green and White (1976, pp. 81–5).

9. Several different terminologies are commonly used in the literature. A degree of hierarchy is implied. For example, marketing 'strategy' refers to the *ex ante* statement of marketing activities at the firm level. Marketing 'process' usually refers to a higher level of aggregation than the firm level – i.e. industry level. Marketing 'system' still refers to a higher level of aggregation than that of the industry. It refers to the entire marketing system of a country. This paper adheres to the above terminology.

10. In Bartels's original paper, 'A' denoted marketing process. In Jaffe's extension, however 'A' denotes marketing system. It is not entirely clear whether Jaffe's terminology refers to the identical marketing activities with the same level of aggregation, or whether there is a true difference between Bartels's marketing process and Jaffe's marketing system. See Etemad (1981) for further discussion.

11. Ansoff (1969) and Ackoff (1974) originated and expanded the suggestion that all 'stake holders' should be included in a firm's environment. They characterized environment by including all stakeholders and accounting for their potential influences. Such a definition of an environment is task oriented, and its degree of complexity is directly related to the complexity (or simplicity) of the task at hand.

12. If the relationship between the technical aspects of marketing (AT) and the technical components of the environment in a given country ($C^{it}$) is characterized by $AT = f[C^{it}]$ then $AT \cdot (C^{it})^{-1}$ will symbolize the degree of correspondence in that country. Theoretically, and barring measurement problems, the degree of correspondence can be compared across countries (i.e. $AT \cdot (C^{it})^{-1}$ vs $BT \cdot (D^{it})^{-1}$). Symbolically, a general comparison would be $[AT \cdot (C^{it})^{-1}]_j$ vs $[AT \cdot (C^{it})^{-1}]_k$ vs $[AT \cdot (C^{it})^{-1}]_N$ vs ...

# References

Ackoff, R. *Redesigning the Future*, John Wiley & Sons, New York, 1974

Ansoff, Igor *Corporate Strategy*, McGraw-Hill, New York, 1969

Arndt, John 'Temporal Lags in Comparative Retailing', *Journal of Marketing, 36*, October 1972, 40–5

Baldwin, K.D.S. *The Marketing of Cocoa in Western Nigeria with Special Reference to the Position of the Middleman*, Oxford University Press, London, 1954

Barksdale, H.C. and Anderson, McTier 'Comparative Marketing: A Program for the Future', *Journal of Macromarketing*, Fall 1982, 52–8

Barnes, W.N. 'International Marketing Indicators', *Journal of European Marketing*, vol. 14, no. 2, 1980, 90–136

Bartels, Robert (ed.) *Comparative Marketing: Wholesaling in Fifteen Countries*, Irwin, Homewood, Ill., 1963

—— 'Are Domestic and International Marketing Dissimilar?' *Journal of Marketing*, July 1968, 56–61

Bauer, P.T. 'The Economics of Marketing Reform', *Journal of Political Economy*, vol. LXII, June 1954, 210–35

Boddewyn, Jean 'A Construct for Comparative Marketing Research', *Journal of Marketing Research*, vol. 3, May 1966, 149–53

—— *Comparative Management and Marketing*, Scott, Foresman and Co., Glenview, Ill., 1969

—— 'The Comparative Approach to the Study of Business Administration', *Academy of Management Journal*, vol. 8, December 1969

—— 'Comparative Marketing: The First Twenty Five Years', *Journal of International Business Studies*, Spring/Summer 1981, 61–79

—— and Hollander, S.C. (eds) *Public Policy Toward Retailing: An International Symposium*, Lexington Books, Lexington, Mass., 1972

—— and Nath, R. 'Comparative Management Studies: An Assessment', *Management International Review*, vol. 10, no. 1, 1970, 3–5

Bonnen, J.T., Eigher, C.K. and Schmid, A.A. 'Marketing in Economic Development', in V.L. Sorenson (ed.), *Agricultural Market Analysis*, East Lansing, Michigan, 1964, pp. 35–8

Boulding, K. and Singh, Pritam 'The Role of Price Structure in Economic Development', *Economic Review*, vol. LII, May 1962, 28–38

Brislin, R.W., Lornner, W.J. and Thorndike, R.M. *Cross Cultural Research Methods*, John Wiley & Sons, New York, 1973

Buxton, Graham 'The Role of Comparative Analysis Approach in Social Marketing', *European Journal of Marketing*, vol. 7, no. 1, 1973, 57 ff

Carman, J. and March, R.M. 'How Important For Marketing Are Cultural Differences Between Similar Nations?' *Australian Marketing Researcher*, vol. 3, no. 1, Summer 1979, 5–20

Carson, David 'Present State of Art of Comparative Marketing', in Thomas Greer (ed.), *Increasing Marketing Productivity and Conceptual and Methodological Foundations of Marketing*, AMA, 1973 Combined Proceedings Series, no. 35, 1974, pp. 67–70

Cox, Reavis 'The Search for Universals in Comparative Studies of Domestic Marketing Systems', in Peter D. Bennett (ed.), *Marketing and Economic Development*, American Marketing Association, 1965

Cundiff, E.W. 'Concepts in Comparative Retailing', *Journal of Marketing*, vol. 29, January 1965, 59–63

Demetrescu, M.C. 'Comparative Marketing Systems-Conceptual Outline', in Done Izraeli *et al.* (eds), *Marketing Systems for Developing Countries*, John Wiley & Sons, New York, 1976, pp. 111–17

Dholakia, N. and Firat, F.A. 'The Role of Marketing in the Development of Nonmarket Sectors and Condition Necessary for Success', in Israeli *et al.* (eds), *Marketing Systems for Developing Countries*, John Wiley and Sons, New York, 1976, pp. 50–62

—— and Dholakia, R. 'Marketing and Newer Theories of Development', a paper presented at American Marketing Association 1982 Annual Meetings, Chicago, Ill., 1982

Douglas, S.P. 'Patterns and Parallels of Marketing Structure in Several Countries', MSU Business Topics, Spring 1971, pp. 38–48

—— and Dobois, B. 'Looking at the Cultural Environment for International Marketing Opportunities', *Columbia Journal of World Business*, Winter 1977, 102–8

—— and Urban, C.D. 'Life Style Analysis to Profile Women in International Markets', *Journal of Marketing*, July 1977, 46–54

—— and. Wind, Y. 'Environmental Factors and Marketing Practices', *European Journal of Marketing*, vol. 7, no. 3, 1977, 46–54

Drucker, P. 'Marketing and Economic Development', *Journal of Marketing*, January 1958, 252–9

Ehrenberg, A.S.C. and Goodhart, G.J. 'A Comparison of American and British Repeat Buying Habits', *Journal of Marketing Research*, vol. 5, 1968, 20–34

El-Ansary, A.I. and Liebrenz, M. 'A Multistage Approach to Comparative Marketing Analysis', *Journal of Macromarketing*, Fall 1982, 59–65

Etemad, H. 'Are Domestic and International Marketing Dissimilar? A Reexamination and Extension', *1981 ASAC-IB Proceedings*, ASAC Halifax, Nova Scotia, 1981
—— 'Marketing: The Catalyst in Economic Development Process', a paper presented at the Seventh Annual Macro-Marketing Seminar, College of Business Administration, University of Colorado, Boulder, Colorado, August 1982
Firat, A.F. and Dholakia, N. 'Consumption Choices at the Macro Level', *Journal of Macro Marketing*, Fall 1982, 6–15
Fisher, Allen 'Marketing Structure and Economic Development: Comment', *Quarterly Journal of Economics*, vol. LXVIII, February 1954, 151–4
Fisk, George *Marketing System: An Introductory Analysis*, Harper & Row, New York, 1967
Goldman, W.I. 'A Cross Cultural Comparison of the Soviet and American Consumer', in Reed Moyer (ed.), *Changing Marketing Systems*, 1967 Winter Conference Proceedings, American Marketing Association, Washington, DC, 1967, 195 ff
Goodnow, J.D. and Hansz, J.E. 'Environmental Determinants Overseas Market Entry Strategies', *Journal of International Business Studies*, Spring 1972, 33–50
Green, R.T. and White, P.D. 'Methodological Considerations in Cross-National Consumer Research', *Journal of International Business Studies*, Fall/Winter 1976, 81–7
Hall, M., Knapp, J. and Winston, C. *Distribution in Great Britain and North America*, Oxford University Press, London, 1961
Haring, Robert C. 'Marketing in Economic Growth in Alaska', in Peter D. Bennette (ed.), *Marketing and Economic Development*, Proceedings of 1965 Fall Conference of American Marketing Association, 1965, pp. 38–43
Harris, C., Still, R. and Grask, M. 'A Comparison of Australian and U.S. Marketing Strategies', *Columbia Journal of World Business*, Summer 1978, 87–94
Holt, R. and Turner, J.E. (eds) *The Methodology of Comparative Research*, Free Press, New York, 1970
Holton, R. 'Marketing Structure and Economic Development', *Quarterly Journal of Economics*, August 1953, 344–61
Holton, Richard 'Marketing Policies in Multinational Corporations', *Journal of International Business Studies*, Summer 1970, 1–20
Jaffe, Eugene D. 'A Flow Approach to Comparative Study of Marketing Systems', in J. Boddewyn (ed.), *Comparative Management and Marketing*, Scott Foresman & Co., Glenview, Ill., 1969
—— 'Comparative Marketing Revisited', *Marketing Business Review*, Winter 1976, 143–53
—— 'Are Domestic and International Marketing Dissimilar? An Assessment', *Management International Review*, vol. 20, no. 3, 1980, 83–6
Jeffreys, J.B. and Knee, D. *Retailing in Europe: Present Structure and Future Trends*, Macmillan, London, 1962
Kelejian, H.R. and Oates, W.E. *Introduction to Econometrics, Principles and Applications*, Harper and Row, New York, 1974
Kmenta, J. *Elements of Econometrics*, Macmillan Co., New York, 1971
Liander, Bertil *et al. Comparative Analysis for International Marketing*, Allyn and Bacon, Boston, Mass., 1967
Litvak, I.A. and Banting, P. 'A Conceptual Framework for International Business Arrangements', in Robert L. King (ed.), *Marketing and the New Science of Planning*, 1968 American Marketing Association Fall Conference Proceedings, AMA, Chicago, Ill., 1968

Mentzer, J. and Samli, A.D. 'A Model for Marketing In Economic Development', *Columbia Journal of World Business*, Fall 1981, 91–101

McNair, M.P., Teele, S.F. and Mulhean, F.G. *Distribution Cost – An International Digest*, Harvard Business School, Boston, 1941

Miller, C.J. (ed.) *Marketing and Economic Development*, University of Nebraska Press, Lincoln, Nebraska, 1967

Nagashima, A. 'A Comparison of Japanese and US Attitudes Toward Foreign Products', *Journal of Marketing*, vol. 34, 1970, 68–74

—— 'A Comparative Model in Product Image Survey Among Japanese Businessmen', *Journal of Marketing*, vol. 41, no. 3, July 1977, 95–100

Pindyck, R. and Rubinfeld, D.L. *Econometric Models and Economic Forecasts*, McGraw-Hill, New York, 1976

Riley, H. *et al.*, 'Food Marketing in Economic Development of Puerto Rico', Chapter 4. Michigan State University, East Lansing, July 1970

Sethi, S.P. and Etemad, H. 'Marketing: The Missing Link in Economic Development', in Jerald Hampton and A. Van Gent (eds), *Marketing Aspects of International Business*, Nijhoff Publishing, Boston, 1984, pp. 95–117

Shapiro, S.H. 'Comparative Marketing and Economic Development', in G. Schartz (ed.), *Science in Marketing*, John Wiley & Sons, New York, 1965, pp. 398–429

Sherbini, Abdel Aziz 'Marketing in the Industrialisation of Under-developed Countries', *Journal of Marketing*, vol. XXIX, January 1965, 28–32

Sheth, J.N. and Sethi, S.P. 'A Theory of Cross Cultural Buyer Behaviour', in A.G. Woodside, J.N. Sheth and P.D. Bennett (eds), *Consumer and Industrial Buyer Behaviour*, North-Holland, NY, 1977

Shimaguchi, M. and Lazer, William 'Japanese Distribution Channels: Invisible Barriers to Market Entry', *MSU Business Topics*, Winter 1979, 49–62

Slater, Charles, C. 'The Role of Food Marketing in Latin American Economic Development', in Peter D. Bennett (ed.), *Marketing and Economic Development*, Proceedings of the 1965 Fall Conference of the American Marketing Association, American Marketing Association, Chicago, 1965, pp. 30–7

—— 'A Catalyst for Development', in D. Israeli *et al.* (eds), *Marketing Systems for Developing Countries*, John Wiley & Sons, New York, 1976, pp. 3–18

—— 'A Theory of Market Processes', in *Macro Marketing: A Distributive Process for A Social Perspective*, Graduate School of Business Administration, University of Colorado, Boulder, 1977, 117–40

Sommers, M. and J. Kernan 'Why Products Flourish Here, Fizzle There', *Columbia Journal of World Business*, Winter 1977, 53–64

Terpstra, Vern *International Marketing*, Dryden Press, Hinsdale, Ill., 1978

Urban, C.D. 'A Cross-National Comparison of Consumer Media Use Pattern', *Columbia Journal of World Business*, Winter 1977, 53–64

Van Raaij, W.F. 'Cross Cultural Research Methodology as a Case of Construct Validity', in H.K. Hunt (ed.), *Advances in Consumer Research*, vol. 5, Association for Consumer Research, Ann Arbor, Michigan, 1978, 693–701

Wadinambiaratchi, George 'Channels of Distribution in Developing Economies', • *Business Quarterly*, Winter 1965, 74–82

Wind, Y. and Douglas, S. 'On the Meaning of Comparison: A Methodology for Cross Cultural Studies', *Quarterly Journal of Management Development*, vol. 2, no. 4, June 1971, 108–10

—— and —— 'Environmental Factors and Marketing Practices', *European Journal of Marketing*, vol. 7, no. 3, 1973, 155–65

—— and Perlmutter, H. 'On the Identification of Frontier Issues in Multi-national Marketing', *Columbia Journal of World Business*, 1977, 131–9

—— and Douglas, S. 'Comparative Methodology and Marketing Theory', in

C.W. Lamb Jr. and D.M. Dunne (eds), *Theoretical Developments in Marketing*, American Marketing Association, Chicago, 1980
—— and Douglas, S. 'Comparative Consumer Research: The Next Frontier', *European Journal of Marketing*, June 1981

# 13 STATE ENTERPRISES: A MARKETING PERSPECTIVE

## Durariraj Maheswaran

### What is a State-owned Enterprise?

Hanson (1965) defines a state-owned enterprise (SOE) as 'state ownership and operation of industrial, agricultural, financial and commercial enterprises'. Fernandes (1980) provides an elaborate definition:

> a public enterprise is an organisation, wholly or by a majority publicly owned, engaged in economic activities with the sphere of agriculture, industry, commerce or services, involving investment and returns. They should also be involved in selling goods or services and whose affairs are capable of being stated in terms of balance sheets and profit and loss accounts.

Most LDCs have adopted a pattern of mixed economy, where both private as well as state resources are utilized for development; there is both public and private ownership and use of resources. The mix of the public and private capital and ownership varies from country to country. The economic policy is often shaped by the political and historical circumstances, and the relative importance of the two sectors determined accordingly. In general, most of the LDCs in Latin America place a large emphasis on the private sector for economic development, while the Afro-Asian LDCs resort to state intervention to shape the process of development.

It has been observed that even within a system of mixed economy, state ownership may range from a minority participation, direct or through financial institutions, to exclusive ownership and control by statute. The degree of government control assumes importance since the priorities of the organizations and the business orientation of the firms vary, depending on the government's role in administration.

## Why Does the State Decide to Set Up SOEs?

There are many reasons why the state decides to set up public enterprises, and these reasons can be broadly classified into the following three categories: ideological, economic rationale, and historical.

### Ideological Reasons

The ideological arguments concerning the merits of public enterprise are often based on the ownership of property (Carey-Jones, 1974). It is often centered around the question of the accrued benefits from private or state ownership of property. In most LDCs public ownership is preferred to private control because of the ideological considerations of the perceived benefits of a socialistic pattern of society. There are different levels of ideological patterns that determine the extent and degree of state participation in economic development.

The socialist countries of the East European bloc adopted a policy of state control of the means of production as the sole method of industrial development. Countries like India, Burma and many in the Arab bloc highlight the role of the state in core sectors, viz, power, oil, mass transportation, etc. Cyprus, Korea and many Latin American countries believe that the role of the public sector is to help the private sector grow, at least a complementary role in a predominantly private-sector-owned industrial sector. In short, there is no LDC in which a dominant ideological pattern does not shape the structure of industrial development, determine the relative importance and mix of the ownership, and set the guidelines for economic development.

Nationalization is conceptually similar to ideological motivation for setting up public enterprises. In most of the LDCs, after independence, many state enterprises have been set up by nationalizing private foreign investments. Egypt nationalized foreign-owned enterprises following the Suez war. Indonesia resorted to nationalization of large Dutch companies to consolidate Sukharno's political interests. In Sri Lanka the insurance industry was nationalized to stop large-scale remittance of potential development funds abroad. While the driving force behind nationalization appears to be consolidation of political or economic power, there seem to be underlying ideological considerations for decisions to establish public enterprises to replace foreign investment.

### Reasons of Economic Rationale

State intervention has long since been an effective economic measure in the hands of the governments of many LDCs. They are primarily used to restructure the economy and exercise control over the growth of the economy. In certain cases government control and takeover is needed to revitalize ailing privately owned units and to prevent their closing down. Many socialistically inclined governments prefer to use public ownership as an instrument to gain control of economic resources and monitor the growth of basic industries, viz. banking, insurance, utilities, etc. A number of the Third World countries like Tanzania, Ghana, Nigeria, etc. have resorted to state control of an economy that has essentially been controlled by foreign investors.

The major economic reasons that motivate the creation of state enterprises are:

(1) To spearhead the industrial growth by providing the capital needed for heavy industries, and making available other economic input and infrastructure which could not be mobilized by the private investors.

(2) To reduce the dependence on imports, regulate raw-material exports, develop indigenous substitutes for imported industrial goods, and to foster self-sufficiency and self reliance.

(3) To restructure economic development and monitor the growth in line with ideological considerations and national policies.

(4) To promote uniform development in the socio-cultural and geographical spheres by initiating projects that do not attract private investors, viz. development of backward areas, underprivileged groups, etc.

(5) To effectively utilize the surplus inputs like land and labor by efficient allocation of scarce resources, viz. capital and foreign exchange.

(6) To provide a better standard of living by establishing standards in wages, prices and quality.

(7) In many import-dependent economies as well as socialistic economies, state enterprises are often geared towards earning much-needed foreign exchange.

The Indian Industrial Resolution (Industrial Policy Resolution of India, 1956) states that all industries of basic and strategic importance or in the nature of public utility services should be in the public sector. The Korean guidelines on the other hand emphasize the role of the private sector in economic development. The role of state enterprises will be one of controlling private investment to protect public welfare.

Joint ventures are another means of fostering economic development through the limited participation of the public enterprises. Usually the state encourages foreign investors to collaborate in many key areas to facilitate technology transfer, foster high-risk industries as well as to monitor foreign interests. Countries like Ghana and Zambia have a stipulation that all foreign investment in the key sectors should have the state as a partner. Many governments in LDCs prefer foreign investors to collaborate with the state so as to effectively control the sensitive problem of tradeoff between the social and developmental objectives of the host country and the profitability goals of the foreign investors.

*Historical Reasons*

Most of the LDCs, before their independence, were colonies of developed nations. Most of the investment was controlled by foreign investors and the indigenous entrepreneurship was a rare commodity during colonial periods. Many governments had no option but to take over control of industry as an *ad hoc* emergency measure after independence. While this was conceived as a short-term measure, as the enterprises continued being state owned over a significant period of time a strong inertia developed that kept them permanently as public enterprises. This phenomenon was more pronounced in countries like Chile, Ecuador, etc. with an unstable political climate. The public enterprise then became an instrument of political power in the hands of subsequent regimes.

A country might establish its first refinery or heavy industry in the public sector because of lack of a competent private sector. However, this firm might continue to be controlled by the state even after many years — even when strong and competent private capabilities have developed. This is a widely observed phenomenon in countries like India, Singapore, etc.

## Classification of State-owned Enterprises

Many classification attempts have been made to group the SOEs under broad categories and Friedman (1951) classifies them as:

1. Industrial or commercial corporations
2. Social service corporations
3. Supervisory or regulatory corporations

Griffith and Street (1963) suggest that public corporations be

Table 13.1: The Portfolio Framework

| Market growth | Market share | |
|---|---|---|
| | High | Low |
| High | D | C |
| Low | B | A |

divided as:

1. Managerial economic bodies
2. Managerial social bodies
3. Regulatory social bodies

Zif (1983) suggests a classification scheme placing the public enterprises along a continuum with 'business orientation' at one end of the scale and 'political orientation' at the other. Business orientation of SOEs entails functional management of the enterprise adhering to commercial norms and goals. Political orientation refers to the establishment of coordination and harmony between the enterprise and powerful public groups.

Capon (1981) advances a portfolio model to classify both private and public corporations. This classification using market share and market growth as the criteria variables is illustrated in Table 13.1. The private corporations considered for cell entry are typically individual units, and the state corporations are relatively undiversified whole enterprises. The relevant market used for the business unit is the environment considered.

Two general propositions are advanced by Capon:

(1) The SOEs and private corporations have widely differing objectives. These differences are a function of the relative portfolio positions of the business concerned.
(2) Private enterprises are established across all the four matrix cells while SOEs are often concentrated in low-growth areas.

The following is a fairly comprehensive scheme of classification based on autonomy and control provided by Dias (1976):

(1) *Departmental Undertakings* These are essentially government departments headed by a minister. The Cabinet and the Parliament exercise full control over this department through the minister. This is

a rather unwieldy arrangement for a public corporation, since it is totally controlled by government and functioning according to market conditions is ruled out. Due to excessive control it is also incapable of adopting commercial trade practices or swift decision-making.

(2) *Quasi Corporation* This is an extension of the government department. It retains the same degree of government control but the crucial difference lies in the hierarchy. The decision-making is entrusted to an autonomous board, established as a corporate body. It should be noted that this board is autonomous within government guidelines.

(3) *Public Corporation* This emerged as a tradeoff between autonomy and control. It has a statutory entity, separate from the state as well as management. It is wholly owned by the state, but the state intervention in its management is minimal. It is managed by an autonomous board and the executives are not necessarily public servants. Since the public corporation is established by legislation, any structural changes require legislative approval.

(4) *Mixed Corporations* These are public corporations that allow the participation of private capital. However, the state retains control of the corporation in the policy and developmental spheres. The transfer of shares, voting rights and extent of equity participation are strictly controlled by the state.

(5) *Government Companies* These are essentially a majority state-owned enterprise. The state controls at least 51 percent of the shares either through direct participation or through financial institutions. This provides opportunity for both small and large investors in the private sector to participate in the company's operations. It has the flexibility of the private enterprise, since the necessary changes in structure and organization need not be approved by government legislation. It permits the creation of a separate commercial body, and thereby provides the opportunity to adopt commercial practices. It provides adequate autonomy for the management and has a management style akin to the private sector. There are no restrictions on the transfer of shares, limitation on the number of shareholders and the hiring of executives from outside the organization.

(6) *Mixed Companies* These are forms of organization where the government is a minority participant. It combines both public and private ownership and control. While it has the advantages of both public and private-sector resource utilization in terms of capital and management talent, problems often arise regarding distribution of power, functions and controls. Dual participation in management of the public as well as private sector managers often leads to conflict that undermines efficiency.

*Operating Contracts* are a collaboration of the state with private organizations. The state may retain full ownership or partial ownership, but leaves the management to the private organization. The state enters into contract with a private organization which has total control over organizational policies and day-to-day affairs. This has a number of shortcomings and is rarely used.

Another form of the mixed company is the joint stock company, where the state is a minority participant and provides a part of the capital while the majority of the capital is raised by public issue and private investment. The management is entrusted to the private shareholders, and policy decisions are taken independent of state interference.

## How Extensive are the SOEs?

State ownership has always been a major factor in the economic development of the LDCs. While the extent of state participation in economic development varies across different countries, the need for state participation in shaping the economy of LDCs has clearly been established. Thus, an economy may be oriented predominantly to private ownership with the state playing a supplementary role, or an economy may be oriented more towards public enterprise, relegating private participation to a secondary position.

The extent of state participation in different countries varies considerably.

### Korea

Korean public enterprises have an output-market concentration. In 1972 76 percent of the value added was in markets that had imperfect competition environment, viz. monopoly, monopsony, bilateral monopoly, etc. They are essentially in highly concentrated industries like mining and manufactured goods. The Korean economy has about eleven high-capital-oriented sectors. Public enterprises monopolize four of these sectors, and have a high market share in another six sectors. It was also observed that the public enterprises are more dominant in non-export-oriented industries. Virtually all industries that are large relative to product and factor markets, and capital intensive, have high forward linkages, and are in the public sector.

## *Venezuela*

In Venezuela, of the gross fixed investment 55 percent is from private enterprise and 45 percent from the government. Government ownership extends to the following industries: telephone, telegraph, water supply, iron ore and steel. One of the two domestic airlines is owned by the government. In the non-essential sector the government also owns a hotel chain.

## *Cyprus*

The public sector in Cyprus is entrusted with the role of helping to develop the private sector. The SOEs play a multidimensional role by regulating, supplementing and reinforcing the private sector in economic development. The government participates in development by means of semi-government agencies. The public sector is essentially small, day-to-day management being controlled by autonomous boards. These public-sector enterprises show a considerable flexibility and autonomy compared to other SOEs in most of the LDCs.

## *Malaysia*

Malaysia has a long tradition of public enterprises. In 1948 the Malayan railways were formed to control rail transport. When Malaysia gained independence in 1957, there were already about 29 public enterprises. After independence the Malayan government extensively promoted public enterprises as a means of redistributing economic power, and by 1972 there were as many as 15 new public enterprises. Many of those established in Malaysia are of recent creation, and are geared towards implementing the National Economic Policy of eradicating poverty and restructuring the Malaysian society to correct economic imbalances. State enterprises have been established to run commercial and industrial activities. Specialized institutions like PERNAS have been established to train personnel for the finance, banking and commercial advisory services, marketing schemes and research. The National Electricity board has been especially geared towards providing rural electrification (Herbert, 1976).

## *Sri Lanka*

Sri Lanka has shown a preference for public enterprises since independence. Successive governments have continued to use public corporations as a means for economic development. A public enterprise may be a public corporation established by a law of legislature, or an ordinary company incorporated under the companies' ordinance, with the state having an interest (not necessarily a controlling one). By 1973 there were as many as 84 public corporations and statutory boards totally controlled by the state. The SOEs are often found in sectors with monopoly characteristics such as rail transport, to cultural and educational fields (universities, science councils, etc.), the defense sector, and industries that need heavy capital outlay, for example, Air Lanka (Sanmuganathan, 1976).

## Bangladesh

The industrial sector of Bangladesh, was dominated by West Pakistan entrepreneurs before the country's liberation. When they left the government resorted to total nationalization, and this has created a large number of small and consumer-oriented SOEs. These are ineffectively managed and scattered across the country. Due to the lack of private entrepreneurship these industries continue to be controlled by the state.

## India

The Industrial Policy Resolution of 1956 has laid down the guidelines for public-sector participation. The Industries are classified into three categories:

(1) *Schedule A* This covers industries to be developed by the state exclusively. These include all basic industries like iron and steel, coal, mineral oils, etc. and industries of strategic importance, viz. arms and ammunition, aircraft and shipbuilding, and atomic energy.
(2) *Schedule B* This consists of industries that will be progressively state owned and in which the state will generally take the initiative of establishing new industries. The private sector, however, will supplement the effort of the state, viz. chemicals and fertilizers, petroleum and petrochemicals, heavy industries, etc.
(3) The remaining sectors are open to the private sector.

In 1975 India had about 129 public enterprises with a total investment of Rs 72,610 million (Raj, 1978). These undertakings were in almost all fields of activity. The major functional areas were (i) finance, (ii) transport, (iii) communication, (iv) marketing, and (v) utilities. Electricity and other utilities including power are also controlled by the government. Transportation, including railroad, air and sea are predominantly or exclusively state owned. Public services like post and telegraph service, and food distribution are in the control of the state.

*Indonesia*

Public enterprises in Indonesia have a history reaching as far back as 1925, when the Dutch East Indies administration established them. When Indonesia was still under colonial rule most of the agricultural (primary) and natural-resource-oriented industries were state owned. There were about twenty industries in the areas of salt, soda, tin and plantations. In the 1950s the Sukharno government nationalized all Dutch companies. This move was both politically and economically motivated and the state acquired exclusive control over the economic sector. Present government policy is one of moderation in state ownership as opposed to the extreme nationalization policies of Sukharno. Currently, the SOEs play a pivotal role in the economic development, controlling key sectors like transportation, communications, utilities and heavy industries. They also produce most of the country's mineral ore, coal, oil, etc. State enterprises are also involved in banking and insurance. It is estimated that there are about 149 totally state-controlled enterprises in a wide variety of fields (Prasetya and Hamilton, 1976).

The extent of state participations is highlighted by the 1978 *Fortune* (1979) list of the largest 500 corporations outside the USA. The 34 from LDCs were all state owned.

In Brazil the three largest corporations, and in Mexico two of the three largest are state owned. The developing country SOEs that have established a name outside the country are Petrobas (oil) and CVRD (mining) of Brazil, the National Iranian Oil Co. and Engineering Project of India Ltd (Gillis, 1980).

## Objectives of State-owned Enterprises

SOEs, unlike purely commercial enterprises, have multiple objectives ranging from social benefits to surplus generation. The combination of these objectives varies, depending on the type of industry or the nature of economic and political environment in which the enterprises are operating. However, the underlying motives and general guiding principles of the SOEs are uniform across countries and across industries.

The objectives of the SOEs could be broadly classified into three categories:

    (a)  Commercial goals
    (b)  Socio-political goals
    (c)  Economic goals

## Commercial Goals

Most of the LDCs are faced with inadequate capital formation for re-investment in priority sectors. They rely essentially on foreign capital and other external sources of revenue. Internal revenue, scarce to begin with, is often controlled by private groups which do not reinvest the earnings in accordance with the needs of society. So often SOEs are created with the objective of creating surplus for reinvestment and earning precious foreign exchange. SOEs have to be effectively and efficiently managed so as to generate profits and surpluses.

## Socio-Political Goals

Public enterprises are committed to providing *public services* which enhance the 'quality of life' for society. Societal welfare deals in terms of creation of opportunities for education, social mobility, employment and other aspects of public welfare, essentially to ensure that the basic needs of the people are satisfied efficiently.

## Economic Goals

The economic objective is essentially to restructure the economy and thereby accelerate the growth of the economy. SOEs are used as economic instruments to redistribute income and efficient utilization of economic inputs, viz. land, capital and labor. SOEs also help stimulate growth by providing infrastructure for the private sector to grow. The industrial-development goals of SOEs in the manufacturing sector depend on the existing policy of the government regarding private sectors. The various possible alternatives are:

(1) To establish joint-sector enterprises in collaboration with the private sector.
(2) To undertake operations in sectors that are left unexplored by private sectors due to lack of capital or returns.
(3) To phase out private sectors by restricting their entry and nationalization of key or strategic sectors.
(4) To help private sector enterprises by providing scarce raw materials, efficient allocation, etc.

State enterprises may be created to provide local partners for foreign investors. In Indonesia, for example, foreign banks which operate in areas of resource mobilization and merchant banking cannot do so without collaborating with state-owned banks.

In some of the fairly industrialized countries, SOEs are often created in sectors where private enterprises are well established. This helps to stimulate competition, thereby improving operational efficiency and reducing costs of production. This is also motivated by economic considerations, like diversifying the sources of national income and government revenues and to stabilize prices.

The scope of public enterprise in any country is a function of the nature of the development program the government envisages for the country. The emphasis may be placed on developing the existing agricultural sector with industrial development being accorded a secondary role. The manufacturing sector may be geared to providing infrastructure facilities rather than for directly productive purposes. The industrial sector may be restructured to emphasize the growth of heavy industries or light/small industries.

In most of the LDCs the colonial pattern of SOE growth has emphasized infrastructural development and public utilities. In recent years international trade is being controlled by SOEs to regulate foreign-exchange earnings. This helps in price stabilization for many primary-product exporting countries. In the internal economy, public sectors are effectively used to stabilize prices and enhance public welfare.

However, there seems to be a general trend that most LDCs create SOEs with the objective of promoting development in terms of social benefits and strategic considerations, rather than with the primary objective of surplus generation.

**How Efficient are the SOEs?**

By whatever standard employed, state-owned enterprises now play a more critical role in the development process of a greater number of developing countries than do multinationals, and their relative importance is likely to grow in the future. (Gillis, 1980)

The growth of SOEs has been very spectacular during the last two decades. SOEs have contributed significantly to industrial production and development in countries like India, Sri Lanka, Nepal, Egypt and Turkey. State-owned enterprises control over 75 percent of non-agricultural investment in Bangladesh, Bolivia and Mexico. SOEs have contributed largely to the import-substitution and export-expansion programs in a number of LDCs and across a wide range of industries. Indigenous steel-making in India, Indonesia and South Korea has been effectively established in SOEs. The petrochemicals industries in Brazil,

Mexico and Venezuela are state owned, and all among the major contributors to the growth of the national economy of each of these countries. Shipbuilding and textiles are other areas in which the SOEs have done well in the developing countries (Ballance, Ansari and Singer, 1982).

Even in countries like Brazil, Pakistan and Cyprus, which are by philosophy the exponents of private-sector economy with private ownership and control of property, the role of the state owned enterprises has been pivotal. In many industries in these countries the SOEs have participated in stabilizing market conditions, generating funds for reinvestment, controlling prices, etc. It is also clear that the participation of SOEs is extremely necessary for growth and survival in many newly liberated African nations.

In the Indian context, the performance of the SOEs has been mixed. In some of the key sectors, viz. electricity, water supply, mining, etc., the economic efficiency of the SOEs has been far below expectations. The public sector has never succeeded in generating a reasonable surplus. Especially in the late 1960s the financial and economic performance of the public-sector enterprises, reflected in the return on investment to the enterprise or value added, has been very poor. In a survey of the SOEs conducted in India in the early 1970s it was concluded that, despite more than two decades of existence, many were still 'in the red' and operating at low levels of capacity utilization. Inefficient management and lack of planning were seen as the major problems (Raj, 1978). In recent years India has redefined her policy of managing SOEs to improve their efficiency and competitiveness by placing a higher emphasis on exports. Some of the public-sector undertakings have performed well since then (Ballance *et al.*, 1982).

Notable among the efficiently run and internationally successful SOEs are BHEL, which manufactures heavy machinery such as thermal reactors, transformers and compressors; HMT, which produces machine tools and a host of other consumer durables like watches, bulbs, etc.; and PEC, which manufactures and exports bicycle parts, textile machinery and tools. In the fields of construction and consultancy, many public-sector firms like Engineers India Ltd, Engineering Projects India Ltd, NBCC and MECON have done exceedingly well, and have successfully competed with international firms. Some of the SOEs have collaborated with Japanese multinationals to secure projects in the Middle East (*Public Enterprise Survey*, 1978-79).

Even though many of the large SOEs in the LDCs are monopolies operating natural-resource-based industries, their performance in generating savings for reinvestment has been dismal. Except for a few of them, most of the natural monopolies show huge operating losses. Pemes of Mexico and Timah of Indonesia show sizable profits in their operation. Natural-resource-based SOEs such as Comibol (tin) in Bolivia, Gecamines (cobalt and copper) in Zaire and CVRD (iron ore) in Brazil have made nominal operating profits. On the other hand, many of the natural monopolies like Turkey Petroleum of Turkey, Ecopetrol (oil) in Columbia, Petamina (petroleum) in Indonesia and Zambia Industrial and Mining are always in the red (Gillis, 1980).

In terms of general profitability, the performance of SOEs varies from country to country and also across industries. In countries like Egypt, Somalia, Ghana, Zambia and Turkey, the public sector is operating under chronic losses, thereby representing a major drain on the governmental resources. While the state corporations in Sri Lanka, Bangladesh, Sudan and Panama are not necessarily dependent on the government for their survival, their profit history is virtually non-existent. The performance of the public sector is mixed in countries like Brazil, Indonesia, Chile, Uruguay, Thailand and India. These economies are marked by chronically inefficient SOEs on one extreme and highly profitable, export-oriented SOEs on the other. Of the 41 largest state enterprises in Brazil, 14 showed net operating losses in 1977 (*Brazilian Business*, 1979). On the other hand, the export-oriented economies of Korea, Taiwan and Singapore have relatively profitable state sectors (Gillis, 1980).

It is seen that the performances of the SOEs during the last two decades have been mixed. There seems to be a trend that most large SOEs based on natural monopolies, in spite of their environmental advantages, perform far below expectations. However, the SOEs in the mixed sectors, competing with privately owned firms, are reasonably efficient and often more profitable.

Many explanations have been advanced for the relatively disappointing performance of state enterprises. They center essentially around two major issues (i) inefficient management and (ii) lack of planning. These issues are aggravated by the intervention of the state in the management of SOEs and the social accountability of the publicly owned corporations. An analysis of the contrast between the public sector and private-sector organization is undertaken in the next section to highlight the influence of these factors on public-sector performances.

**How Should the Marketing Function be Performed?**

State-owned enterprises have been set up for a variety of reasons. They operate under a wide range of economic and market conditions. The marketing policies and the relevant strategies to be followed by SOEs will also differ according to the type of industry and nature of competition. Different strategies need to be adopted for a 'public service' industry, a technologically advanced industry or an export-oriented industry. A SOE operating under monopolistic or quasi-monopolistic conditions will adopt a pricing policy based only on social objectives. It may not take into consideration future market share or demand estimates. If a SOE is in a market where it is forced to compete with private firms for market share, then its strategies and policies need to be comparable to the purely commercial enterprises. Renault is one of the four car manufacturers in France. Even though it is a SOE, its products are not especially low-priced or aimed at the lower-income target group. Its marketing mix and policies are indistinguishable from other commercial enterprises. Air Canada is a SOE, it operates in a market with other privately owned international airlines and domestic airlines, viz. Canadian Pacific. The marketing activities of Air Canada differ very little from other private airlines. It maintains a good level of in-flight service, offers competitive fares and carries out heavy promotion activities. Air India is another example of a SOE competing in a mixed market. Although these airlines have social commitments and receive government subsidies, they do not significantly alter their marketing mix. They are active competitors in the industry.

It is seen that the key determinant of the marketing strategies to be adopted is the nature of competition in the industry rather than the nature of ownership *per se*. However, in most mixed economies of the LDCs, the nature of ownership influences the priorities of the organization. In other words, marketing strategies will be determined by the interaction of two variables:

(1) nature of competition in the industry;
(2) priority of objectives — social or commercial.

The behavior of the firm differs depending on its position in the matrix shown in Table 13.2.

*Monopoly — Social Objectives (A)*

This is the classical position of many large SOEs in LDCs. Due to

Table 13.2: The Competition-objective Matrix

| Nature of Competition | Objectives Social | Priority Commercial |
|---|---|---|
| Monopoly | A | B |
| Competition | C | D |

ideological considerations and the policy of nationalization to protect scarce developmental funds being remitted abroad, many LDCs have created large monopolies that operate in this cell. The dominant objective of these SOEs is often the fulfillment of existing demand for economic goods and services. In India and Burma the core sectors, viz. power, water and transportation, have such monopolies.

The marketing mix to be adopted in a situation of this nature is discussed below.

(1) *Product Strategy* In the existing public enterprises, the 'form' utility of the product is decided by the state considering the available level of technology and skilled manpower, the level and nature of investment capital and the degree of sophistication of the consumed public. In most cases the type of product available is highly standardized, often based on utility considerations rather than appeal. Product differentiation is not encouraged. Provision of utilities follow this pattern. Public services like rural health services and educational programs also follow this pattern. The objective is to provide the minimum necessary levels of service to a large population. The emphasis is on satisfying as much demand as possible at a minimum cost.

(2) *Pricing Strategy* Under monopolistic conditions the public-sector units have the advantage of setting their prices. While this may be an acceptable strategy ideologically and politically, in the long run it may be economically unsound. The state enterprises normally adopt two kinds of pricing policies:

(a) social-benefit pricing
(b) cost pricing

*Social-benefit Pricing* This is a strategy of providing essential commodities and services at below the cost of production. The only consideration is the delivery of the product to satisfy the demand. The state often provides subsidies for the unit to continue producing. However, to make up the deficit, the state has to divert resources from other sectors. Most of these industries are in the nature of providing utilities. When their sales/extent of coverage increases, the state subsidy also has to grow proportionately. Eventually a stage will be reached when the unit can no longer be supported without reduction of quality and good will. Even from the management point of view, a perennially losing unit will be a bad example as it will undermine the morale of its workers. Lack of incentives and worker motivation will also lead to loss of efficiency. This in turn will be reflected in higher costs and higher subsidies. So a social-benefit pricing policy is, at best, problematic.

The pricing policy should be based on realistic estimates of social benefits derived. Quantification of perceived social costs can be undertaken, i.e. costs incurred in meeting social objectives, in order to provide a datum level for evaluation of costs over and above social costs ('Pricing Policies in Public Enterprises', 1980).

*Cost Pricing* This strategy fixes prices at the cost of production. While this may be in tune with the state's objective of promoting public welfare, it also suffers from the inherent weaknesses of social-benefit pricing. Most government monopolies have been found to operate with low efficiency, low quality and high operating costs. This is also enhanced by lack of incentives due to the non-profit emphasis of the organization (profit levels often decide incentive structures). The decrease in efficiency increases cost of production, resulting in higher prices to the public. In the long run, the public pays a higher price.

It is suggested that the government takes into consideration the following variables before adopting the pricing policies:

(i)   minimum levels of efficiency
(ii)  standard costs
(iii) minimum levels of capacity utilization
(iv)  quantification of social costs.

(3) *Promotional Strategies* Since the major emphasis is on social objectives, two types of communication strategies are in order: consumer relations and consumer education.

The promotional activities of the state should be in the nature of informing the public about the development and growth of the various core sectors. This is also necessary since state-owned enterprises are subject to greater public scrutiny and are ultimately accountable to the whole of society. Another aspect of the communication strategy should be marketing to the enterprise's own employees. This becomes important particularly when wage levels need to be kept motivated.

The consumer-education aspect assumes importance in LDCs where the level of consumer awareness and literacy are exceedingly low. If the SOEs provide goods which are considered desirable from the long-term point of view of society, then the consumers may have to be persuaded to use the product/services and also to do so effectively.

(4) *Channel Strategies* The basic objective of the channel decision is to minimize the total cost of the channel (Bucklin, 1966). The profit element should be eliminated in transferring goods from the production point to the consumers. This will rule out the participation of privately owned channel organizations. So the distribution needs to be retained by the government. The levels of the channel outputs, viz. market de-centralization, product differentiation, waiting time and lot size should be standardized and fixed at a level where the cost to the manufacturer is reduced (since an increased cost to the manufacturer will automatic-ally mean an increased cost to the consumer). Since the criterion is to increase the coverage rather than the depth of the usage, minimum levels of output will be in line with the policies of the government. In some cases the state may 'demarket' the product usage by fixing limits to usage or making access difficult by increasing waiting time to provide the service.

## Monopoly – Commercial (B)

Commercial state monopolies can be classified into two categories, external orientation and internal orientation.

*External Orientation* In countries like Korea and Taiwan the economy is dependent on the export of both manufactured goods and raw materials. The state owns at least 30 percent of the export industry and in many sectors is a monopoly. The international air travel industry is a classic example of state monopolies with commercial objectives.

*Product Strategies* The type of product to be marketed will be determined by the demands of the market. Product design needs to be undertaken with the preferences and consumption-pattern considera-tions of the consumers. Due to international competition, the quality of the product has to be at par with others on the market. The ideal strategy will be to incorporate unique characteristics in the product to establish an identity. Product differentiation will thus help to broaden the target market.

*Pricing Strategies* In most cases they are determined by two crucial factors, i.e. balance of payment position and dependence on foreign aid.

Since in most LDCs foreign exchange is a very precious commodity, pricing strategies are often governed by a desire to maximize export earnings. In some cases dumping in the international market is resorted to in order to earn foreign exchange. Another aspect to be considered is the gap between the cost of manufacturing the product and external prices. However, due to low labor costs, the internal costs will often be lower than external prices. It has been proven that short-term subsidies by the state to help lower the prices and establish the product are helpful in the long run.

*Promotional Strategies* Communication strategies will be in tune with the state of the art in the market. They will have to be aimed at creating a national identity and quality image. It is often rewarding to do promotional activities that are culture-based and unique. 'Exotic', 'oriental' or 'African' emphasis often tend to capture the imagination of the audience in most developed nations.

*Channel Decisions* The channel decision depends on a host of factors, viz. the nature of the enterprise, the line of its products and their usage. The decision must be to reduce the cost to the consumer. Products should be provided at higher levels of channel output. Since this is likely to be in conflict with the objective of reduction in cost to consumer, a balance needs to be arrived at. However, in most cases, market forces will determine the level of channel outputs.

*Internal Orientation* The role of the state as a commercial monopoly within the country is a recent phenomenon in many LDCs. Non-essential sectors are slowly being taken over by the state in order to reap the excess surplus it is often possible to generate in these sectors. Tourism, luxury hotels, internal air travel are some of the areas which are run as commercial monopolies by the state. The state will behave exactly like a commercial enterprise in its marketing-mix decisions. The major objective will be to maximize earnings. It is also seen that in many SOEs in this sector, efficiency is very low and high prices are charged for low standards of service.

Another type of commercial state monopoly is the state trading corporation that controls the import of industrial raw materials and intermediaries. While these are not strictly commercial, having been set up with the objective of streamlining imports and helping in stimulating growth by efficient allocation of scarce imports, their pricing policies need to be looked at. They normally adopt a 'cost-plus' orientation. They also use the 'landed cost' as the base cost. However, the landed cost is often influenced by variations in the export policies of the different countries, the nature of the international political situation, uncertain exchange rates, etc. This variability will tend to increase the cost of the raw material and the cost of the product.

### Competition – Social Objective (C)

This is often a sector where the SOEs are in competition, since very few private-sector firms are set up with primarily social objectives. The public enterprises producing products of high demand, viz. power, steel, oil, etc., are often in competition with one another. However, in most LDCs such industries are set up in decentralized locations with clearly demarcated markets. Since these sectors involve products that are of strategic importance, the prices are often fixed by the government. Promotional and distribution policies will be standardized for the industry as a whole. Product mixes will also be predetermined to cater to different segments. In most cases these SOEs, even though in a competition situation, will play a complementary role due to government control. The areas of operation will hardly overlap – either geographically or by product specification.

### Competition – Commercial (D)

This cell is essentially a preserve of multinationals and private-sector firms. The state may be in this market either to regulate the market conditions, viz. price stabilization, or to take over sick units.

The state monopoly may also be relaxed to let private-sector firms enter.

Since this is a competitive condition it is argued that the market forces will shape the behavior of the firms. However, the degree of competition and the market share of the SOE will determine the orientation of the market forces. The higher the market share of SOE, the closer the industry will be to a state monopoly situation.

Capon (1981) hypothesizes some of the deficiencies that are likely to be present in the strategies of public and private-sector enterprises:

*Product Strategy* Under low-market-growth conditions, the SOEs will exhibit greater product differentiation than will private corporations. The SOEs are also likely to enjoy higher government benefits than their private competitors.

*Pricing Strategy* SOEs, under low-market-share conditions, will price more aggressively than private corporations.

*Promoting Strategy* Except under certain circumstances where the government restricts advertising, the promotional strategies of the

SOEs and private corporations will be similar.

*Distribution Strategy* Both private and public corporations choose what combination of distribution methods will be appropriate regardless of their portfolio positions.

## Conclusion

Whatever the combination of primary objectives and the market forces, SOEs have to arrive at a tradeoff between their social benefits and commercial viability. The marketing mix should be carefully chosen so that the emphasis on the social or commercial objective does not jeopardize the effective survival of the firm or the goodwill of the public. The state should evaluate its policies taking into consideration both its economic and social roles as an organization. It is recommended that consideration of efficiency and financial viability be represented in pricing-control decisions based on social benefit. Also social costs should be considered in commercial decisions.

## References

Ballance, R.H., Ansari, J.H. and Singer, H.W. *The International Economy and Industrial Development*, Wheat Sheaf Books, Brighton, UK, 1982

*Brazilian Business* April 1979

Bucklin, L.P. *A Theory of Distribution Channel Structure*, IBER Publications, Berkeley, Ca., 1966

Capon, Noel 'Marketing Strategy Differences between State and Privately owned Corporations: An Exploratory Analysis', *Journal of Marketing*, vol. 45, Spring 1981

Carey-Jones, N.S., Patanker, S.M. and Boodhoo, M.J. *Politics, Public Enterprise and the Industrial Development Agency*, Croom Helm, London, 1974

Dias, C.J. 'Public Corporations in India I', *Law and Public Enterprise in Asia*, Praeger Publishers, New York, 1976

Fernandes, P. 'Public Enterprise — "A Word and a Vision" ', *Public Enterprise*, vol. 1, no. 2, 1980

*Fortune* 'Directory of the 500 Largest Industrial Corporations Outside the US', 13 August 1979

Friedmann, M. 'The Legal Status of Organization of the Public Corporation', *Law and Contemporary Problems*, Autumn 1951

Gillis, M. 'The Role of State Enterprises in Economic Development', *Social Research, 47*, Summer 1980

Griffith, J.A.G. and Street, H. *Principles of Administrative Law*, Pitman, London, 1963

Hanson, A.H. *Public Enterprise and Economic Development*, Routledge & Kegan Paul, London, 1965

Herbert, C.F. 'The Organization and Management of the Public Enterprises in Malaysia', *Law and Public Enterprise in Asia*, ILC, Praeger Publishers, New York, 1976

*Industrial Policy Resolution of India* Government of India Publications, Schedules A & B, New Delhi, 1956

Prasetya, R. and Hamilton, N. 'The Regulation of Indonesian State Enterprises', *Law and Public Enterprise in Asia*, ILC, Praeger, New York

*Public Enterprise Survey* Bureau of Public Enterprise, New Delhi, 1978–9

Raj, A.B.C. *Public Enterprise Investment Decisions in India*, Macmillan Company of India, New Delhi, 1978

Sanmuganathan, M. 'Public Corporations in Sri Lanka', *Law and Public Enterprise in Asia*, ILC, Praeger, New York, 1976

Zif, J. 'Explanatory Concepts of Managerial Strategic Behavior in State-owned Enterprises: A Multinational Study', *JIBS*, Spring/Summer 1983

## Further Reading

Administrative Reform Commission *Public Sector Undertakings Report*, GOI Publications, New Delhi, 1981

Gantt, A.H. and Dutto, G. 'Financial Performance of Government-owned Corporations', in LDC-IMF Staff Papers, 1968

Green, R. 'The Parastatal Corporation as an Element in the Quest for National Development – Tanzania 1967–72', Seminar on the Role of Public Sector, Cairo, May-June 1972

Jones, L.P. (ed.), *Public Enterprises in LDCs*, Cambridge University Press, Cambridge, 1982

Kemikumba, C.B. 'Public Management Training: The Tanzanian Experience', in S.A. Seshan (ed.), *Professionalization of Management in Developing Countries*, Praeger Publishers, New York, 1978

Lovell, E.B. 'Appraising Foreign Licensing Performance', in Sethi and Seth (eds), *Multinational Business Operations*, Goodyear, 1973

Pradhan, P. 'Management Challenges and Institutions in Nepal', in S.A. Seshan (ed.), *Professionalization of Management in Developing Countries*, IIMA, 1978

'Pricing Policies in Public Enterprises', *Public Enterprise*, vol. 1, no. 2, 1980

Ramanadham, V.V. *The Finances of Public Enterprises*, Asia Publishing House, London, 1963

Richman, B.M. and Copen, Melvyn *International Management and Economic Development*, McGraw-Hill, New York, 1972

Sheahan, J.B. 'Public Enterprise in Developing Countries', in W.G. Sheperd (ed.), *Public Enterprise*, Lexington Books, 1976

# 14 MARKETING-RESEARCH TECHNIQUES AND APPROACHES FOR LDCs

Erdener Kaynak

## Introduction

In recent years many multinational companies, small and large, have looked toward the less-developed-country markets for newer, larger markets for their products and services. In order to venture and penetrate into these growing and lucrative overseas markets, a sound knowledge of the market and its socio-economic, cultural and behavioral characteristics is needed. However, only a select number of companies study thoroughly the LDC markets they are planning to enter. International marketing decision-makers at all levels, as well as public policy-makers, need factual information to reduce the amount of uncertainty surrounding their decision-making process.

As the structure of economy of a LDC alters from production to consumption, society in a competitive environment places greater emphasis on marketing as a decision-making tool (Bauer, 1976). The last few years have witnessed a growing recognition of the importance that marketing can play in economically developing countries, and how marketing strategies can complement the macro-economic approaches of development planning on the micro-economic levels of the managerial decision process (Morton, 1966). Such a marketing system can only be preserved by having a closer contact with the customers themselves, as they are the focal point of company activities. This is where marketing research enters the scene as the best helper of the LDC marketing manager in his policy-making and in designing his marketing strategy. However, a sizable segment of the LDC business community still refuses to accept marketing research as a management tool.

Marketing research is expected to contribute to market expansion and thus to the economic development of the LDC. Marketing research in LDC markets is needed to determine the areas in which comparative advantage exists; to study the consumer preferences of final consumers or of the consumers of intermediate products; to set up standards of pricing and marketing efficiency; and to seek out complementaries and externalities which can expand industries based upon changing factor endowments (Abbott, 1961).

Although marketing research proves to be the best tool of the international marketing manager in developed countries, the usefulness and reliability of it in Third World markets depends on certain factors. A well-organized and highly talented team of interviewers well acquainted with the respondents, a correctly chosen representative sample, and a carefully designed survey questionnaire appear to be the boundary conditions to achieving valid research results which can be fruitful for the marketing manager marketing his products in Third World countries. Furthermore, the researcher needs to be well acquainted with the unique characteristics of the area, namely: religion, culture and norms, population trends, buying behavior, customs and traditions, export wealth and available local research expertise.

So far, little marketing research has been done in LDCs. Public officials and economic program planners in these countries believe, however, that much of the growth and development in the developed countries is due to the application of superior marketing techniques. If markets have failed to expand or have declined in LDCs, marketing research should seek the causes of market stagnation and suggest remedies. If the products themselves face diminishing demand because of changes in demand, demand for substitute products, the opening up of new and better resources through discovery or development, or because of restrictions imposed by importing countries, marketing research should be directed towards the discovery of substitute products or industries in which the LDC or region can exercise some degree of marketing advantage (Folz, 1967).

In LDCs the entire market structure should be analyzed to determine inefficiencies which place the industry in a less favorable competitive position over other producing areas. In these countries marketing inefficiencies which result in cost increases are only one type. Inefficiencies caused by the prevailing market conditions are equally important. Furthermore, analyses of the demand profiles of firms as well as customers should be conducted in the major markets of LDCs. These analyses would indicate whether or not the product policy, the quality of the commodity and the marketing methods are changing in such a manner as to necessitate changes in the market structure or in the production process.

This chapter is the outcome of a comprehensive literature survey of marketing research, and empirical research undertaken by the author in a number of LDCs of the Near East, North Africa and Latin America.

An attempt will be made first to expand on the various problems and constraints faced by the marketing researcher in LDCs. Secondly, the chapter will enlighten the marketing managers of LDC-based firms as to the optimum ways and means of eliminating or reducing the impact of the problems identified.

## Current Problems of Marketing Research in LDCs

Marketing research for balanced socio-economic development in LDCs needs to focus on answering the following fundamental question: 'Which type of market system or configuration of distribution methods and techniques do LDCs need in order to adequately support an efficient and equitable socio-economic development process?' A marketing system is a social network of elements dealing with an exchange of information, property titles, goods and value units, and the transformation of goods in space, time, quality and quantity (Schmid and Shaffer, 1964). In this process, marketing research information helps managers in LDCs to match what is offered by companies with what is demanded by customers. Parallel with this recognition has appeared an increasing interest in the various aspects of marketing research ranging all the way from consumer research to the systematic study of industrial markets (Sherbini, 1965). In addition to the micro role of marketing-research function at individual-firm level, the process also offers certain additional benefits at macro (societal) level to public policy-makers and economic-development planners. Table 14.1 provides a list of common marketing-research problems encountered in LDCs. Let us now look at the marketing research problems at these two different levels.

### *Macro Problems (Country Specific)*

In most cases, conducting surveys in developing countries is difficult because of the countries' socio-economic, technological and cultural structures which hinder the utilization of certain market-research techniques and methods. These countries are in a period of rapid transition — demographically, economically and culturally. There is great mobility, particularly from rural to urban areas. With the advent of increased income and educational levels, consumer purchasing behavior is changing. Also, with the rapid developments in mass-media communications and the influx of consumer goods from the developed world, consumers in LDCs are emulating the tastes and shopping

## Table 14.1: Uses and Problems of Marketing Research in LDCs

| Micro use | Macro use |
|---|---|
| Increase market share and profitability of individual firms (facilitatory tool to meet individual company objectives) | Facilitate socio-economic development process (facilitatory tool to meet developmental objectives) |

Collection of primary and secondary data

| Firm-specific problems encountered (Technical) | Country-specific problems encountered (non-technical) |
|---|---|
| Probability sampling very difficult (kept at rudimentary level) | Lack of good research facilities |
| Inaccessibility to respondents | Lack of trained researchers, research organizations, interviews and supervisors |
| Interviewing difficult | Cultural and societal factors hinder data collection |
| Widespread sampling errors | |
| Telephone and mail surveys are very difficult to conduct | Technical staff dominate the marketing-research process |
| | Poor transportation network |
| Many dwelling units are unidentified | |
| | No common language in most cases |
| High response errors and non-existent sampling-frames | Low literacy rates |
| Use of outdated, incomplete or non-existent sampling-frames | Family structures are extended and complexly interwoven |
| Measurement errors are involved | |
| Lack of sufficient or accurate basic background data | |

Source: Compiled by the author from: R. Brislin, W. Lonner and R. Throndibe, *Cross-Cultural Research Methods*, Wiley & Sons, New York, 1973; D.H. Casley and D.A. Lury, *Data Collection in Developing Countries*, Clarendon Press, Oxford, 1981.

behaviors of their counterparts in the West. All of these changes will, of course, have an impact on the way surveys are conducted in developing countries (Casley and Lury, 1981).

To relate marketing to economic and social-development objectives and conditions in LDCs requires consideration of the following four factors, as well as the interactions among them (Smith, 1966):

(1) interaction between various sectors of the economy relevant to development;
(2) workable diagnosis of marketing problems of each sector;
(3) definition of relevant performance criteria related to development;
(4) evaluation and terminal text of marketing research as a basis for devising more effective and workable institutions for development.

A satisfactory type of solution to the integration of the above-mentioned factors in LDCs necessitates the undertaking of original empirically oriented work, including fact-finding field surveys. The need for empirical marketing research is justified in these countries on at least six counts (Kraemar, 1973):

(1) Statistical documentation is often unsatisfactory in LDCs because of insufficient facilities for collection and retrieval of relevant data and limited financial funds available to the universities and other research institutions.
(2) The importance of empirically obtained information and its relevance to development policies is acknowledged both by research institutions and policy-makers in many LDCs. Yet domestic research capacity is frequently underutilized, and qualified research workers are often assigned to other management tasks. There is an unreasonable and unfounded distrust of the knowledge of native marketing researchers and their studies and published reports.
(3) Whatever market research and analyses are available are frequently limited to macro and global aspects, while fundamental problems (micro-level) at the grass-roots level are overlooked and not deemed important.
(4) Market-research studies often concentrate on planning organization and target settings while neglecting the execution and implementation stages of the research process.
(5) Core issues like socio-economic and cultural context of the problems tend to be neglected.
(6) The chief failure in research methodology pertains to store audits. Marketing researchers in LDCs try methodologies successfully used in other countries, but problems peculiar to LDC trade outlets limit the utility of the audit results. Among the main problems are the incompleteness or total lack of sales receipts and purchase orders in the trade outlets. Many LDC small-store owners, furthermore, keep two sets of books for the purpose of tax evasion, and would not show the

accurate one to the revenue man, much less to a marketing researcher (*Australian Journal of Marketing Research*, 1968).

In order to achieve fruitful and objective results in marketing research, a competent organization is required. A general look at LDCs reveals that most marketing organizations are government sponsored and few specialize in marketing research. The critical role of marketing in the socio-economic development of Third World countries has been underestimated by management and policy-makers. Why has marketing been undervalued like this? Perhaps the major obstacle to marketing research in LDCs is the prevailing attitude of those government administrators who view marketing as a mechanistic process, unrelated to the production-oriented character of the prevailing LDC economy. Since the demand typically exceeds the supply for most products there is little concern about profits through customer satisfaction.

In LDCs most of the firms are either small or medium-sized establishments, and many are owner-managed or family owned. The prevailing attitude among these types of firms is one of maintaining the *status quo*. As long as they attain a certain level of sales and profit, they do not want to grow and expand their markets to make even higher profits for fear that they may lose control over the operation and running of their firms. This is a serious hindrance to the growth and development of small and medium-sized firms in LDCs. As a result, managers and/or owners have no interest in spending money and time for research and development. As far as the product is concerned there is little, if any, effort in the area of product design, testing and research since most are copies of Western products. Although these firm owners lack the managerial talent to utilize the tools of marketing and marketing research effectively, they very seldom think of obtaining qualified help from outside.

The people who are qualified to conduct marketing research in LDCs are associated either with the government or the universities. Access to these qualified people is limited. First, the 'bureaucratic attitude' of the government environment proves a major obstacle to obtaining advice from civil servants. Secondly, the gap between academic and business life is greater than in the West. As a result firms do not refer to academics as a source of expert advice.

Although there is lack of marketing orientation in most LDCs in line with the rapidly expanding LDC economy, public officials in these countries increasingly expect to adopt and use more marketing-research techniques and methods in industry and the private sector. Through such techniques, analyses can be made profiling the demand of firms as well as consumers in the main markets. These analyses will determine whether or not the product policy, the quality of the commodity and the marketing methods are changing in a manner so as to necessitate changes in market structures. In the process, marketing research is expected to contribute to market expansion, and through market expansion to the economic development of LDCs. When one considers the circumstances prevailing in a planned economy, marketing research is not only a means of market information, but is also a indispensable factor in the formulation of plans for the national economy and for supervision of the fulfillment of economic development plans (Szabo, 1973). In such economies the need for large-scale macro-economic market research is emphasized while market research by manufacturing units is narrowly concerned with the sales possibilities of individual products. Macro-economic market research, however, has yet to extend to in-depth production, consumption and public opinion (Szabo, 1979).

As cooperation increases between highly industrialized nations and newly industrialized ones, empirical marketing-research methods based on motives, opinions, and behavior patterns for populations in Europe and North America are being applied in LDCs. There seems to be some doubt whether research methods elaborated in highly industrialized countries are suitable because of educational and socio-cultural differences. For example, the level of illiteracy is much higher in less-developed countries, and as a result fewer people can articulate their personal opinions. The concept of individuality is more or less a recent urban phenomenon. Group personality seems to be characteristic of the people living in villages and non-urban areas. In many rural cultures for example, the eldest male directs the opinions of the households.

It is quite different, therefore, to use existing information gathered from Western culture and to try to adapt this to LDCs for purposes of secondary analysis (Dickensheets, 1963). However, it is of particular importance to evaluate the weak and the strong parts of the existing materials to establish a sound basis for collecting original data. There are certain important characteristics of the LDC environment which impinge on the role of marketing research. This role of marketing research cannot be fully assessed unless one elaborates on the micro (firm-specific) factors which hinder the use of marketing research at the individual firm level in LDCs (Neelankavil, 1979).

*Micro Problems (Firm Specific)*

Among other factors the success of any survey work relies upon a well-selected sample. Many of the sophisticated and improved sampling procedures and techniques commonly used in developed countries are difficult to implement in LDCs. First, there is the problem of inadequate sampling frames. Detailed maps of urban or rural areas are available in relatively few countries of the Third World. The absence of population registers also hinders the use of pre-listings in sample selection (Yavas and Kaynak, 1980). Such lists may be available in municipalities, but unless a 'friend' is located in some key office it is almost impossible to obtain the data. For instance, high birth-rates in Africa make census data quickly obsolete. Population shifts from towns and villages into the urban areas causes urban area statistics to be unreliable in Turkey and Zambia (Horder, 1978). Naturally, it becomes very difficult to measure the exact nature and extent of sampling bias under such circumstances.

There seems to be a good reason to question the competence of the interviewing-sampling staffs in many LDCs of the world (Yavas and Alessandra, 1977); and dishonest interviewing practices are quite frequent. One often finds that research agencies manage to establish their sample figures comparable with the known-universe data. They achieve this by using various weighing procedures or returning to the field to interview extra respondents for particular population segments. Samples drawn by government agencies are much better in quality, but these are rarely available to people involved in non-governmental research.

In fact, very few developing countries have adequate sampling information. Outdated maps and the absence of population registers are not uncommon (Boyd, Frank, Massy and Zoheir, 1964). In non-urban areas the interviewers often apply the random-walk procedures and become the sampler at the same time. As regards to specification of the sampling frame, adequate lists of respondents in Latin America are often not available. Telephone ownership listings are not often found as appropriate frames either (Stanton, Chandran and Hernandex, 1982). This is due to out dated directories and the fact that only one out of thirty or so households own telephone equipment in most LDCs.

The lack of sampling resources available in LDCs, and the sampling obstacles created by the poor and mobile population prevent the sampling of large segments of the population. Therefore, international comparisons are really not possible because of non-comparable sampling frames (Gaither, 1966). Often, when sampling material is available it is less specific than similar data gathered in the West. For example, although fairly complete street and area maps are available for Taipei, and less complete city maps of Taiwan's other four or five major cities, the kinds of materials useful for systematic area-probability samples common in Europe and North America are simply not available. In Taiwan marketing researchers are forced to abandon more precise sampling techniques in favor of stratified, quota, area and convenience-sampling techniques which may be based on relatively incomplete maps and population information (Andrus, 1975).

Due to the lack of adequate parameter data in LDCs, the marketing researcher is not able to infer the exact nature and extent of the sampling biases in his materials. Therefore, it is not an uncommon practice for the marketing-research agencies and individual researchers to use outdated frames. The prevalence of extended families with many relatives sharing a house also makes it difficult for interviewers to select a specific interviewee in a household. In many cases more than one person matches the characteristics of a pre-established quota-sampling unit. Furthermore, many dwellings are inhabited by several family units. This author while researching in Turkey had considerable difficulty locating, in a dwelling unit, the individual who made the majority of food-shopping decisions (Kaynak, 1974).

Besides the difficulties of sampling frames, obstacles created by non-response bias due to social and cultural inaccessibilities appear to be important. For example, quite a number of studies have shown that in Asia, women are culturally and socially inaccessible to interviewers. Accessibility varies within the same nation, depending on the regional, social and cultural development (Redding, 1982). In different LDC environments different non-response rates are encountered either for the total questionnaire or for individual items within a questionnaire. This, of course, causes a non-response bias and affects the validity of survey results considerably. Several studies have pointed out such differences. For instance, according to Mitchell (1968) in a Mexican study, 64 percent of the respondents were female while comparable census statistics showed that females accounted for only 52 percent of the population. Further, in India, 80 percent of those interviewed were male. In a five-country study Almond and Verba (1963) reported a non-response variation from 17 to 41 percent.

Measurement errors are also possible while undertaking market research in LDCs. It is found, especially in tradition-directed, less developed societies, that opinion formation seems to be absent in the lower class, and it is rather difficult to explore the harbored opinions of the ordinary people. Preliminary research suggests that sophisticated questions framed by marketing researchers obtain meaningless responses from respondents who have no opinion or only very unstable opinions. It is also suggested that different cultures have different response styles. In Malaysia, for instance, the Chinese tend to be reticent and are more likely to say 'no', while the Indians are more talkative and more likely to say 'yes' (Mayer, 1978).

In order to reduce such biases a clear distinction should be made between the topics on which the respondent has no opinion, topics which are culturally sensitive, and topics which require greater conceptual and linguistic capability (Brislin, 1978).

Although personal interview is the most favored data-collection method in most LDCs, it suffers from another form of socio-cultural inaccessibility (Lenrow, 1963). In Mexico upper socio-economic classes are difficult to reach because of the housing structures of walls, gates and intervening servants (Loudon, 1974). Because of these difficulties and owing to the increased costs of personal and telephone interviews, increased attention has been focused on mail surveys in LDCs. It is suggested that a monetary incentive and reminder postcard can achieve acceptable response rates at moderate cost (Jaffe, 1982).

Refusals to cooperate with the marketing researcher in LDCs are considerably higher than they are in the developed countries of the world. In LDCs there is a general mistrust of strangers, and this produces considerable difficulties in conducting satisfactory interviews. There is also a great reluctance among both men and women to discuss certain subjects with strangers.

It is common practice in the developed countries of the West to use female interviewers in consumer surveys. The use of female field workers in LDCs would preclude the application of a geographically dispersed sample and the possibility of evening calls, both of which are essential to a rigid random-sampling application. Because of poor transportation, women in LDCs refuse to travel alone and to enter poor areas with inadequate lighting and a high crime-rate. Thus, the use of male field workers is a substantial modification of research in the LDCs (Kaynak, 1978).

Another bias, particularly common in the Middle East and Asia, might be termed the courtesy bias. In this situation the respondent tries to provide the information that he feels the interviewer will want to hear rather than his real motives and opinions. Exaggeration, especially in the Middle East, forms another source of bias. For instance, in one study quite a few of the respondents told this author that they purchased meat every day and that they could not do without meat at every meal. Yet those respondents lived in low-income neighborhoods where the purchase of meat for every meal was beyond their income level (Kaynak, 1976). By training the interviewers and using carefully designed questions, it is possible to reduce the effects of this kind of bias.

The status characteristics of the interviewers and the respondents give rise to yet another kind of bias. In some developed countries the interviewers are judged to be government employees; respondents are often reluctant to provide accurate information believing that the information will be used against them. These suspicions can be eliminated by obtaining academic sponsorship for the survey and denying any government connection. Besides these difficulties in communication, there are certain taboo subjects such as sex, personal hygiene, finances, household expenditures − the degree of objection varying from one LDC to another. Marketing researchers should be fully aware of these taboos and modify research techniques and procedures accordingly.

## How to Conduct Effective Marketing Research in LDCs

The technical and social difficulties both at macro and micro levels of marketing research in LDCs are quite evident. Difficulties due to governmental organization, social and cultural inaccessibility, unavailability of competent organizations, differently structured sampling frames, and lack of understanding of the importance of research, are major obstacles to expanding marketing research in emerging nations. Yet these countries badly need information about the market in order to effectively plan and control their socio-economic development. Even though there are numerous difficulties involved in the research process in these countries, the need to initiate and encourage the process is paramount (Kurtulus, 1980).

Once this is accepted by managers of firms and public policy-makers, then the question 'How' surfaces. This chapter proposed the following steps to achieve objective results while undertaking marketing research in the LDCs of the world:

(1) If marketing research is to become an effective tool for business analysis leading to market expansion in LDCs, specialists will have to devote more time to devising effective research tools. Some of the methods used in developed countries will require considerable

modification in procedures and technique.

(2) If LDCs are to be assisted in socio-economic development, marketing research will have to point the way in a specific manner, and not merely set the conditions for development. A good way to provide such specificity in approach would be to devise micro and macro models in marketing which the LDCs will have to simulate if they are to be competitive in world markets.

(3) There is an urgent need to disrupt the 'vicious circle' found at present in the applications of research to marketing management in LDCs (Ogunmodede, 1979). What we regard as a vicious circle arises as follows. While many marketing companies in LDCs complain of 'bad research' from technically weak and characteristically pretentious research suppliers, the latter complain of 'bad clients' who do not appreciate the role of research and therefore want to pay as little as possible for as detailed and authentic a market survey as possible. Thus, the quality of many marketing-research projects in LDCs suffers as a result of this antagonistic relationship.

(4) The managers of LDCs should be aware that marketing research is a 'must' for socio-economic development.

(5) Competent organizations must be established with qualified researchers and talented interviewers. Such organizations may have an academic basis or be encouraged at the private-sector level. To enhance the available research facilities, government and private entrepreneurs should sponsor research organizations.

(6) The samples must be carefully chosen and the basis for comparative analysis with information obtained in developed nations should have a common framework. Specifications should be reduced to the smallest detail to prevent poor field procedures.

(7) Educational, psychological and sociological factors have to be taken into consideration when drafting a questionnaire. The questionnaire has to be adapted to the level of the population group. Questions have to be clearly stated so that they are understood by the target group. Offering a monetary reward may maximize the return rate, thus decreasing the marginal cost of undertaking surveys in LDCs (Francel, 1966).

(8) Interviewers must be thoroughly acquainted with the mannerisms and customs of the country. One should obtain respondents' confidence prior to administering an interview. Prior contacts in this regard can be very helpful.

(9) In order to determine marketing-research priorities, the rate of increase in the purchasing power of the general population should be

carefully observed. The factors which cause changes in consumer buying habits should be delineated. A well organized team with sufficient marketing background should be used, and adequate financial resources should be made available. Tests should be carried out to determine the competitive position in the market. A close contact with households must be maintained over a long period of time to enable the researchers to observe the changes in buyer attitudes.

## Conclusions

In LDCs marketing research has three major roles to play. The first is the closing of the gap between production possibilities and demand in the internal market. The discovery, the measurement and the direction of marketing efforts to satisfy such segments are important aspects of marketing research (Savitt, 1973). The second role of marketing research in LDCs lies in the coordination of activities within the marketing channel. The third role lies in the evaluation of external demand for the country's output, either in the form of exportable products or importables such as tourism. Also, the development of foreign markets must be considered in more sophisticated terms than simply finding ways to export goods and services for which the country has a comparative advantage.

For LDCs there are sociological, psychological and cultural difficulties, and technical complexities involved in the marketing-research process. In most LDCs the initial marketing research can be done since a competent group to conduct surveys is present. Managers who are aware of the marketing environment should start finding ways and means to initiate marketing studies for the benefit of the economy and the benefit of the individual firms.

## References

Abbott, J.C. 'Information Sources on Foreign Marketing', *Journal of Marketing*, vol. 25, no. 1, January 1961

Almond, Gabriel A. and Verba, Sidney *The Civic Culture*, Princeton University Press, Princeton, NJ, 1963, p. 77

Andrus, Roman R. 'Marketing Research in a Developing Nation Taiwan: A Case Example', *University of Washington Business Review*, Spring 1969, 42; and 'World Population: Recent Demographic Estimates for the Countries and Regions of the World', US Bureau of the Census International Statistical Programs Center, Washington, DC, 1975

Bauer, P.T. 'State Control of Marketing in Developing Countries', in Dov Izraeli, Dafna N. Izraeli and Frank Meissner (eds), *Agricultural Marketing for Developing Countries*, Halsted Press Book, 1976, p. 30

Boyd, Harper W., Frank, Ronald E., Massy, William F. and Zoheir, Mostafa 'On the Use of Marketing Research in the Emerging Economics', *Journal of Marketing Research*, November 1964, 19–23

Brislin, Richard W. 'Back-Translation for Cross-Cultural Research', *Journal of Cross-Cultural Psychology*, vol. 1, no. 3, September 1970, 185–216; and Mayer, Charles S. 'Multinational Marketing Research: The Magnifying Glass of Methodological Problems', *European Research*, vol. 6, no. 2, March 1978, 79

Casley, D.J. and Lury, D.A. *Data Collection in Developing Countries*, Clarendon Press, Oxford, 1981

Cranch, Graeme A. 'Modern Marketing Techniques Applied to Developing Countries', in Becker and Becker (eds), *Marketing Education and the Real World and Dynamic Marketing in a Changing World*, AMA Combined Proceedings, no. 34, pp. 183–6

Dickensheets, R.J. 'Basic and Economical Approaches to International Marketing Research', in the Proceedings of the American Marketing Association, no. 38, 1963, pp. 359–77

Folz, William E. 'The Relevance of Marketing Research to Economic Development', in C.J. Miller (ed.), *Marketing and Economic Development*, University of Nebraska Press, 1967, pp. 60–81

Francel, E.G. 'Mail Administered Questionnaires: A Success Story', *Journal of Marketing Research*, vol. 3, February 1966, 89–91

Gaither, George M. 'Researching Latin America', in Frederick E. Webster (ed.), *New Directions in Marketing*, Proceedings of the American Marketing Association, 14–16 June 1965, New York, pp. 538–47; and Webster, Lucy L, 'Comparability in Multi-Country Surveys', *Journal of Advertising Research*, vol. 6, no. 4, December 1966, 14–18

Horder, C.H. 'Problems of Pitfalls in Conducting Marketing Research in Africa', Paper presented at American Marketing Association Conference, Philadelphia, 1978, in *Marketing Expansion in a Shrinking World*, pp. 86–90

Jaffe, Eugene D. 'The Efficacy of Mail Surveys in Developing Countries – The Case of Israel', *European Research*, vol. 10, no. 2, April 1982, 102–4

Kaynak, Erdener *Comparative Analysis of Food Retailing Systems in Urban Turkey*, unpublished PhD Dissertation, Cranfield Institute of Technology, 1974, pp. 69–75

——— 'Shopping Practices for Food: Some Cross-Cultural Comparisons', in M.J. Baker (ed.), *Buyer Behavior*, Glasgow, 1976, pp. 132–45

——— 'Difficulties of Undertaking Marketing Research in the Developing Countries', *European Research*, vol. 6, no. 6, November 1978, 256

Kracmar, John Z. *Marketing Research in the Developing Countries*, Praeger Publishers, New York, 1973, pp. 4–28

Kurtulus, Kemal 'Development of Marketing Research in Turkey', *European Research*, vol. 8, no. 1, January 1980, pp. 42–8

Lenrow, Morten M. (For more information on the topic see:), 'Why Are You Afraid to do International Research When You Are Already Halfway Home'!, in Edward M. Mazze (ed.), *1975 Combined Proceedings AMA*, 1975, pp. 302–4; and Calbriele Wuelker 'Questionnaires in Asia', *International Social Sciences Journal*, 1963, 35–47

Loudon, David L. 'A Survey of Marketing Research Practices Among Selected Mexican Consumer Goods Manufacturers', in Barnett A. Greenberg (ed.), *Proceedings of the Southern Marketing Association 1974 Conference*, p. 41

Mayer, Charles, S. 'The Lessons of Multinational Marketing Research', *Business Horizons*, vol. 21, no. 6, December 1978, 12

Mitchell, Robert E. 'Survey Materials Collected in the Developing Countries: Obstacles to Comparison', in S. Rokkan (ed.), *Comparative Research Across Cultures and Nations*, Mouton, The Hague, 1968, p. 223

Morton, J.E. 'The Potential of Econometrics for Marketing Research in Developing Countries', *The Philippine Review of Business and Economics*, vol. 3, no. 1, May 1966, 17–25

Neelankavil, James P. 'A Coming of Age: Marketing Research in Developing Countries: The Case of Singapore', in *Proceedings of the Academy of International Business*, Honolulu, Hawaii, 18–20 December 1979, pp. 612–17

Ogunmodede, A.O. 'The Role of Research Marketing', in Julius O. Onah (ed.), *Marketing in Nigeria*, Cassell, London, 1979, pp. 95–6

Redding, S.G. 'Cultural Effects on the Marketing Process in Southeast Asia', *Journal of the Market Research Society*, vol. 24, no. 2, 1982, 98–114

Savitt, Ronald 'Marketing Research in a Developing Economy – A Luxury or a Necessity?', in *Marketing and Economic Development: The Case of Turkey*, Bogazici University, Istanbul, May 1973, pp. 17–37

Schmid, A.A. and Shaffer, J.D. 'Marketing in Social Perspective', in V.L. Sorensen (ed.), *Agricultural Market Analysis: Development, Performance, Process*, Michigan State University, East Lansing, 1964, p. 16

Sherbini, A.A. 'Marketing in the Industrialisation of Underdeveloped Countries', *Journal of Marketing*, vol. 29, January 1965, 28

Smith, E.D. 'Agricultural Marketing Research for Less-Developed Areas', *American Journal of Agricultural Economics*, November 1966, 666

Stanton, John L., Chandran, R. and Hernandex, S.A. 'Marketing Research Problems in Latin America', *Journal of the Market Research Society*, vol. 24, no. 2, February 1982, 131–2

Szabo, Laszlo 'Market Research in the European Socialist Countries', in *Marketing East/West: A Comparative View*, ESOMAR/WAPOR Congress 1973, Budapest, 1973, pp. 191–203

—— 'Market Research in Hungary', *European Research*, vol. 7, no. 2, March 1979, 71

'The Problems of Marketing Research in the Philippines' *Australian Journal of Marketing Research*, vol. 1, no. 2, September 1968, 96–8

Yavas, Ugur and Alessandra, A.J. 'Marketing Research in Turkey: A Comparative Perspective', in H.W. Nash and D.P. Robin (eds), *Southern Marketing Association Conference 1977*, p. 81

—— and Kaynak, Erdener 'Current Status of Marketing Research in Developing Countries: Problems and Opportunities', *Journal of International Marketing and Marketing Research*, vol. 5, no. 2, June 1980, 82–3

# ABOUT THE EDITOR AND CONTRIBUTORS

GURPRIT KINDRA is Assistant Professor and Coordinator of Marketing at University of Ottawa. His current research interests lie in the areas of marketing and development, technology diffusion, and international marketing. He has contributed to numerous national and international conference proceedings and publications like the *International Journal of Production Research*. Dr Kindra recently spent several months in Sri Lanka in connection with a management training program under the auspices of Canadian International Development Agency. Professor Kindra, holds a MA and PhD from the University of Iowa and a MBA from Northwest Missouri State University.

RUBY ROY DHOLAKIA is an Associate Professor of Marketing at the University of Rhode Island, Kingston, Rhode Island. Dr Dholakia's research interests are in the areas of consumer behavior, marketing in developing countries and macro marketing. Her publications have appeared in *Journal of Consumer Research, Journal of Macromarketing, Journal of Business Research, and Public Opinion Quarterly*. Dr Dholakia holds a BSc and MBA from University of California, Berkeley and a PhD from Northwestern University.

NIKHILESH DHOLAKIA is Associate Professor of Marketing at University of Rhode Island. His research interest lies in the areas of macro marketing, marketing and development, and international business. He has written or edited three books and published over 50 papers in his areas of interest. Dr Dholakia obtained a BTech from Indian Institute of Technology, Delhi, and MBA from India Institute of Management, Ahmedabad, and a PhD from Northwestern University.

HAMID ETEMAD is Associate Professor of Marketing and International Business at the Faculty of Management, McGill University. He received his engineering degrees from University of Tehran, his MSc, MIBA and PhD, all from the University of California at Berkeley. His research interests include topics in international and comparative marketing,

253

economic development, industrial strategy, and multinational enterprise-host country relations. He has travelled extensively, and is currently involved in the management education of future management professors in the People's Republic of China.

TAIEB HAFSI teaches strategic management at École Superieure des Sciences Economiques et Commerciales, Paris, France. His research has focused on strategic decision-making in state-owned enterprises. He holds an engineering degree from l'École Nationale de la Météorologie in Paris, and MS in Management from MIT, and a DBA from Harvard University.

C.L. HUNG is a Research Associate at the Institute of Asian Research, University of British Columbia. He has researched and published widely on foreign investment in Southeast Asia. Dr Hung holds an MA from Hong Kong and an MSc and PhD from British Columbia.

JAN J. JORGENSEN is Assistant Professor in Policy in the Faculty of Management, McGill University, Montreal. He is the author of *Uganda: A Modern History* (London, Croom Helm, 1981) and is currently conducting research on entrepreneurship in Kenya and on the management of state-owned enterprises in East Africa. He earned his PhD in political science from McGill University.

ERDENER KAYNAK is Associate Professor of Marketing and Chairman of the Department of Business Administration in Mount Saint Vincent University, Halifax, Nova Scotia, Canada. He is the author of six marketing and management books and has published over fifty scholarly articles. Dr Kaynak holds a BEcon from Istanbul University, an MA from the University of Lancaster and a PhD from Cranfield School of Management.

MOSES N. KIGGUNDU is Associate Professor of Human Resource Management at Carleton University, Ottawa. His research interests include work motivation, socio-technical systems theory, and the transferability of management theory and practice to developing countries. He earned his PhD in organization behavior from University of Toronto.

DURAIRAJ MAHESWARAN is a doctoral candidate in Marketing at the Kellogs Graduate School of Management, Northwestern University.

He has extensive technical and Marketing experience and has worked as a Market Research Consultant for the Sarabhai Group and SSC&B Lintas Ltd, India. He holds a BS in Engineering and MBA from Indian Institute of Management, Calcutta.

ESSAM MAHMOND is Assistant Professor of Quantitative Methods at Concordia University. He received his MBA and PhD from the State University of New York at Buffalo (SUNY). Dr Mahmond's research interest lies in the area of political-risk forecasting, and international marketing. He is the author of a forthcoming article in the *Journal of Forecasting, Technological Forecasting and Social Change*, and *Management International Review*.

RONALD McTAVISH is Professor of Marketing at Concordia University, Montreal, Canada. Dr McTavish's research covers the areas of Third World marketing education, industrial marketing and new product development. He is the author (with A. Maitland) of *Industrial Marketing* (London: Macmillan, 1980) and has published in the *Journal of Management Studies*, and the *European Journal of Marketing*. Dr McTavish has a BSc (Economics) from London University, and an MA and PhD from Strathclyde University.

PREM PANGOTRA is a doctoral candidate in Urban and Regional Planning at the University of Wisconsin, Madison, USA. He is presently engaged in research on the economic impacts of alternative rural energy systems in developing countries. Mr Pangotra holds a BTech from I.I.T. Delhi and MBA from I.I.M. Calcutta.

GILLIAN RICE is an Assistant Professor of Marketing at Concordia University. She obtained her PhD from the University of Bradford. Her research interests are political-risk-forecasting and export promotion. She has published in the *Journal of Business Forecasting Methods and Systems* and has forthcoming articles in *Management Decision and the Journal of Forecasting*.

CHRISTOPHER ROSS is an Associate Professor of Marketing at Concordia University, Montreal, Canada. Dr Ross's main research interests are in the area of export management and marketing in developing countries. He is the author of a forthcoming article in the *Journal of Marketing Education* and numerous papers in a variety of conference proceedings. Dr Ross holds a BSc from the University of the West Indies and an MBa and PhD from the University of Western Ontario.

FRANÇOISE SIMON-MILLER is Adjunct Professor of Marketing at the Graduate School of Business, University of Chicago. Her articles have appeared in various psychology and marketing journals. Dr Simon-Miller holds an MBa from Northwestern University and a PhD from Yale University.

# INDEX

advertising 18, 20, 83, 86, 87, 90, 101, 124-6, 161, 165, 199, 235
AGRIPAC 117, 121-2

birth control *see* population control
black-marketeering 124
bureaucratic problems 80-2, 90, 91, 176, 181, 243
business laws and regulations 79, 104-6, 199, 221, 224

CEAO (Communauté Economique de l'Afrique de l'Ouest) 115
central countries 66
CIDA (Canadian International Development Agency) 1
comparative marketing 7, 188-92, 208
  generalized model of 200-8
  history of 188-91
  statement of 199-204, 208
consumer emancipation 118
consumer price index 79
corporate taxes 104, 108
courtesy bias 86, 247

demand manipulation 1
dependence on imports 79, 99, 110, 218
descriptive marketing 7, 192
  extended model of 194-200
development 57-8, 61-72, 177, 119,
  alternative concepts of 3, 13, 57, 61-2, 67-8, 70-1
  growth view of 61, 63-4
  growth with diversification view of 62, 64
  growth with equity view of 62, 64, 65
  hard variant 62, 64
  implications of alternative views for marketing 3, 63-4
  multidimensional view of 12, 62-4
  soft variant 62-4
  theories of the process of 3, 63, 67-71

views of 11-13, 61
  *see also* development models, development options, economic development process
development models 2, 14-16, 20-5, 70-1
  autonomous development model 14, 21-3, 25
  minor world mode 14, 16, 21
  miracle export model 14, 20-1, 24
developmental options 10
  extrapolating status quo 13-14, 19-20
  future of 19
Dholakia, N. 1-2, 10, 20, 72, 196, 200
Dholakia, R.R. 4-5, 10, 17, 20, 200
distribution systems 6, 35, 37-40, 60-1, 90, 119-22, 161, 162, 189-90, 236
  horizontally integrated 120
  vertically integrated 64, 85, 120, 122
dualism (economic) 12, 16, 17, 76, 77, 89, 119
  dependent structure 17
  monopolistic power 17
dysconsumption 118

economic change 217, 226
  governments' role 217, 223, 225
  need for marketing 25
economic colonialism 115
economic cycles 180
economic development 2, 19, 29-51, 122, 159, 169, 189, 196, 200, 222, 244
economic development process 2, 16, 29, 42-9
  classification of people for 45-6
  classification of products for 44-5
  inward orientation 2, 31, 234
  organizing for 48-9
  outward orientation 2, 31,

257